Shoshana

Memoirs of Shoshana Shoubin Cardin

Foreword by Robert I. Hiller
Introduction by Rabbi Joel H. Zaiman

Edited by Karen L. Falk

Jewish Museum of Maryland
Baltimore

The Jewish Museum of Maryland is an agency of
THE ASSOCIATED: Jewish Community Federation of Baltimore

Book and jacket design by Amy Freese/Stonehouse Design.

ISBN-10: 1-883312-09-4
ISBN-13: 978-1-883312-09-1

THE **Jewish**Museum
OF MARYLAND

15 Lloyd Street, Baltimore, Maryland 21202
410-732-6400 / www.jewishmuseummd.org

Table of Contents

Foreword

arly in 1965, in the first months of my tenure as the executive director of the Associated Jewish Charities, Baltimore's Jewish federation, I was asked to assist our Women's Division in solving a jurisdictional dispute with the unrelated Federation of Women's Organizations. On a heavily snowy day, unusual for Baltimore, I appeared at Women's Division headquarters in northwest Baltimore, and watched the coated, booted, and hatted entrance of the very striking Shoshana S. Cardin, recently elected president of the Federation of Women's Organizations. As we negotiated a constructive outcome to the dispute, I was overwhelmed by Shoshana's cool, respectful savvy. We exited Women's Division offices together, and I told her that this meeting could be viewed by her as a beginning step in a professional relationship that I knew would be beneficial to her and to the Jewish community.

In the 1960s, it took time and patience for even the most skilled woman to achieve community recognition. This was particularly true in the Jewish community of Baltimore, which was blessed with a large, energetic group of able men seeking to be community leaders. But in 1983, nearly twenty years after first entering the ranks of Women's Division leadership, Shoshana became the first woman president of the Associated. So outstanding and so successful were the twenty years leading to her presidency that her reputation was national. In fact, during the final six months of her presidency, she became the first woman to be elected president of the Council of Jewish Federations—at the time, the central body of Jewish federations in North America—and she served simultaneously in both positions for six months. Yes, she was the first woman president of the Associated Jewish Charities in Baltimore and the first woman president of the Council of Jewish Federations at the same time!

Shoshana has leadership qualities possessed by many, but she has several that are unique. She is respectful of other people, from the security guard at the Associated offices to the president of the United States. All who work with her feel this respect and at the same time recognize her humility. One must know her to know the very strong ego that goes with respect and humility. She knows how to listen and to use what she hears. She is very bright and adept and a consummate communicator. These qualities make her a great negotiator and advocate whether in private sessions or in meetings with world leaders such as George H. W. Bush, Mikhail S. Gorbachev, or Yitzhak Shamir.

There is a great deal more than leadership skills to Shoshana Cardin. She is a loyal and caring person who knows how to seek guidance and take counsel. I was asked twice by nominating committees of the most significant organizations to help secure her acceptance to lead the organizations. Both times I met first with her husband, Jerry Cardin. I knew him very well, since we worked together when he was chairman of the Associated annual campaign. These meetings were held with Shoshana's full knowledge. Jerry had to be convinced that what was being asked was good for Shoshana, for his family, for him, and, finally, for the Jewish community.

Shoshana's love of family is basic and primary to her sense of self. When her husband, Jerry, faced legal adversity, I spoke to her frequently. She always shared the facts, and she was steadfast. Even after he lost the legal battle she never wavered, out of love as well as a conviction that the facts never were allowed to surface. She carried on much of her communal responsibility throughout the ordeal, but her life was altered.

Jerry served penal time, and when he was released he was sick and broken. My wife, Marianne, and I had Jerry and Shoshana to dinner in our small retirement home in Florida. Jerry was breathing with a portable oxygen tank. We talked away the evening, as old friends do, sharing views of past events. I had always felt great pride in Shoshana's achievements, but that night in our home I felt her willingness to sacrifice, and knew her greatness was founded on her love of family, love of community, and love of the Jewish people.

For the sake of history, a principal participant in critical meetings and negotiations affecting people worldwide should provide a first-hand account of such events. Shoshana has written her story, as she must, and it is the story of a truly remarkable person. She serves as a model—for men and for women—for the kind of future leadership the Jewish community needs to inspire. Her story not only provides substance for future historians but offers inspiration to much-needed future leaders.

—Robert I. Hiller

Robert I. Hiller was Executive Vice President of the Associated Jewish Charities and Welfare Fund from 1965 to 1978 and Executive Vice President of the Council of Jewish Federations from 1978 to 1981.

Introduction: Profile of Leadership

*S*hoshana S. Cardin exudes "presence." She is an orator, a mediator, an adept learner, a passionate human being, and, most of all, a great leader.

What makes a great leader? Are some people born leaders, or can they be trained? What does it mean to be a Jewish leader? Others possess qualities of character and mind similar to Shoshana's, yet they are not great leaders. So what does it take to become the first woman to hold the most significant leadership positions in the Baltimore and American Jewish communities? These and other questions are at the heart of Shoshana's autobiography.

Like many great Jewish leaders in the past, Shoshana began her life in modest circumstances. Hers was not an "entitled" family. Her father was a dreamer, her mother stronger and more grounded. Her parents clearly articulated their values and lived them. Behavioral parameters abounded. It seems that they were more concerned that Shoshana respect them as parents rather than be close to them as friends. They also wanted Shoshana to develop a strong sense of self and not be governed by the opinions of others. Others, they taught her, may and should inform you, but never dominate you.

From an early age, Shoshana felt herself to be an outsider, different from those in the neighborhood. By virtue of an innate and developed sense of personal worth, she was able to deal with it, even to build upon it. Education was vital in her parents' home, particularly Jewish education, which always had an ethical and moral component and carried behavioral expectations. A full and meaningful life, Shoshana was taught, was one of passionate commitment.

Shoshana took these lessons to heart. As she moved slowly but firmly up the leadership chain, Shoshana never forgot her origins. To this day, she has not lost touch with childhood friends. Her tolerance for difference—different backgrounds, different perspectives, different opinions—is great. Her tolerance for Jewish ignorance is limited, although sadly, she has encountered it regularly. Throughout her career, she has tried hard to introduce and strengthen the "Jewish" part of "Jewish leadership." It has been an uphill struggle, but she has partially succeeded. Unlike many American Jewish leaders, she routinely uses the Hebrew language to underscore Jewish values. More importantly, she is a role model, living a fully Jewish life: *Shabbat. Kashrut. Mitzvot. Gemilut hasadim. Avodah.*[1] All of it.

If you read this book carefully, you will notice that Shoshana equates leadership with communal activism. To her mind, the function of a leader is not to delight in how wonderful things are, thus maintaining the status quo; the function of a leader is to identify problems, to envision solutions, and to lead the community to a better future.

Likewise, she is always committed to *amcha* (her people)—Jews. Shoshana is concerned with all Jews, whoever and wherever they are, and they, in turn, have adored her. A most compelling speaker with a need to be heard, her messages burned in her. In turn, Shoshana has always known how to listen carefully and to hear. To be a great leader one must be able to listen and change minds, sometimes even your own.

She knows how to bring people together. She uses words carefully—never to push others away, always to draw them near. She is a master at working out compromises. Uniquely, she never forgets when a solution is a compromise so when the matter is discussed again, she can begin from the original ideal position. That is leadership.

Most important, Shoshana understands the source of her authority. It lies not in her person, not in those who encouraged and helped her as she moved step by step up the Jewish leadership ladder, certainly not in those of wealth. Standing toe-to-toe with world leaders, speaking her mind as she always did, she never flinched, even though her power did not compute when measured against theirs. The source of Shoshana's authority—and she knows it in the marrow of her bones—is the Jewish people. Sitting at the head of some of American Jewry's most influential organizations, she represented a people with a glorious past, which she had studied and knows well, and a very significant present that she also knows in her grounded way. Furthermore, the future she envisaged for our people was always before her as she acted on the international stage. It wasn't about her. It was about us, the Jewish people. That, too, is leadership.

The *paytan* (poet), in describing the *Shabbat*, suggests, "First in God's planning, though fashioned the last...." If you must, peek at the last chapter before reading the entire book. It is one of the keys to understanding Shoshana Cardin. After an amazing and illustrious career in the Jewish community her greatest achievement from her own perspective is starting an independent Jewish community high school that bears her name. Therein lies the future she still dreams about—a knowledgeable, pluralistic community dedicated to *Torah, avodah* and *gemilut hasadim*.

—Rabbi Joel H. Zaiman

Rabbi Joel H. Zaiman is rabbi emeritus of Chizuk Amuno Congregation in Baltimore.

Acknowledgments

hroughout my career, I have said much but written little. Most often I approached a podium with a clear purpose for my speech but only a few notes. I am a speaker, not a writer. Therefore, I must acknowledge several people who have contributed to the writing of this memoir. First, there were the organizations and interviewers who have at various times recorded my oral history, and who have generously allowed me access to their transcripts.

Hya Heine interviewed me twice in 1990 and 1991, once for the Jewish Historical Society of Maryland, and once for the Associated. Stephen Steiner interviewed me on behalf of the Council of Jewish Federations in 1992. Elisheva Urbas conducted further interviews with me in 1999. Her copious notes helped me organize my thoughts for this book. Elaine Eff did the honors in 2001 for the Jewish Women's Archive, a wonderful and growing resource for Jewish women's history. Peter Golden mined these transcripts and notes, adding his excellent historical research and our wide-ranging conversations to produce a draft of this book for me in 2003. I am grateful to all of these individuals and organizations for their assistance and their interest in my life and work.

In addition to these recorded discussions—done when events were fresher in my memory than they are today—I have made extensive use of my personal archive of documents and photographs collected while I was in the thick of things. I kept agendas and notes, diaries and scrapbooks, all carefully filed by organization and by date, and available to verify my remembered version of events. It has been my pleasure to acknowledge several photographers, many of whom I came to know well as we repeatedly worked together, when including images throughout this book. Photographs not otherwise credited are from my personal archives.

Finally, I must thank Karen Falk and the Jewish Museum of Maryland, my editor and publisher. Karen, the Museum's Curator, has been my principal collaborator in shaping (and re-shaping) this book—questioning, verifying, revising, editing, and managing the design and publication. Her patience, prodding and encouragement were essential for its completion. The Museum believed in this publication. Without this commitment, my book might never have come to fruition.

It was particularly meaningful to be praying at the Western Wall at the start of the Gulf War, February 1991.
Photo by Robert Cumins. Reprinted with permission.

Prologue:
Living in Interesting Times

*I*t was early 1991, three weeks into my term as chairman of the Conference of Presidents of Major American Jewish Organizations. Iraqi President Saddam Hussein had invaded Kuwait, the United States was preparing to force his retreat, and everyone expected that Israel would be threatened or targeted in the coming conflict. I knew the weeks ahead would be demanding, on world political leaders, on the organized American Jewish community, which was rallying in support of Israel, and on me.

My week would be spent in New York, so I was packing my suitcase. My calendar was also packed: on Monday, I would preside over a meeting of the Conference of Presidents, meet with Israeli Ambassador Zalman Shoval, sit in on a United Jewish Appeal meeting, and attend an evening reception to dedicate the new office building that was to house the Conference of Presidents and several other Jewish organizations. On Tuesday, I would meet with Executive Director Martin Wenick to take care of business for the National Conference on Soviet Jewry (of which I was also the chairman), make a presentation at a press briefing on the United Nations and Israel, try to schedule a meeting with Israeli Prime Minister Yitzhak Shamir for later in the month, and have dinner with my children and grandchildren in New Jersey. Still in New York on Wednesday morning, my schedule showed an early morning strategy briefing with members of the American Israel Public Affairs Committee (AIPAC), an afternoon meeting with Deputy Secretary of State Lawrence Eagleburger (we were to discuss Israel's request for loan guarantees from the United States government, as well as the United States' request that Israel not retaliate should it be attacked by Iraq in the brewing hostilities), and dinner at the home of Israeli Consul General Uri Savir.

It was on that Wednesday night that the first Persian Gulf War began, and the rest of my week's plans were completely altered. Thursday morning I headed back to the Conference of Presidents office where we held an emergency briefing— with Ambassador Shoval weighing in by phone—after which we attended an anti-terrorism seminar. On Friday, we fleshed out our plans for a Conference of Presidents-sponsored mission to Israel, and I made a formal call to Prime Minister Shamir to assure him that the thoughts and prayers of America's Jews were with him and all of Israel. On Sunday I attended an Israel solidarity rally, and then it was off to Florida to be with my husband. And the year was just beginning.

By then, I had been traveling the world for years to advance Jewish communal objectives. I was used to spending long hours on airplanes, speaking to crowds, meeting with leaders of government and captains of industry. But by any standard, the year 1991 surpassed these experiences. In that year I became the spokesperson for the organized American Jewish community, disagreed publicly with President George H. W. Bush, witnessed the repeal of the United Nations' infamous resolution equating Zionism with racism, and told Soviet President Mikhail Gorbachev to disavow anti-Semitism.

At times, this life felt unreal. How had I, child of the Great Depression, daughter of immigrants who struggled to make a living, a woman, become someone whose opinions were heard at the highest echelons of power? My youthful ambition was simply to help people in need, but I didn't know how I would achieve that. I did not set a clear course, never made a conscious decision to pursue a particular profession. I never sought to take command, but somehow, that's just what I did.

It was not my original intention in writing this memoir to answer that question. Rather, I began this tale to explain to my grandchildren where I went and what I did while so far away from them. It grew to become a record of my role in events that shaped the Jewish world in the late twentieth century, a way for me to provide a glimpse into the political intrigue of Jewish organizations, and to share my perspective on issues we still grapple with today. Luckily, I kept scrapbooks and files from each organization for which I worked, saving agendas, minutes, talking points, and publications for future reference. I also kept my daily calendars, and today, when I re-read my notes and schedules, I can close my eyes and see again events unfolding before me, hear conversations as if they were held yesterday. Follow me, then, as I remember and re-live these things, as I did, indeed, live in "interesting times."

TEL-AVIV. General view of Jaffa & Tel-Aviv.   תל-אביב   מראה כללי של   HAIFA, The Beach   חיפה יחוף

לשנה טובה

תכתבו

1928

חיפה

ארץ ישראל

תל-אביב

Above: My grandmother, Miriam Barbalot, on a Rosh Hashanah greeting card sent from Palestine to my parents in Baltimore in 1928. Opposite page: Abba (seated in front) with his fellow kibbutzniks, c. 1921.

I
Palestine: Molded by History

Although I only lived there for the barest fraction of my life, my future was molded by my birth in Palestine.

My parents did not arrive in Palestine together. My mother came first, at an impressionable age, and stayed the longest of us all. Chana—I called her Imma—emigrated from Bessarabia in 1913, at the age of six, together with her parents Abraham and Miriam Barbalot, three sisters and two brothers.[1] Their start in the Holy Land was inauspicious. First, they learned upon arrival that they did not have clear title to the land they had purchased from an itinerant rabbi with the last of their savings. Without connections of any kind in Palestine and no place to live, the family moved from place to place until they settled in the northern grape-growing region of Binyamina. Then, they survived a widespread famine, sometimes subsisting on grass, a diet that caused health problems that plagued Imma forever. Finally, the Turks began conscripting the young men of the *Yishuv* (as the Jewish community in Palestine was known) at the onset of World War I, and Imma's brothers began dodging the authorities.[2] This was not the life the family had anticipated when they left Europe for *Eretz Yisrael*.

Neither Imma nor her two older sisters were able to finish school. They each left at about the age of twelve, moving to Tel Aviv where jobs were more plentiful, hoping to help support their parents and siblings. The older sisters, Shoshana and Chaya, found work, married, and moved into an abandoned British barracks (sited not far from where Dizengoff Circle is now located in the center of Tel Aviv). Living conditions in the barracks were primitive, but the girls counted themselves lucky to have secured shelter. They hung sheets and blankets from wall to wall to divide the large open space of the barracks into separate living quarters for each couple, and carved out a similar space for their single, younger sister when she joined them. Imma started working in a bakery, and not long after her sixteenth birthday, her brothers-in-law introduced her to my father, Sraiah Shoubin.

My father, whom I called Abba, followed his adventurous older sister, Devora, from their home in Riga, Latvia, to Palestine. He was only seventeen when he left home in 1920, taking with him youth and vigor, an optimistic outlook, and a sharp mind already well educated in Jewish and secular literature and languages. He was also fascinated by politics, and his ardent Zionism—along with the threat of induction into the Latvian army—drew him halfway across the world. Abba told me with some measure of pride that by his estimate he covered over 3,000 miles on his journey from Latvia to Palestine, walking much of the way. My guess is that he was slightly amazed that he made it at all.

His journey to Palestine, as best he could recollect, lasted somewhere between six months and a year. As he wandered, he saw people working the fields and pastures. If they were friendly and needed help he stopped to take on a laborer's job in exchange for food and a place to sleep and maybe some small payment. When he was rested and full he would push on to the south, keeping a wary eye on the local peasantry, who were sometimes friendly and sometimes not. He had no memory of feeling frightened as he covered the vast distance, but he was invariably relieved to wander into a town with a cluster of Jewish families. His route took him across Russia, Romania, Bulgaria, and Turkey; then he headed down into Syria and along the shimmering blue coastline of Lebanon into Palestine.

At last, here he was, Sraiah Shoubin, late of Riga, young and able and ready to put his shoulder to the wheel on behalf of that wildest of dreams, a Jewish homeland. He had dreamt of this day, when he would become part of the *Yishuv*, but crossing that border was a good deal less dramatic than he had envisioned. He traveled farther still, hiking through the heat and dust and blazing sun, across hills and barren fields until he located a *kibbutz*. The *kibbutzniks* gladly accepted him: they could always use another pair of hands.

I like to imagine the joy he must have felt falling asleep that first night on the kibbutz, having finally arrived in this Jewish place. Then, before dawn the following day, my father learned what it meant to put Zionist theory into practice. After eating breakfast in the dark, someone issued him a sledgehammer, and sent him to clear rocks from a field.

For months, my father cleared fields, planted trees and crops, and stood guard against the nuisance of Arab bandits. He grew into a slender, handsome man, his brown hair streaked with red from the sun and his eyes a merry blue-green. He was energetic, high-spirited, physically agile, and never lacked *chalutsiut*—the idealistic pioneering spirit so necessary to survive in those early days of deprivation in the *Yishuv*. But emotionally, my father wasn't well-suited to the repetitive, mind-numbing

Abba's passport shows he left Riga on December 29, 1920.

work of pioneering an arid land. He wasn't physically or intellectually lazy—far from it. The problem had more to do with who he was as an individual and the nature of his Jewishness.

Abba was attached to Judaism on two levels. First was his conviction, formed as a boy and solidified as he grew older, that Jews in Eastern Europe were encircled by a hostile Christian culture and even though this hostility fluctuated in its perniciousness, in the end it seemed to be a permanent feature of existence for Jews. This belief logically led him to Zionism and the conclusion that the only viable answer for a Jew who craved the same normality as his Gentile neighbors was to reside in a Jewish country.

Second, Abba had an equally strong attachment to the intellectual component of his Jewishness—an unbounded, lifelong love for its literature, mystical speculations, Talmudic intricacies, and languages, Hebrew and Yiddish. Working on the kibbutz was indeed noble, but his mind wasn't engaged. Since, by necessity, cerebral pursuits didn't play a central role in kibbutz life, Abba knew that he would have to find another way to earn his keep, preferably in a city where he would find the kind of people who shared his interests. So, after nearly a year on the kibbutz, my father turned in his shovel and headed toward Tel Aviv.

Originally a suburb of the Arab port city of Jaffa, Tel Aviv was then becoming the metropolitan center of Jewish Palestine, attracting a wide variety of businesses and industry. The first job Abba found was as a tutor. He loved the work, but it didn't pay much, and finally, after he taught himself to speak and read and write English, he secured employment as a clerk at the Palestine Lloyd Shipping Company. The money was an improvement over tutoring, but barely enough to support him.

Every day Abba watched the ships entering and leaving the harbor, but despite the economic hardships he suffered he never entertained ideas about boarding one of the boats and sailing to the United States. Many who had settled in Palestine had already tired of the challenges they faced by remaining in the *Yishuv*, Abba's sister, my Aunt Devora, among them. She and her husband had left for America and were living in New Jersey. My father, on the other hand, loved life amid the sun-splashed hills and valleys of *Eretz Yisrael*, and he did not intend to leave. Then, through fellow ex-kibbutzniks, he met and he fell in love with Chana Barbalot, and his plans changed.

My parents married in 1925. Abba held onto his clerk's job at the shipping company, and Imma worked until her pregnancy was a few months along. I was born in 1926, in a Hadassah clinic located between Tel Aviv and Ramat Gan. My birth should have ushered in one of the happiest periods in my parents' lives but instead marked the beginning of terrible trouble. Imma suddenly took sick.

Her illness, which probably had its roots in the malnourishment she had endured during the famine of her childhood years, had begun to cause serious problems a couple of years earlier. A doctor in Palestine removed her gall bladder and at first, her pain went away, but then she developed adhesions. This not-unheard-of-complication left Imma doubled up in pain, and by the winter of 1927, my mother's condition had gone precipitously downhill. She became so ill that she could hardly care for me, and I, having been stricken with dysentery, required constant care.

My father was beside himself. The one piece of medical advice he trusted was that my mother was in need of more advanced medical care than she could receive in Palestine. With sisters and brothers-in-law on both sides already residing in America (Imma's older sisters had decided that life was too difficult and had left Palestine with their husbands just months after my birth), their course was clear: they would go to America. Abba had no

This may be Abba and Imma's wedding portrait, taken in Tel Aviv in 1925.

intention of permanently leaving *Eretz Yisrael*, however. All he wanted to do was take a temporary trip to get his wife the help she needed.

But how to get there? My father didn't have any savings, and the princely sum of $500 was needed to book three of the cheapest spaces on board, in steerage. Abba wrote to his brothers-in-law in New York asking for help. Luckily, one of them had a successful uncle, a furrier, and from him my father secured a loan. Abba booked passage on the *Patria*, and in September 1927 we sailed to America.

In later years, my parents rarely spoke of our ocean voyage on the *Patria*. I'm certain that it wasn't a pleasant experience, since they were booked into steerage, the hot, seemingly airless bowels of the ship, near the rudder and steering gear. In order to maximize profits for the shipping line, passengers were crowded into steerage like big sardines in a small can. Needless to say, the food was bad, and there was a notable shortage of drinking water and toilets.

The lack of basic comforts made it very difficult to relieve Imma's terrible pain

Our exit visa shows we left Palestine on September 6, 1927. I was eleven months old.

from the adhesions and worsened the generally fragile state of her health. I had recovered from my bout of dysentery, but I was less than a year old and required the regular and exhausting care needed by infants living in far more comfortable surroundings than below the deck of an old ship. Imma managed the best she could, and my father comforted himself with the idea that our move was a temporary one. Soon, his wife would receive the medical attention she needed, and then we would all be back on a ship heading home to the *Yishuv*. I wonder now what my father would have felt sailing across the cold, gray Atlantic, if he knew that he would live the rest of his life in America.

My parents' first glimpse of the United States came on a brilliant fall day as the *Patria* docked in Providence, Rhode Island. We filed down the gangway along with hundreds of other passengers, Abba holding me in his arms. Long lines began to form on the pier. Uniformed men directed people toward the appropriate gates. My parents handed their passports and visas to officials and then waited while their papers were checked and stamped.

As part of the long, tiring process, my father was interviewed by an official who wanted to know why Abba had come to America. In 1927, one had to have special talents to be allowed to enter this country, and my father decided that he would pass as a chicken specialist. He had worked for a chicken farmer in Palestine and knew something about the varieties of chickens and how to raise them, but I recall my father telling me he really didn't know much about chickens other than what he read: he certainly was not a fully qualified poultry professional! Luckily, Abba's interviewer had not done his homework. The inspector did not understand Abba's answers and our family was admitted to America.

We immediately caught a train to New York City and moved in with Aunt Chaya and Uncle Shimon. Abba and Imma planned to rent their own apartment as soon as Abba could find employment, but things did not work out so well. My father found and quit or lost three jobs in three months. My mother, still in chronic pain, did not have the opportunity to visit with an American doctor. It was going to take some time to get settled.

Never doubting it would be possible to establish himself in some rewarding and remunerative line of work, Abba searched high and low until he overheard an attractive rumbling on the immigrant grapevine: there was an opening for a Hebrew teacher in Baltimore. My parents were taking a risk: they didn't know a soul in that city and the salary would be small, but what did they have to lose? And, as I said, my father's deepest love was language and literature. So, after ninety days in New York, we moved south in the winter of 1928.

Above: Left to right, me, Imma, Abba, and Zvi, around 1935. Opposite page: A decorative detail from my parents' *ketubah* (marriage certificate), signed in Palestine, September 19, 1925.

II
East Baltimore: Molded by Family

כּוֹל שָׂשׂוֹן וְקוֹל שִׂמְחָה קוֹל חָתָן וְקוֹל כַּלָּה

בְּסִימָן טוֹב 🕊 וּבְמַזָּל טוֹב

וַיִּפְרֹן וִיִרְבֶּן וְהָיָה

וַאֲשֶׁ שָׁ יְבָרֵךְ לָקְהַל עַמִּים

Abba took a job as a teacher at the Broadway Talmud Torah, where Jewish boys and girls of East Baltimore could go after school to learn Bible, Jewish history, and Hebrew. We moved to an apartment very near his school, in the 1700 block of East Baltimore Street. The apartment was on the third floor of a row house that had a confectionary on the ground floor, and since teaching at the Talmud Torah was part-time work, the opportunity to manage this confectionary appeared to be an ideal way for Abba to supplement his income.

This store was not successful, so he tried selling cheese-slicing machines, which didn't prove to be any more profitable. Next, he started putting lending libraries in the local pharmacies, and at last he seemed to be onto something. With his contacts and his easy, open way with people, my father made friends with the store owners and soon he was also putting pinball machines into their establishments as well. The winking and blinking machines did even better than the books, finally earning my father enough money that he could spend a little more and worry a lot less.

We were soon joined by my Uncle Jack, my father's younger brother, who is a bright spot in my memories of those years. Curious to see if he could make a future here, Uncle Jack had emigrated from Latvia to Canada, then illegally crossed the border into the United States. After deciding that he would finish up his studies in Baltimore he went back to Canada and legally re-entered the country (at which time the immigration officer managed to change the spelling of his last name to "Shobin"). When he wasn't in school, Uncle Jack helped Abba in his business and at night he shared my bedroom, tiptoeing in after I had gone to sleep.

My father had decided that moving up meant moving down a flight of stairs, so as soon as he could afford it, we left our tiny apartment at the top of three flights of narrow stairs and took a second floor flat in a corner house. I particularly liked that apartment because it had large, sunny windows on two sides, and because it was above a Democratic club where Jewish young adults would meet and lively political debate would flow late into the night. Most exciting was the fact that this club had a piano. Uncle Jack used to spend time down there. Sometimes, he would bring me—a four-year-old—with him in the early part of the evening, and I would sit on the bench next to him while he played the piano.

The American Shoubins: left to right, Aunt Devorah Kram, Uncle Jack Shobin, and Abba in an undated photo that I believe was taken in the 1930s.

We were still living in the third-floor apartment when my brother Zvi was born in 1928. In Palestine a physician had warned Imma that it was too risky for her to have any more children. The adhesions from the gall-bladder operation had left her vulnerable to infection—a dangerous possibility before the advent of antibiotics. My mother, however, disregarded this advice. She had little confidence in the doctors who had treated her in Palestine—after all, none of them had been able to alleviate her pain.

More importantly, however, she wanted desperately to succeed in her role as wife and mother. Imma was petite and pretty, with brown hair, dreaming dark eyes, and lovely, soft features, but she was a deeply insecure woman who always felt that her marriage was tenuous. She lacked formal education, a source of discomfort that kept her on the edge of the lively discussions my father enjoyed with his intellectual friends. She was private and withdrawn, fearful of a disaster lurking around every bend. My father, on the other hand, was gregarious and adventurous, perpetually seeking out new places, new experiences, and new friends. I do not believe that Abba gave Imma real cause to feel that he might abandon her in this new land. But I can imagine her wondering how she, depressed and chronically ill, could please such an effervescent man. And I can understand her feeling that her marriage would be strengthened if she had a second child—hopefully a son.

Unfortunately, Zvi's birth raised the panic quotient in the Shoubin household. Although my mother came through the delivery without further injury to her health, Zvi suffered from chronic bronchitis and soon developed such severe allergies that he had to be hospitalized on a number of occasions. He would break out in hives, his tongue would swell, and he would choke. Once, I remember a doctor being summoned in the middle of the night to give my brother a shot of adrenaline so he could breathe. Zvi was sick on and off until he was eleven years old, and his illnesses, combined with my mother's own bouts of pain and depression, were a source of endless worry.

Between the anxiety over my brother's health and my mother's delicate emotional balance, the atmosphere at home was often strained. For another child, it might not have been an easy childhood, but I developed a precocious maturity. My father would say to me, "It's up to the two of us." I had to help run our household, and, when my father was at work and my mother busy taking the baby to the doctor and sitting with him in the hospital, I had to stay at the homes of others, leaving my home without making a complaint.

I was frequently cared for by our very kind third-floor neighbors, the Ainellas. A rather odd couple, he was Italian, short and dark, and she was Irish, tall and redheaded. They had no children of their own, but they treated their dog as lovingly as a child, and they were very good to me. They fed me each evening and took me downstairs, put me to bed, and stayed with me until my parents came home from the hospital.

This kind of "visiting" with other families was something I did frequently, staying sometimes with the Ainellas, sometimes with other friends of my parents. As I recall, these friends were wonderful about having me, and I learned from everyone. I learned small things, like how to give a manicure; and I learned important things, developing a sense of independence and to treat everyone with respect. That was drummed into me: respect. I was taught that no matter what other adults said, no

I can still hear the sounds and smell the odors of the Lombard Street markets when I look at this picture from the collection of the Jewish Museum of Maryland, c. 1930. JMM 1998.017.001, gift of Jack Lerner.

matter what they asked, I could not lose my calm. I must remain very cool and respect what they asked of me. "They are your elders," I was told. "They deserve your respect." I had to learn to put up with other people's uncomfortable rules and ways of doing things because they were doing my family a favor by taking me in. That's a lot to learn before one is ten years old.

Nevertheless, I also remember lots of nurturing warmth, at home and all around us. We lived in a neighborhood of immigrant families. All of us were adjusting to America; all of us were struggling to make ends meet. As I walked along East Baltimore Street, Fayette Street, Chester Street, and Broadway, I would pass the Talmud Torah where I attended and my father taught, businesses such as my father's confectionary, drugstores, groceries and tailor shops, and row houses interspersed with synagogues, all owned and run by the people who lived around me. The Jewish Educational Alliance—our JCC—Hendler's Creamery, and Smelkinson's Dairy were on East Baltimore Street, while delicatessens and kosher butchers selling smoked meats and live chickens were on Lombard Street. Imma's best friend was the daughter of a *shochet* (butcher) there, and I can remember smelling the blood and seeing feathers in the air as they slaughtered the chickens while the women visited. Down the block, the pungent aroma of baking rye bread filled the air. And the delicatessens were always packed with people, because rich, heavy food was thought to be healthy for you back then.

Jewish sights, sounds, and smells pervaded the entire area. I saw market stalls holding big wooden barrels of pickles floating in brine, crates piled high with the vividly colored fruits and vegetables, and silver-skinned, fresh fish resting on beds of crushed ice. I saw men with *kippot* (head coverings) and women dressed with traditional modesty; I saw other men and women dressed in the latest American fashions. I listened to them haggling, chatting, gossiping, and debating in Yiddish and English, with some Hebrew mixed in. I learned to distinguish differences among these Jews, and I came to understand that not everybody acts the same way and not everybody believes the same things. On Saturdays and the High Holidays, the whole neighborhood was out on the street, many walking to *shul* (synagogue) out of respect for tradition.

At home, my life was very much like my neighbors', yet different. Searching the dimmest reaches of my memory, I can call up a hazy image of Abba standing over my crib singing to me in Hebrew, which was my first language. My mother, father, and I spoke mostly Hebrew and English with some Yiddish, while few of our neighbors were fluent in Hebrew. I switched so easily between the languages that I sometimes didn't realize I was doing it: if the word didn't come to me in Hebrew, it came in Yiddish; if it didn't come in Yiddish, it came in English. But at the age of four, Zvi still wasn't speaking and the doctor told my parents that we would have to speak one language only at home. Of course, we chose then to speak English, and my facility with Hebrew and Yiddish slipped away, retained only on a subconscious level (until I visited my remaining family in Israel in the 1960s and found myself speaking a stumbling, archaic Hebrew that surprised us all).

Like many of our neighbors, our home was kosher. Imma was a wonderful cook. I helped her in the kitchen and she taught me how to prepare blintzes, borscht, eggplant, brisket, and her *Shabbat* fricassee—chicken gizzards, necks, and feet mixed with meatballs and tomato sauce. I learned to bake what my brother and I called "Imma-cookies," light as air and coated with sugar and cinnamon, and the twelve-egg sponge cake that she prepared for *Pesach*. On Friday nights, we lit candles, recited *kiddush* and *motzi* (blessings over wine and bread), and sat down to a family meal. And we sang—even though there were just the four of us, we raised the roof singing our favorite *Shabbat* songs.

Even with all that, we really weren't very traditional. Abba was an *apikoris*. He did not believe that God was responsible for what we did on this earth. He was a very learned man: he knew all of the prayers, and if you mentioned a book of Torah or Talmud he could quote from it, literally giving you chapter and verse. But praying in the synagogue was not for him, and unlike many of our neighbors, we went to *shul* only on the holidays. Instead, Zvi and I celebrated Saturday mornings in East Baltimore by climbing into bed with my parents, where we would play games and sing together.

What mainly set us apart from our neighbors was that my parents were Hebrew-speaking Labor Zionists. This was the ideology my brother and I were raised with, as well as our family's social milieu. My mother became a member of the Pioneer Women and my father of Poale Zion and the Labor Zionist group. Were it not for Imma's painful memories of famine and poverty, my father was ready at any time to return to *Eretz Yisrael*. They both supported "the Homeland" to the fullest, because they knew it to be important.

The community of Labor Zionists in Baltimore wasn't large, but it was dedicated. On Saturday nights our whole family went to the *ulam*, the Labor Zionists' hall located on Eutaw Place. The adults usually met in the first-floor rooms, the women in one room, the men in another, or together if there was a speaker or a lecturer. The children occupied other rooms. There was a group for teenagers fourteen-years-old and over; and there were other groups for the younger children. We children had *madrichim*, leaders, who came over from Palestine to indoctrinate us and teach us songs and dances. We learned Israeli dance (as we call it today), Hebrew poetry and what it meant to be a Labor Zionist.

We were taught to follow the very different political dreams of both Theodore Herzl, who worked to achieve a sovereign state where Jews would be the majority population and determine their own fate as Jews, and Achad Ha-Am—who believed that *Eretz Yisrael* should be the cultural center for world Jewry, not a nation.[1] We learned an egalitarian social philosophy. All of us could be *chalutzim*, working to reclaim the land, fostering the rebirth of the Hebrew language, and practicing the values of Judaism—justice, *tzedakah* (charity), *gemilut hasadim* (acts of kindness), and the whole system of human values critical to the development of a country.

The egalitarian Labor Zionist ideology created a remarkable link between men regardless of where they lived or what their occupation was. The group included accountants and attorneys and university professors, as well as those just barely scratching out a living. It fostered a sense of sisterhood among the women as well. Caring for those who could not take care of themselves and offering respite to those who needed assistance was a hallmark of *Na'amat*, or Pioneer Women, where my mother was a mainstay. She baked for the meetings. She and Abba supported the group financially, in spite of their own meager income. If someone became ill, one of the women immediately came to help, support we appreciated when my mother and brother took sick together.

Often we entertained friends from the *ulam* at home. When they came to our house they would speak Hebrew, discussing how the language was growing and, always, the political situation in the Middle East. We also received *sh'lichim* (emissaries) from overseas. And, whether they were from the *Yishuv* or Europe or Germany, when they were here the adults would have meetings to share information. I was never excluded, but I confess that as a child I wasn't always that interested, either. To keep up, my brother and I would discuss with my parents—usually over dinner—what we heard going on around us. My father would explain to us who the guests were and what they represented. In this way, our home was always connected to the rest of the world.

Abba's involvement with the Labor Zionist community led him to write on occasion for the Yiddish-language newspaper, the *Forverts*, the Hebrew-language journal, *HaDoar*, and sometimes a letter to the English-language press. He used to sit at the kitchen table and write, and then he would take me on his lap, let me read what he was writing, and explain it to me. Once, when I was about ten or so, he wrote a letter to the editor of the Baltimore *Sun*. I was skeptical when he showed me the letter, thinking, "They'll never print this letter because my father is unimportant, he's just another American." Lo and behold, the letter was printed, and I was very proud. I told him then how I had doubted, and he explained to me that in the world of well-expressed ideas we were all equal. Abba had written his letter as an act of protest against an injustice he had witnessed, and he had been heard, his point of view respected.

In retrospect, I feel that our household was somewhat different from the other immigrant households around us—we were less interested in assimilating and more committed to the world we had come from. My brother and I were raised as Europeans are raised, not as American children were being raised, and that was clear even when I was too young to recognize the distinction. In our home the relationship between the parents and children was one of respect for authority, not the permissiveness of friendship. Abba and Imma established parameters for our behavior, confident that we would perform our expected responsibilities. I did not see that same level of expectation in the other apartments I visited or among the children with whom I played. My family did not want to become Americanized; we wanted to be a Jewish family, located in America. Looking back, I can see that this distinction shaped my whole life.

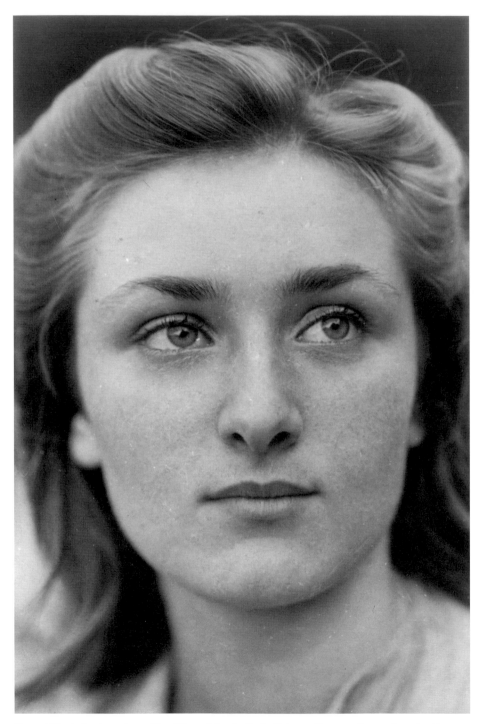

Above: This photo of me at age 14 or 15 was taken by Hayim Kutzer, a German refugee who arrived in Baltimore around 1940. He was just starting out as a photographer and was testing his equipment on this portrait. JMM1987.196.001. Gift of Hayim Kutzer. Opposite page: From my Western High School yearbook, the girls from the "A Course," 1942. That's me in the third row.

III
Lessons Learned in the World

y the time I entered school, we were living in the ground-floor flat of a row house at 2225 East Baltimore Street, across the street from Patterson Park. That mid-block house wasn't as filled with light as our previous, corner apartment farther up the street, but it did have almost floor-to-ceiling windows that admitted the noise of the traffic and the occasional breezes of a hot Baltimore summer. Often, we would sleep on the floor in front of those windows; on the hottest nights the whole family (and lots of our neighbors) would take pillows and blankets out into the park to sleep. In a way, that might be one of my earliest memories of being "out in the world."

Besides the Ainellas, I didn't know of another non-Jewish family in the 2200 block of East Baltimore Street—it seemed to me that everyone was Jewish, from Broadway to Patterson Park Avenue. Patterson Park was a dividing line where the Jewish community ended, however—a geographical barrier. East of the park there were mostly Germans and Poles, mainly immigrants like us. My brother and I went to Public School 27, a sturdy building located at Fayette and Chester Streets, with children from the German immigrant community, the Polish immigrant community, and the Jewish immigrant community.

I was a well-behaved pupil and an apt student who was promoted quickly semester by semester until I was a full year younger than the other students in my grade. My one dissatisfaction with school was that when we enrolled, the principal insisted my brother and I change our first names as part of her plan to promote the Americanization of her students. My mother translated my name as "Rose," and my brother became "Harry." Zvi didn't mind the change—he continued to use his English name until his mid-30s or 40s—but I detested it. I mentally divided the world into two kinds of people: children and adults who called me Shoshana, Shana, or some derived nickname could be my friends; those who called me Rose were not. Young as I was, I couldn't articulate that I felt my identity was being taken away from me, but I knew I wasn't "Rose."

Attending School 27 was my first experience with people who were not Jews (the Ainellas didn't "count" as Gentiles, in my mind: they were part of "our" neighborhood, and they cared for me like family). Although it was only a seven-block walk from our apartment to the school, the neighborhood where I lived was a close and sheltered environment where almost all my needs could be met. I left that neighborhood behind when I entered the school; there, I learned about all the other people with whom I needed to connect. However, these relationships ended with the school day. We Jews, Germans, and Poles each lived in our own communities; I never invited them to our apartment, and they never invited me to theirs.

To get to school, I walked through an alley where I learned that there was another community nearby with which we didn't interact and about which I knew nothing. The alley was lined with rowhouses like ours, but while the steps leading to our front doors were marble, the houses in the alley had wooden front steps. It wasn't until I was in the third or fourth grade that I realized all the houses in the alley were the homes of black families. This was how Baltimore was segregated in those days. We lived in East Baltimore until 1936 and I don't think I saw a child outside of those houses more than two or three times the entire time we lived there. Of course, the schools were segregated also, and to this day I have no idea where these children went to school. Nobody ever mentioned this community—it was as if it didn't exist. Even then, I wondered how it felt for those children to be living as though invisible.

The one experience that stands out from my years at School 27 was the time I was chosen to play the king in a play that was presented to the entire school. I don't recall the play, but I do remember that the part required me to wear pants, which I did not have at the time. That meant I'd have to convince my mother to spend some of our precious household money to buy me a pair of pants to wear onstage. I almost didn't make it to the performance. I carelessly broke a vase at home, and Imma was ready to replace the vase instead of buying my pants. It's funny: I know that the show went on, but I have absolutely no memory of the performance; instead, I remember only how fearful I was that at the last minute I would not be allowed to perform.

During these early school years, the fortunes of the Shoubins were on the rise. Abba had been so successful with his pinball-machine business that a local racketeer decided that Abba should sell it to him. With the proceeds from the sale, my father bought the Pic Theater in Southwest Baltimore. It was a second-run movie house, which meant that my father could only book films that had already played the first-run circuit. In those days, when a first-run movie could play a theater for weeks, the audience was somewhat less choosy about what they saw and how many times they saw it. For the most part, my father could fill his 400-seat theater with the second-run features, and the string of shorter films he showed on Saturday afternoons. Whenever receipts grew thin and we needed to sell more tickets, we ran King Kong, and people lined up around the block.

I was probably about fourteen when this picture of me working the cashier's window at Abba's movie theater, The Pic, was taken. This is a single print with a close up and slightly wider angle image side-by-side.

In 1936, with the sale of the pinball business and the success of the movie theater, we were able to rent a two-story row house on Norfolk Avenue, in the Forest Park section of Baltimore. Forest Park was a lovely residential area mostly filled with those of us who were working our way up from East Baltimore apartments. The houses had small lawns offering the possibility of a garden. There were two streetcar lines about six or seven blocks away and the main neighborhood shopping area was an easy walk—maybe a mile—away. We could find almost everything we needed in the shopping district: drugstores, children's clothing stores, a shoe store, a movie theater, a butcher—it was all in the neighborhood.

My family moved to Forest Park while I was away for the summer, living with my cousins in West Orange, New Jersey. Zvi was sick again, and the move was planned, so I was sent away to make things easier on Imma. Spending the summer

Here's Imma standing in front of our house at 4157 Fairview Avenue, in the Forest Park section of Baltimore, c. 1938.

with my cousin Ruth, who was just six months older than I, and her brother Daniel, who was a couple of years older than the two of us, was certainly no hardship; it's what I had instead of sleep-away camp! My Aunt Devorah, Abba's older sister, and Uncle Grisha lived in a beautiful house surrounded by woods. They had a little farm where we children all had chores: it became my job that summer to feed the chickens and collect their eggs in the morning. After the chores were done, the three of us played in the fresh air all day long.

By the time I came back to Baltimore my family had moved into the house on Norfolk Avenue. The house had a little lawn and porch in front, an area for a garden in back, and I finally had a room of my own. When I saw it, I cried for joy.

After renting on Norfolk Avenue for two years, in 1938 my father bought a house one block away, on Fairview Avenue, at the end of the housing tract. The street ended in woods, an undeveloped area that seemed to us kids a kind of natural paradise. The trees were host to long vines we swung on and called "monkey vines," and there were little streams to jump over, and huge blackberries, which grew wild. My father paid somewhere around $2,000 for the house, taking out a mortgage. I still think with some wonder about the achievement this represented: within a very short time we went from living in an apartment in a row house, to renting an entire house, to a row house we owned. We had succeeded in America.

I entered fifth grade at Public School 64 the year we first moved to Forest Park. There were very few non-Jewish children in my class, which was typical of the school. I found the changes at school difficult at first. I was young—not even ten years old. In addition, quite a few of the children at school came from the elite families of the Jewish community. If there had been tracks, we would have said that those families lived on one side, and my family lived "on the wrong side of the tracks." I felt like an outsider, and it took some time to get into the group.

We were a busy young family, similar to many Jewish families of that time and place. I continued to do well at school, though I remember little of what went on inside the classrooms. Our family remained involved in Labor Zionist activities, and my father made sure Zvi and I attended Jewish Sunday school. When I was about eleven or twelve, I collected the most money of any Hebrew school student in the entire Baltimore system on Jewish National Fund (or *Keren Kayemet*) Day. The organizers of the drive encouraged the students to collect money door-to-door or in front of stores or theaters. Hundreds of us went out to collect money holding round canisters with a slot on the top—not the typical metal *pushkes* (charity boxes) that we now identify with Jewish National Fund. I selected as my "territory" a building that housed two theaters, one above the other, and I worked there the entire Sunday, with my parents' blessing, collecting money from the theater-goers and passers-by. There was no thought then of danger to children or to anyone on the streets having a canister full of money. To my surprise, when the contest was over, I had won. I hadn't been thinking about winning a prize; instead, I was intent on helping my family in Palestine. Looking back, it is fun to think that contest may have helped launch my fund-raising career. However, what I really learned on that long day in front of the theaters, approaching strangers who might be kind or curt, was that patience and courtesy are essential qualities in the world.

Imma was responsible for teaching me another formative lesson in those years. Every now and then she would arrange for programs at the meetings of her Pioneer Women group. On one occasion, a speaker canceled at the last minute and my mother recruited me to fill in. I protested vehemently, but Imma insisted. "We don't have a program and you're going to be there anyway, so you will recite Hebrew and Yiddish poetry for the women." I was terrified—so nervous it was unbelievable. But I found out that while I may have been in turmoil on the inside, it didn't show on the outside—my knees didn't knock and my voice didn't tremble. My "performance" started off fine. I distinctly remember reciting in Hebrew, a language in which I then was still quite comfortable. But when I came to the Yiddish part, my mind went blank in the third stanza. I wanted to absolutely disappear! I somehow recovered; I have no idea what I said except that it wasn't part of the poem. Whatever it was, the women were indulgent of their friend's daughter. They applauded, the program was a success, and I survived.

By this time, I was ready to graduate from the sixth grade at School 64. Our homeroom teacher, who also taught us English, gave us a gift upon graduation: she wrote a couplet for each one of us, predicting what our future would hold. One boy was going to be a movie star, and another was going to be an author. Mine went something like, "In 1960, when television is here, we will watch you in old London while you broadcast from Algiers." She predicted that I would be on television! At the time, I didn't really know what television was. She not only knew about this very new invention, she could imagine how the technology would fit into our lives. I actually forgot all about this little rhyme until many years later when I was waiting in the wings, miked and ready to be interviewed on television for the first time, and then it suddenly came flooding back to me, word for word.

At Garrison Junior High School, I was able to form a bond with some of the girls who had been with me in the fifth and sixth grades. Then, at the beginning of the eighth grade, some of us were offered an opportunity to go to the all-girls Western High School to take what was known as the "A Course," an academically rigorous, college preparatory curriculum. I don't recall discussing at home whether or not I should accept this offer; it was taken for granted that I would attend college. There were twenty-six of us in the ninth grade when we started at Western High School, and there were sixteen of us as we began the tenth grade. The others dropped out and picked up the regular Western High curriculum.

I worked hard at my studies, but I recall taking part in some school activities: I was an alto in the glee club (I particularly remember learning to sing the *Hallelujah Chorus*), and I played ping pong and basketball. Most important to me, however, was a group of girlfriends who were also members of the "A Course" class. We all lived within ten or twelve blocks of each other, so we could easily walk to each other's houses for visits. We planned outings once a month or so, usually going downtown to the Hippodrome for an afternoon movie and ice cream. We had a wonderful time together—I remember a lot of giggling. We named our group the "Happy-Go-Lucky Club," which we thought described exactly who we were: friends who just wanted to enjoy life, in and out of school. We even had a club pin. In retrospect, however, we were a pretty serious bunch who depended on one another to maintain the high level of concentration needed to excel in our studies. Because our special classes and demanding academic schedule isolated us, to some degree, from the rest of the school, we also came to depend on each other for our social outlet.

The A Course meant taking five or six major subjects, instead of the usual four majors and three study periods. Then, because the United States had entered World War II and teachers were scarce, those of us in the A-course were offered the chance to graduate early as part of a "Victory class," in 1942 instead of 1943. To finish graduation requirements on time, we had to take the one college prep course we hadn't yet taken—chemistry—in summer school. Even though it meant that I would only be fifteen years old upon graduation, I elected to join the Victory class.

Western prepared me well for college, but it was also the place where I received my first face-to-face exposure to anti-Semitism. There were only three or four of us who were Jewish in our small, A-level class, and of these I was the only one who observed the second days of the *chagim* (Jewish holidays). My math teacher, Miss Arnold, seemed to take my absence as a personal affront. In her resentment, she deliberately gave tests and collected assignments on the second day of holidays. When I returned to school after a two-day holiday she always reminded me "nobody else in this class missed [the day]," and made other comments that demonstrated her dislike of Jewish religious observance.

I had been taught by my parents to respect teachers, but I found it impossible to respect Miss Arnold, and she maintained an ongoing hostility toward me. When I complained about the situation, Abba and Imma seemed neither surprised nor inclined to speak to the principal—I would have to adjust. When I found out that she was to be my teacher again in the eleventh grade, there was nothing I could do but suffer another year with her. This experience taught me a painful but very important lesson. I had always thought that anti-Semitism might be understandable in a person who wasn't educated, hadn't learned history, and didn't know any Jews; but to meet someone who was well-educated—a teacher in a high school—and who was anti-Semitic? This meant that anybody, at any time, could be an anti-Semite.

In spite of Miss Arnold, I remember my Western years very fondly, but they composed only one part of my life. Outside of Western I had another life with my Labor Zionist friends. When I was about fourteen years old, Imma said, "You should run for president of *Habonim*," which was the name of the Labor Zionist youth group. I had been in the youth group for two or three years, so I knew everybody, but running for president had not been on my agenda. I was by far the youngest in the group—somewhere between one-and-a-half and two years younger than the others. Just as when Imma had suggested I recite for the Pioneer Women, I balked. I made excuses: "I don't think that they're going to have any Number One" (which is what we called our president) and, "I don't know whether I want it." Somehow, the next thing I knew, I was president.

My awareness of the world was growing. Abba had never shielded us children from ugliness such as the anti-Semitic ranting and raving of Father Coughlin, the early enactment of Nazi policies against German Jews, or the killing of Jews by Arabs in Palestine. In 1939 or 1940, brothers Manfred and Carl Wolfsohn moved in with our next-door neighbors. The boys were sent from Germany to the United States by their parents, who wanted to keep their children safe but were themselves unable to leave. Though I knew no German, and the boys knew no English, we used to meet at night and talk—they on their porch and I on our porch—getting by with my broken Yiddish. They explained to me what was going on in Germany at the time, and I remember thinking that the world was becoming a terrible place.

By the time I became president of *Habonim*, it was becoming clear to those of us who were ready to listen that the Holocaust was taking place. They hadn't yet begun the mass slaughter, but there was enough anti-Semitism in Europe to frighten everyone. And I remember that the Labor Zionist Movement sent us an emissary, a *shaliach*, from the *Yishuv*, who brought material—which some people called "propaganda" but which we called "literature to read so you can understand what is going on" in Palestine. For the first time, we went on the air to broadcast our point of view about the importance of Palestine. Radio scripts were developed, and another *Habonim* member, Marvin Braiterman, and I were chosen to read them on a series of Sunday morning broadcasts.

I was glad to be in a position to let people know what was going on. We had relatives overseas. Abba's parents, several of his siblings, and their families were still living in Latvia until the war started, at which time they fled east, deep into Russia. His parents died in the Holocaust but other family members managed to survive the war. Imma's parents had died in Palestine, but her brothers and her younger sister, Rachel, were married and raising families there. Manfred and Carl's parents had been deported (they were killed). The events taking place in Europe and the Middle East directly and drastically affected my family and the families of my friends. Thus the greatest political lesson I learned in my youth: for Jews, politics is often personal.

In my high-school years, my life was very full. Besides attending school and activities with friends and my *Habonim* cohort, I was working, and these jobs provided additional experiences that broadened my understanding of the world outside my little community. At twelve, I began to help out as a relief cashier and office clerk on Saturdays and Sundays at the Pic, Abba's movie theater. The theater was in southwest Baltimore, near Pigtown, a totally Christian community with an economic level and way of life very different from what I knew in Forest Park. Because of this experience, at fifteen I was qualified to land a job as a cashier at the very grand Hutzler's department store.

Hutzler's was a fascinating place to be an employee or a customer. Their elegant Tea Room was where the elite would meet—very fine-looking ladies with hats and gloves and genteel manners—and where food was served that was different from that which we prepared at home. An appointment there was the epitome of a social afternoon. When I worked as a cashier, I was decades younger than anyone else on the very well-trained staff. It was my responsibility to go to each of the cash registers to collect the cash that had not been sent up to the office through the vacuum tubes, starting in the basement and working my way up to the cashier's office on the seventh floor. There were two buildings at the time that I began working at Hutzler's, one with an entrance on Saratoga Street and one with an entrance on Howard Street. I had to collect from both buildings, and I was told, "You must never take an elevator when you have money. You have to use the stairwells," which is why the older women didn't want to do this job. I had very good exercise that summer!

At Hutzler's we were highly entertained, and I was just a little shocked, by the way customers would pull cash to pay their bills—sometimes two dollars, or twenty dollars, or fifty dollars—out of the weirdest places on their body. The money came from everywhere—bras, panties, shoes. They were just hiding it, or making certain they didn't lose it. The cashier's booth was above waist height, but we could see everything that was going on as they reached around to find their money, and it was quite an interesting experience to stand there watching them.

At Hutzler's I also learned the difference between what I had been doing in the movie theater, handling eleven-cent and fifteen-cent admission fees, and a large business, where I opened up a drawer that held hundreds of dollars. By the end of the day, our hands were black from handling the money. As we counted the money that came from the bank every morning, and recounted it before depositing it each night—tens of thousands of dollars—money lost its aura of power and mystery and became just dirty paper.

At the end of that summer, approaching my sixteenth birthday, I enrolled at McCoy College, Johns Hopkins University's college for women. Classes at McCoy began at four p.m. so women who were working as schoolteachers could attend. This was wartime, however—September 1942—and the number of men at the university was diminishing every day. Since student enrollment was down, we women were permitted to take courses at Hopkins. Classes were small, filled with motivated students and taught by the excellent Hopkins faculty rather than the mostly adjunct McCoy faculty. It turned out that for a woman, wartime was a good time to be in college.

In spite of this temporary relaxation of the rules, Hopkins was essentially a men's college. Some campus facilities, including the student center in Levering Hall, were run by the Young Men's Christian Association (YMCA). The cafeteria there was co-ed, but there were other rooms in the building that were set aside for male students only. At some point during my first term at Hopkins, I heard piano music in Levering Hall, and I went into the room and sat down to listen to the young man who was playing. Soon, however, I was told that the area was off-limits to me; in order to use the room one had to be a member of the YMCA. I thought that was unfair since I paid tuition to McCoy College and this was the only student center on campus. I wouldn't accept that answer, so I asked the young man to find out what I could do to rectify the situation. I found out that I could apply for membership in the Y, and the following week I put down my two dollars and became a member of the Young Men's Christian Association. After that I could sit down and listen to this young man play. None of the other women followed me, nor did I try to mobilize them or permanently change university policy. My small foray into activism gained a privilege only for myself.

That's me on the right, in costume for a Johns Hopkins Playshop production, c. 1943. Reprinted with permission of Johns Hopkins University.

When I entered Hopkins I began dating several young men. This was a rather new experience because in high school I had gone out only a few times. My friend Manfred Wolfsohn took me to his senior prom, probably my first date. The following year, I didn't have a date for my Western High School prom. Instead, four other girls and I dressed in our gowns and spent the night eating cotton candy and riding the ferris wheel and other rides at the Lady of Lourdes carnival. One of my close girlfriends arranged occasional dates for me, but all in all, I wasn't very experienced when, in 1944, I began dating the nephew of one of my mother's friends. Jack was a nice man, about eight or nine years older than I, with a good job. I dated him for three or four months, and then one evening, while we were at his mother's house, he gave me an engagement ring and asked me to marry him. I was shocked into speechlessness.

I knew that I wasn't ready for marriage and I wasn't in love, but I couldn't turn him down, not with his mother, brother, and sister all standing there watching us.

My mother was thrilled; my father, thank goodness, didn't care for the fellow, so I knew I'd have an ally when I broke the engagement. Happily, I never had to. After about six weeks, my fiancé contracted a severe case of cold feet, and the next thing I knew, the engagement was off, and I returned the four-carat ring.

Abba and Imma had celebrated their eighteenth wedding anniversary with a trip to Los Angeles. My father enjoyed the California sunshine because it reminded him of Tel Aviv; Imma felt healthier in Los Angeles, where the warm, dry weather soothed her arthritis and her psyche. On vacation together, they were happy and relaxed. Upon returning home to Baltimore, Abba announced that he wanted to move permanently to California. Initially, it was just an idea, but around the time of my engagement he was eager to make the change.

A few years before, Abba had sold the movie theater and bought an apartment building on Eutaw Place. It seemed like a terrific idea at the time; since my father could fix anything, he could serve as the superintendent of the building. Unfortunately, it didn't take Abba long to discover that he didn't enjoy owning an apartment house. He was much more comfortable with abstractions than reality, and in this instance the reality was that his tenants phoned him at all hours of the day and night, complaining that the boiler wasn't working properly or the plumbing needed repair. So even though he had no job in California and no prospects of one, and even though we had no place to live and no family or friends to help us there, he happily sold our house and the apartment building on Eutaw Place to finance the move. My parents gave away their furniture, and in an act of real commitment to their plan, my mother made gifts to her friends and neighbors of the plants that she had nurtured so lovingly.

My brother, a senior in high school, planned to remain in Baltimore, living with family friends until he graduated. I arranged to transfer to UCLA to complete my college education. At the end of January 1945, after trading our food ration stamps for enough gas stamps to take us across the country, my parents and I loaded up the car and drove away from Baltimore, hoping to make it to California in time for the February start of the semester.

We made the drive in five-and-a-half days, taking the southern route because it was wintertime. Each day on the road seemed to bring a new adventure. In Birmingham there were no hotel rooms available so we slept in a hotel ballroom, which had been set up dormitory-style to accommodate the large number of servicemen and women who were then on the move. Luckily, on the night we stayed, there were no other overflow guests, so the three of us had the huge ballroom to ourselves. We drove through several days of bad storms and our car was struck by lightning. We could smell the tires burning and we felt the shock of the lightening bolt, but, other than being terrified for a few moments, we were fine.

In Arizona, we passed a prisoner-of-war camp and picked up a young soldier who was looking for a ride. My mother was hesitant to pick him up because it meant he would be sitting next to me in the back seat for many hours, but it turned out to be very fortunate that we did. After some hours of driving and listening to his very interesting talk of the prisoner-of-war camp where he was stationed, we had driven into the mountains. At the top of a very steep incline and the outside of a sharp curve we had a flat tire. In those days, there were no guardrails—nothing to stop you from going over the side of the road, and falling 1,000 or 2,000 feet. I thought to myself, "It was a *mitzvah* that we picked him up, and he's about to return the *mitzvah*." As Abba and the soldier changed the tire, I prayed no car would come in either direction because it was impossible to see us around that curve. We left him two or three hours later, all of us grateful to have met.

The first thing we did when we got to Los Angeles was head to Boyle Heights, a Jewish section of the city. I didn't like it much; it was dirty, crowded, and noisy, like Baltimore's Lombard Street on a bad day. My mother liked it even less, finding the neighbors and shopkeepers unsophisticated and uncivil. In three or four weeks, Abba found us a cozy house with an orange, clay-tile roof and a yard with palms and fruit trees. The house was on Hudson Avenue near the "Miracle Mile."

This turned out to be a hasty purchase because Hudson Avenue was not in a Jewish neighborhood. It was not far from Fairfax, which was a Jewish section my mother might have enjoyed, but far enough away so that one couldn't walk there— certainly not with groceries. We had no friends or family in the area. We had no phone because of the war. My mother did not know how to drive a car. Isolation became a very serious problem for her because Abba was busy earning a living, having bought an apartment building in Hollywood, and I was busy with classes at UCLA.

Zvi graduated from high school in Baltimore and arrived in L.A. at the end of June 1945. I don't think he was there two, maybe three, weeks when he decided that he didn't like California, which was all my mother needed to hear. She informed my father that she was leaving with Zvi. My father tried to talk her out it, but there was no changing her mind. Had he not gone with her, it would've meant the end of their marriage. We had just left Baltimore in January, and by August the decision was made that my parents and my brother were going back.

I loved everything about living in California, including the way the sunlight lit up our house on Hudson Avenue. (That's me on the front steps.)

In the meanwhile, I had acclimated during my semester at UCLA. I had made friends with some of my classmates, and I loved California. For the teenager I was then, it was a fascinating place to live. On the one hand it was a bustling, optimistic, up-to-the-minute place, where we occasionally ran into celebrities (like the time my father backed into Clark Gable's car). I was particularly impressed with the modernity of the stand-up eatery where I got my breakfast on the way to school each morning. Commuters piled into the coffee shop, picked up coffee, juice, and roll assembly-line style, ate at the counters lining the walls, and left to catch their connecting bus. It was efficient, yet somehow not rushed. People served themselves with the best of humor, which was another thing I liked about Los Angeles: everyone was cheerful, tolerant, and easy-going about social relationships.

Moreover, university rules did not allow students to transfer in the senior year. I would have had to take an additional year of classes if I had returned to McCoy, so I told my parents, "No. I'm not going back with you."

This was a blow to Imma, who was still in pain from the six-month separation from her son and would now endure a year away from her daughter, but it did not dissuade her from her plan to return to Baltimore. Abba sold all of his interests in L.A. and left with my mother and brother. He invested his savings in a stock that promptly collapsed, and soon the family was living once again in a tiny row house with rented furniture. In Los Angeles, I faced an exciting, although uncertain, senior year, having no support system and very little money. I would learn my first lessons of living on my own.

It was not terribly difficult that fall to find somewhere to live. Even though Germany and Japan had surrendered, millions of our soldiers had not yet been mustered out of the service. Rooms were available in a fraternity house in Westwood that had allowed its house to be rented temporarily to women while the fraternity brothers were away at the war. I spent my first semester there in a co-op with thirty other women.

In January, we learned that the fraternity house would be given back to the boys, and it became my top priority to find other living arrangements. There were no dorms for women students, and I was not interested in joining a sorority. The dean of women posted a sign on the bulletin board that read: "The following houses are licensed to accept female students—up to five students per house. Apply," and listed some phone numbers. I was turned down at the first three houses where I applied, quite obviously because I was Jewish. Finally, I was accepted with three other students into the home of a widow who asked me no questions about religion during our interview, although she did specify several house rules. Top on her list was that the girls couldn't use the refrigerator at night, which wouldn't have been possible had we been so inclined because she padlocked it. She also locked herself into her wing of the house, so we didn't see her much.

After about three weeks, I returned from class one afternoon and caught the woman looking through my mail. She began screaming that I was a communist and she wouldn't let any communists into her house.

"Do you mean communist or Jewish?" I asked her, since I had by now figured out that to many Americans that was one and the same thing.

She didn't respond to the question, because she was beyond rational discussion, ranting and raving and throwing her arms in the air. She phoned the police, demanding that they come over immediately and evict me. Minutes later, two policemen pulled up in their squad car. I explained to them that I had no idea what my landlady was talking about, but if they'd let me collect my belongings, I'd be happy to go. I spent several days sleeping on the floor of a classmate's apartment.

My next living situation was in Brentwood, where I was hired by a woman to work as an *au pair* for her young son. I had no idea what an *au pair* did, so I carried out any requests made of me. Less than two weeks later, it was the boy's fourth birthday. I bought a small gift and brought it to his party, at which point his mother exploded.

"How dare you attend a family celebration!" she screamed.

I didn't appreciate her reaction and said, "I don't need this position that much."

"Fine," she said. "Then you may leave."

She wrote a check and handed it to me, whereupon I let my pride get the better of me and made a grand gesture I couldn't afford: I tore up the check, letting the pieces fall to the floor. It wasn't more than fifteen dollars, but I needed every penny of it.

Finally, I moved into a house with a family of whom I grew fond, the Nesters. They were Irish, and Mr. Nester was a policeman. His wife was one of those women who radiate warmth and concern and kindness. They had one child, a daughter, and five female college students living with them. We paid twenty-five or thirty dollars a month for room and board, and those of us who had ration stamps would share them with Mrs. Nester so that she could do the cooking that was necessary.

When I arrived at their home, Mrs. Nester said to me, "I want you to know that we are Catholic. Do you object to living with Catholics?"

"I'm Jewish," I said. "And I have no objections at all."

Mrs. Nester said, "If you're Jewish, you probably have special food that you can and can't eat."

"Yes," I said. "That's true.

"Well," she said. "Let me know what those foods are and I'll accommodate you."

Los Angeles was more to me than a place to go to school, although my courses were fascinating—I was then passionately interested in psychology and was enjoying completing my degree in English. The campus and the city also offered new worlds to be explored. The city bus didn't run on the school schedule, so I regularly hitchhiked between the Nesters' house and school, meeting some pretty interesting people traveling that way. On campus, I encountered a universe I hadn't known existed: gay men and women, pot smoking, couples living together without—as we used to say—the benefit of marriage. I didn't participate in any of this, but it was an invaluable experience because it gave me an idea of the differences among people and highlighted how sheltered I had been in Baltimore. Off campus, I went to Malibu Beach as often as possible—it was the closest thing I'd ever seen to the Garden of Eden.

I found time to get involved in new activities. I auditioned for UCLA's Dance Theater and I was invited to join, becoming executive director of the group a mere two or three months later when the current director wanted to resign. Each year, UCLA would adapt a Broadway show or a well-known movie for a major student production. This was a rather daunting experience for me, but I soon found out that I was a rather capable administrator who could motivate people as well as manage the schedules and the budget. The play that year was *Lady in the Dark*, which was a very successful dramatic musical. The show included several dream sequences that required a number of male dancers. Remember, it was 1946. A number of male students had returned from the war, but they were all much older than the college students at this time. We put out a call for male dancers and, surprisingly, about thirty applied. It was my responsibility to audition them, and accept or reject them, a responsibility that made me feel very uncomfortable. We held auditions on three different days, picked the cast for the dance sequences, and then picked the women dancers, which was somehow easier for me to do. In the end, we had a remarkable play that was very professionally done and garnered rave reviews from audiences.

For a while, I became involved with a political group of Jewish students, thinking they would be similar to my *Habonim* youth group. Then, at one meeting I learned they were ardent communists, and I quit. As a result of these and other activities, however, I cultivated a wide circle of friends, Jews and non-Jews. My closest friend was Shirley Pello, whose father owned several food stores. Her parents were very kind to me, frequently inviting me to their home and becoming like a second family.

The Pellos were Zionist in their thinking, but they were totally assimilated, pure Californians, and I'd never met any Jews quite like them. Once, on the spur of the moment, Shirley brought a group of her friends to the house for a party. Her mother

was unsure what she might cook for them, and I volunteered to make blintzes. Mrs. Pello was amazed; she knew what they were, but had never eaten them before. I was stunned by that information, since I doubt that in Baltimore I'd ever come in contact with a Jew who hadn't eaten a blintz.

In the spring of 1946, at the age of nineteen, I received my B.A. in English from UCLA. From the moment I took off my cap and gown, I was anxious to get out and do something, to make my mark. My goal was to find employment with a radio station.

I'm on the left, having fun in character for a modern dance production at the UCLA Dance Theater, 1945.

There were a host of stations, both big and small, to choose from in California, and with the war over and the peacetime economy picking up steam, I thought odds were good that I'd find something. I wanted to be behind the microphone. From my theater experience I felt that I had a good speaking voice, and I believed that it would transmit well on the air. I was interested in the news and the lives of everyday people. What else did I need?

Before plunging into my adult life, I arranged to visit my family. My brother had written that Imma missed me terribly, crying daily, and I hoped that a visit from me for her birthday, which she celebrated on July first, would cheer her up. When I left Los Angeles I fully intended to return to California the following September, but since I did not know if I would be able to earn enough money to finance the trip, I packed all my things and said goodbye to the Nestors.

I had written to my parents, asking if it made any difference to them whether I took the train or flew home. Abba wrote back that the ticket prices for each were similar enough that it was my decision, but before I could answer his letter there was a major train wreck outside of Chicago, on the *Cross-Country Flyer*. Abba wrote again, saying, "Choose whatever you want, because, obviously one is as bad as the other, if you're in trouble." I chose to fly.

The trip—my first experience with flying—was a twenty-six hour ordeal. It began at two o'clock in the morning, when the airline transported its passengers by bus from the fogged-in Los Angeles airport to the Long Beach airport. Our small plane stopped nine times going cross-country. In those days, any serviceman who was returning home had the right to occupy any seat. Therefore, passengers knew they could be bumped at any stop. The stewardess told me, "If you don't want to lose your seat, fall asleep ten minutes before every landing, because I won't wake you, and I don't think that anyone else will." This was apparently good advice, because I was never bumped. I was supposed to fly into Washington and take the train to Baltimore, but we ran into a terrible storm that grounded us in Pittsburgh. I took a train from Pittsburgh to Washington, then another, finally, to Baltimore. I arrived in the Baltimore train station at four o'clock in the morning, and, fortunately, there was a cab. I took the cab to a house I'd never seen before, where my parents were worried but delighted to see me.

I began to look for a summer job that could finance my return to California. I'd come home with a degree in English, which I soon learned did not open very many doors. I didn't want to be a cashier any more, so I applied for a job as a jewelry repair helper at S. and N. Katz, on Charles Street. I knew nothing about jewelry repair, except that I liked jewelry. I certainly wasn't qualified to repair watches, but I

In my cap and gown for graduation from UCLA, June, 1946.

could repair wristbands, bracelets, and other things, so I said, "I can do this job." They offered me the job at twenty-seven dollars a week and I rather boldly said, "If I work here, it has to be thirty dollars." This was a bit foolhardy because I didn't have any other job. I went home when they didn't offer me the thirty dollars, but the next day I received a phone call. "Come in to work. We'll give you thirty dollars a week." I later learned that they hired me out of dire necessity: the woman who repaired the jewelry was planning to go on vacation, and they had no one to take her place.

In August, I took a weekend off to go to New York City with my cousin Malka, Aunt Shoshana's daughter, who had recently moved to Baltimore. While there I developed abdominal pains so severe I could not stand or sit, and had to lie down on the train all the way home. My mother rushed me to a doctor who diagnosed an appendicitis attack. (The evidence would later point to an ovarian problem.) I was taken into surgery, and it wasn't until the operation was over that the doctors determined that my appendix was fine.

During an especially prolonged recovery period, I not only lost my job in Baltimore, I also lost my opportunity to return to Los Angeles in time to find a job for the fall. I was almost twenty years old, and it was time to make a new plan for my life.

Above: I'm not sure who took this picture of me, posed at the entrance to Southern Junior High "Annex" during my first year teaching at the school. Opposite page: Jerry and me with our families after our wedding in August 1948. Photo by Paul Jordan. Reprinted with permission of Linda Rosenthal Studio.

IV
Choosing a Road

any roads are open to a young person with a brand new university degree. The road I started down at twenty was not the one I chose but the first one to open before me. Thinking that I was taking a temporary detour on my life's journey and that I would shortly be returning to California, I began looking for a job in Baltimore.

The Baltimore City school system was perennially desperate for teachers, so when I applied in early September 1946 to be a substitute teacher, they hired me right away. The school year had already begun when I was assigned to what was known as "the Annex" of Southern Junior/Senior High School. It didn't take long for me to realize I had drawn duty in the school that served the lowest socioeconomic group (of whites, since the school system was then segregated) in the system. The building was in disrepair and the students were troubled. I was to teach English to seven classes of seventh- and eighth-graders, including two classes of truants—one class of thirty boys and one class of twenty-eight girls, all of whom were marking time until they turned sixteen and could legally drop out of school.

As I walked into the classroom for the first time on the seventeenth day of school, the leader of the students in the boys' class informed me that they had had sixteen previous substitutes, each had lasted just one day, and they would be very happy to get rid of me as well. That was all I needed to hear; I immediately resolved to stay, telling them, "I am not a substitute. I am here to be your teacher. I'm not leaving."

The first three weeks on the job were very trying, and I went home every night in tears. The students were much larger than I and thought they were in charge of the classroom. They bullied their way through all of their other subjects and intimidated all their other teachers. I was determined to bring some order to that chaotic classroom—and, eventually, I did. The breakthrough came with a direct challenge from Nelson, the same large, solidly built fifteen-year-old who had promised to send me packing. As usual, he was acting up, disrupting the class, and as usual I said, "You'll have to sit down and behave."

Evidently he had decided it was time for a showdown, so he answered, "I don't have to sit down just because you tell me to." After weeks of frustration, I was more than ready to do battle. With all thirty students staring at me, I walked calmly down the aisle and stood at his desk, silently presenting a counter-challenge.

He glared at me and said, "For a nickel, I'd slap you in the face."

Telling him, "Don't go away," I turned and marched to my desk, where my purse was kept. The class was quiet—it was the first moment of complete silence in that room during all of the weeks I had been teaching there.

I opened up the desk drawer and, in full view of the students, took a nickel out of my change purse. I walked back down the center aisle to Nelson's desk and told him, "Hold out your right hand." He slowly put out his hand and I dropped the nickel into it, waiting to see what he would do.

For an instant, Nelson floated in suspended animation. Then he spun around and threw the nickel on the floor. I stood there, looking up at him, and slowly he sat down.

That was the end—I had "won." I had gained the respect of the class, and after that I was able keep them under control and, on occasion, teach them.

It had been a huge risk, for which the vice principal, who had been in the corridor watching the whole scene, took me to task when the bell rang. He told me I should have sent Nelson to the office for discipline, but I had recognized a moment of truth. Either I accepted that challenge and gained control of the classroom, or I would leave the school in defeat.

The girls were never as difficult to teach. I was left to craft my own curriculum for them, and I tried to teach them some skills for life. We talked about dress, manners, and appropriate behavior, and most seemed to enjoy the required reading list. Many of them were already working to help support their families, and some were even prostitutes. My goal was to help them get through school with enough self-respect and skills to make good decisions for their lives.

The five other classes I taught turned out to be delightful. The students were working at the right level for the seventh and eighth grades, and one class was filled with truly outstanding students. I developed an experimental reading list for them. We started a class newspaper called *Baby Prattle*, which became a school-wide project as students in the Commercial department typed it up and those in the Mechanical Drawing department printed it. I even took them on a visit to the Walters Art Gallery to enhance our unit on "Greek Gods and Goddesses," the first teacher in the school to do so. (The administration thought I was insane to be taking a large class of nearly forty students on a field trip to an art museum!)

I developed a reputation among my fellow teachers for being able, or maybe just willing, to deal with the disruptive students. When someone was acting up in a class, the teachers often sent him or her to my room rather than to the office. I'd direct the student to a seat in the back of the room where I kept a shelf of books, including *Classic Comics* and *Classics Illustrated*. There they could sit and read until the bell rang.

I learned how much these kids needed an ally. One time, I contacted the parents

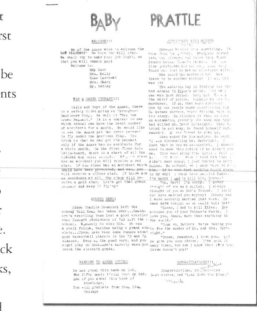

Here's an issue of *Baby Prattle*. The graphics were simple, but the kids worked hard to get the newspaper just right.

of a student who was misbehaving, and they came to meet me at the school. The father said, "You can beat him any time you want, because that's what I do at home." Another time, I sent a note home after I determined that a student who was doing poorly was having difficulties because he couldn't see the blackboard—he needed glasses. I received an unbelievable hate letter in return that said, among the epithets, that their child was not going to wear glasses, and who was I to tell them what to do? I gave it to the principal and to the school nurse who had tested the student. I told them, "He's not going to make it in class if he can't see," but the father was adamant that no son of his would wear glasses.

I taught this way for two years, and then it was time to apply for tenure. To be tenured I had to pass an exam, and I had to be observed in the classroom by a supervisor from the city system. On the first visit, the supervisor arrived unannounced, watched me in the classroom and wrote an unsatisfactory report. She had several problems with what I was doing: I didn't really insist on homework (I knew these students didn't have time to do homework—any learning they were going to do would have to happen in the school) and those *Classic Comics* were definitely out of the question.

My principal, who liked my work a great deal, had a plan. "She has to report to me before going into the classroom to observe; when she does, I will send you a message that she has arrived. That will give you enough time to erase your boards and put up a lesson plan she will approve. Tell your students what is happening; it'll be fine." The next time the supervisor came, the principal sent me a note. I put a lesson plan on the board, and I told the students who was coming. They were eager to cooperate, we had a wonderful lesson, and I received a very good evaluation. I took the exam and passed, and I had tenure.

I came to enjoy teaching. I treated my students with respect, and I felt that they liked and respected me. I know I looked young to them, and in truth, when I began teaching at nineteen, I was not much older than the problem students in my classes. For the first few days I was in class with the boys, there were whistles and catcalls and rude gestures, so I made certain to wear modest skirts and heels, and pulled my hair back in a French twist. There were enough young girls in that school whose clothing was provocative; I didn't need to compete with them! Gradually, the students learned what to expect of me, and my youthful appearance was a positive factor as I became their ally and advocate.

Being young and single, work was not my only pursuit. My social life was very active from the moment I returned to Baltimore from California. I liked social dancing—and I was very good at it—so I went nearly every week with one young man to the Club Charles, where they had a live band. He wanted to marry me; I explained to him quite clearly that I was not getting married, and certainly not to him, but we went dancing together anyway. There was another young man with whom I enjoyed opera and the theater. At the time I began teaching school, I was regularly dating three or four different men.

That first fall I was home a friend, Ben Berman, phoned to say that he wanted to fix me up with Jerry Cardin, a law student. It wasn't exactly a blind date—more like a date with one eye open. Jerry's uncle, Meyer Cardin, was Abba's lawyer. His father, J. L. Cardin, was a well-known attorney in Baltimore, and I had actually seen Jerry once or twice when we were in Hebrew school, where he'd had a reputation as an undisciplined youngster.

The friendly, fun-loving Jerry I fell in love with, c. 1946.

Jerry had red hair, intense eyes, a quick smile, and an infectious laugh. I had fun on our first date, and on the dates that followed. His uninhibited zest for living was exhilarating. He taught me to take life a little less seriously and gave me the freedom to take risks. However, I didn't realize immediately that he was the man I would marry. We began dating in October 1946, and the following April I mentioned to him that I had a ticket for my long-dreamed-of move back to California. Jerry said, "If you go, I won't be here when you get back." Of course, I wasn't planning on coming back at all, but his comment made me sit up and take notice—and what I saw was that I didn't want to lose this man. The route back to Los Angeles, so clear to me just weeks before this, was becoming cloudy. I signed on to teach in Baltimore for another year.

Finally, in June, I discovered that our relationship had also become important to Jerry. Jerry had just brought me home from a date, and he mentioned that on the following Saturday we would be going to a party. Although Jerry and I had by that time been dating pretty heavily for almost a year, I continued going out with several other men so I told him, "I'm sorry, but I have a date on Saturday night."

Jerry looked almost as surprised as Nelson had when I dropped the nickel in his hand. He said, "I don't want you to date anyone else while you're dating me."

"Does that mean we're engaged? Otherwise, that restriction doesn't hold," I told him.

He said, "If that's what you think it means, that's what it means."

A lawyerly answer if ever I heard one, but I said, "Fine," and called out to my parents that I was engaged. I didn't have a ring, but I was in no rush to get one. Having been through that with my first engagement, I knew the ring itself meant nothing. However, when we wanted to set a date, Jerry's mother unexpectedly began to put up roadblocks. First, she insisted that Jerry finish law school before getting married; then, she wanted him to pass the bar exam before the wedding as well. She professed to be worried that I would distract Jerry from his studies or somehow convince him not to finish. This didn't make much sense to me. I would have done just the opposite, since it was in my interest, as well as his parents', that he become a lawyer, but she managed to extract a promise from us. We finally set a date for August 17, 1948. Even though we would not have the results of the bar exam at that point, I was convinced Jerry would pass.

Still, eleven months was a long time to be engaged and although we both felt the obligation of the promise we had made to Jerry's mother, neither of us wanted to wait that long. So when Jerry scheduled a weekend trip to Salisbury, Maryland, in December to look at some investment property and asked me to come along, I was willing to accompany him, but not as a "girlfriend." I suggested we get married right away, and that this marriage would be a one-year trial, with no strings attached if things didn't work out. A "trial marriage" in 1947? Jerry did not expect to hear such a suggestion from me, but I had given this some thought. I didn't want him to think I was marrying him for his money. More important, I sensed that Jerry wanted to marry, but that he was hesitant, his parents were hesitant, and his friends were counseling him not to get married. I thought, "There is a way to get over this." We could try it out; the marriage would either work or it wouldn't. He said, "OK, but it has to be kept quiet"—meaning kept out of the Baltimore newspapers— so without telling our parents we went out to Baltimore County, where a non-Jewish (because we knew none of our Jewish friends would keep the secret from our parents) co-worker and her husband witnessed our marriage.

Except for that one weekend in December, we never lived together until our public wedding. But we spent a great deal of time together at meals, and companionably worked and studied side by side. Jerry even stayed the night at my parents' house quite frequently, sleeping in Zvi's vacant room. We adjusted to one another, learned each other's foibles, and tested our commitment. I, at least, was confident we could make it work.

Finally, after months of being legally wed in secret, Jerry and I had a beautiful wedding at the Belvedere Hotel in Baltimore, with friends and family in attendance. Since my family followed traditional Jewish practices and his family was Reform, we compromised on a Conservative service. Dr. Louis L. Kaplan, a rabbi and dean of Baltimore Hebrew College, performed the ceremony. Jerry and I had a discussion about our vows: would it be, "love, honor, and cherish," as was standard in 1948? Or would I say, "love, honor and obey," as Jerry preferred? Because I felt secure that

Jerry and I were in agreement about the kind of wide intellectual freedom I would need as a wife, I promised to "obey," while he promised to "cherish."

Jerry borrowed his father's convertible, and we drove north for a three-week honeymoon. We stopped in Manhattan for a night, and then headed up through New York State to the Finger Lakes and Niagara Falls. We kept driving into Quebec where we visited Le Manor Richelieu, moved on to Nova Scotia, then came back down through Maine and New England to Baltimore. It was a wonderful trip. We came home three hundred dollars in debt, and it was worth every penny.

Back home in Baltimore, we moved into a three-story walk-up on Auchentoroly Terrace, a very old building owned by my father-in-law. The apartment had high ceilings, huge rooms, and fireplaces in the bedroom and living room. I loved it, with its wonderful architectural detail and expansive spaces. It didn't matter to me at all that it was not in the most convenient location for commuting to work. With only one car in the family (and I didn't have a driver's license anyway) I took two streetcars to get to school. In the afternoons, I would stop downtown on my way home. Often, I would go to Jerry's office, where he clerked for his father's firm at a salary of something like twelve dollars a week, and we would go out to dinner or just ride home together. At other times, I shopped or met friends. Every Friday night we ate dinner at my parents' house, and every other Tuesday night we went to my in-laws' house for dinner. Saturday evening was restaurant night, when no one in the family cooked. It was a pleasantly busy time—we probably averaged only one dinner at home per week in those first months.

In addition to work and pleasant social engagements keeping us away from home on a regular basis, Jerry and I both enjoyed heavy volunteer commitments. The high priority we placed on voluntary work was established even before we married. In 1948, Jerry was serving as president of the revived Nu Beta Epsilon, the national fraternity of Jewish lawyers, which had languished during the war. The fraternity held its first post-war national convention several months before our wedding, and because Jerry was president it was held in Baltimore. The group selected Easter weekend as an appropriate time for a Jewish get-together.

Jerry enlisted my help in the planning. "We're going to have visitors from out of town, and you are going to arrange a trip to Annapolis and a fashion show for the women on Sunday," he told me. I thought, "He's crazy! Who's going to do a fashion show on Easter Sunday? And what do I know about Annapolis?" But being young and in love, I simply agreed when he said, "Let me know when the plans are ready."

The trip to Annapolis was the easy part. I hired a bus, found a guide somewhere, and arranged for a tour of the Naval Academy. Then I called Hutzler's, my former

Officers of Beacon Chapter, Order of the Eastern Star in 1959, the year I became "Worthy Matron."

department store employer, and asked about a fashion show. As expected, I was told, "We don't do fashion shows on Easter Sunday."

"But this is a very special group," I explained. "All are wives of attorneys, and most are from out-of-town." When asked, I told them that 200 people would be attending, and on the strength of that promise, Hutzler's committed to do the show. In fact, I had about twelve people signed up at that moment!

On the morning of Easter Sunday, we still had nowhere near 200 people signed up to attend the show, but I had planned ahead. I instructed the Lord Baltimore Hotel, where the convention was taking place, to prepare tea and set up for an audience of 200 guests. I then asked the hotel telephone operator to leave a call for each guest in the hotel that a free fashion show and tea would be held that afternoon. I also stationed a couple of friends at the Charles and Baltimore Street entrances to the hotel handing out "Free: Easter Sunday Fashion Show!" flyers to passersby. The strategy worked. About 170 people attended the event, and the conventioneers and the Hutzler's department store people were all quite happy. I was relieved, and Jerry's confidence in my "executive" abilities was complete.

Marriage introduced me to a new involvement that proved to be formative. Jerry and all the Cardin men were Masons, and all the Cardin women were members of the Order of the Eastern Star (OES), the Masonic women's auxiliary. Early on, I was "informed" that I would be joining the Order. I had never heard of Eastern Star and would never have joined this group on my own, but it soon became a major component of my social life. A number of the women I met there in the early years of my marriage are still my very close friends.

Our chapter, Beacon Chapter No. 60 OES, was an all-Jewish group. A year or so after I joined, Jerry's aunt became "Worthy Matron," or presiding officer, and she made a point to put me on the leadership track. Aunt Dora (known as "Duckye" Cardin) appointed me to the lowest officer position, so I could work my way through the committee chairs—a ten-year process. Eastern Star rules required that a member of the Masons be present at the biweekly meetings, a role that was usually filled by the husbands of the officers. Jerry happily agreed to serve when it became my turn to lead.

I didn't completely understand or appreciate the attraction of Jewish women to Eastern Star. Even though ours was a Jewish chapter, the group ritual included ceremonial vows taken from Christian liturgies. I was appalled when I entered our meeting room for the first time, to be inducted into the Order, and found that we were expected to kneel at an altar and recite from the New Testament. The name of the group itself had a Christian meaning: the "Eastern Star" referred to the Star of Christ. Still, its appeal in the community was quite strong, and when I joined in 1948 Beacon Chapter had around one thousand members, all of them related by blood or by marriage to a Mason.

Eastern Star was organized into statewide groups known as Grand Lodges, which were divided into local chapters. Maryland's Grand Lodge comprised around 150 chapters, and each performed considerable charitable work in its own community. Beacon Chapter's particular project was to visit and work with the female residents of Pembroke Cottage at Rosewood State Training School, an institution for the mentally disabled. We usually spent one afternoon there each week. Later, we helped found the Alice Rockwell Halfway House for Rosewood residents deemed ready for a more independent living arrangement.

Pembroke Cottage was a locked facility. It was a very odd and somewhat disturbing experience to wait for the door to be unlocked upon our arrival each week, walk through it, and hear it being relocked, knowing no one could leave until the matron returned. As we volunteers entered the facility, the thirty women of the cottage— women of all ages and sizes—would rush toward us screaming, "Mommy, Mommy!"

To the residents, we were all "Mommy." It could be overwhelming, and some volunteers visited once and never returned. But for those of us who could accept that the residents just needed to hug and be held in return, to say "Mommy" and hear a reply in a voice that was soft and soothing, the visits became quite meaningful. We would try to have simple conversations with the women, and we would play games with them. It was possible to establish special relationships with some of them, and we would look forward to seeing each other every week. Sometimes, we were able to make a real difference in people's lives. I remember that another volunteer and I were able to coax speech out of patients who had not spoken for years—that was a great achievement. Later, when some of Pembroke's charges made it to the Rockwell House, we were all very excited.

This work was challenging and rewarding, but it was the social aspect of the organization that attracted most of the membership. Since we met frequently, we women came to know each other quite well. Our husbands would arrive after each meeting to enjoy the refreshments we served, adding to the festive atmosphere. The officers of the group were particularly tight-knit. If any one of us were in trouble, all of the others would come to that person's assistance. The organization rules required it, but we would have done it anyway.

I was a member of Eastern Star until Beacon Chapter went out of business in 1988. In the end, we simply did not have women who were willing to lead the group. Heading the chapter was a major responsibility that included frequent meetings, ritual to be memorized, volunteer work to carry out, and social obligations to the other members of the group. The Worthy Matron visited the sick and the bereaved, made certain that meeting minutes were printed and shared with the rest of the members, and was responsible for money that was collected from the members. These funds were used to run the organization, and were distributed to select causes. Over the years, our membership aged and few younger women joined. Eventually, when we could not find anyone with the energy to assume the leadership, we decided to close shop and donated our remaining money—approximately $25,000—to worthy causes.

There was yet another track that Jerry and I stepped onto during that first decade of our marriage. Jerry's family had long been active in local Democratic politics, and every family affair—even our wedding was attended by local and state notables of the day—had a political side to it. Soon we were caught up in events to support our candidates. We bowled every Wednesday evening with the Citizens Democratic Club, and our home was the site of many strategy and working sessions for political campaigns. In those early years, I brewed a lot of coffee, stuffed a lot of envelopes, and became friendly with many city, county, and state political leaders.

This aspect of our lives was both familiar and newly interesting. As a child I had been used to observing my father and Uncle Jack animatedly talking politics with friends, so strong opinions and heated debates seemed a natural part of daily life. On the other hand, I had never before been so closely connected to those in a position of influence. Now I was being treated to an insider's view of politics. I listened and developed opinions of my own, which I kept mostly to myself since they were often far more liberal than my husband's ideas.

Looking back, it seems to me that all of these activities prepared me in some way for my future career in community activism. However, they were just background scenery to the most important and fulfilling journey Jerry and I took together: the creation of our home and family.

Above: Jerry and me c. 1968. I was always a "stand-behind-your-man" kind of wife. Opposite page: Our children (from left) Ilene, Steven in his school uniform, the baby, Sandy, and Nina in 1957.

V
Family Comes First

As a young woman, I had been told that I could not have children. Doctors said that the ovarian malady that had been misdiagnosed as appendicitis not many years earlier would prevent me from ever becoming pregnant. In the spring of 1950, however, I called my gynecologist—a leading practitioner at Johns Hopkins Hospital—and told him I was pregnant.

"You can't be," he said.

"Well I am, I can feel it," I told him, "and I want an appointment."

I went to see him and his examination confirmed my suspicions. He immediately told me that we would schedule a date for an operation.

"A what?" I asked, becoming alarmed.

He then informed me that these pregnancies are often not viable and can even be cancerous. The pregnancy, he said, should be terminated.

This news brought me as near to hysteria as I have ever been. I had arrived at the doctor's office alone, but now insisted that we call Jerry to join us. His office was not far away, and he rushed over. The doctor then explained to Jerry what he had been telling me, while I sat with my husband and wept. I had been told I could never have children, and then had been surprised and excited to find I was pregnant. The disappointment of losing this new possibility was terrible. Jerry and I determined to get another opinion.

Being young and generally healthy, we did not have a family physician to consult. My parents' doctor recommended Dr. Wharton, of Union Memorial Hospital, and this time Jerry and I visited him together. We explained the situation, and he said, "Yes, there may be problems, but we will watch you very carefully to see how the pregnancy develops before making a decision."

"I'm more interested in my wife than the pregnancy," Jerry told him. "Her health has to come first." Dr. Wharton told us that he understood, and my pregnancy progressed under his watchful eye.

Baltimore Public Schools stipulated that teachers who became pregnant must take a leave of absence or retire from teaching. As there were only a few more months left in the school year, it was easy to keep the pregnancy a secret while we waited to see how things would turn out. Finally, at the end of the term, the principal called me in to tell me how happy he was with the innovative things I had been doing in my classroom, and to offer me a promotion to the high school. I told him then about the baby, and he said, "Here's what you'll do. Take your leave of absence, have your two children, and return as a tenured high school teacher in four years," a scenario endorsed by the school system. However, Jerry and I had agreed that if we were able to afford to live on his income I would not work, and I left teaching without regret at the end of the term.

Our son Steven was born in November 1950, three weeks late but underweight and with respiratory difficulties. I engaged a nurse to help me take care of him, and I rubbed his wrinkled, dry, and cracked skin with Vaseline every day. It was six weeks until he was well enough to have a *bris*, long past the eighth day of life on which that tradition is usually observed.

When Steven was six months old, Dr. Wharton told us that if we wanted to have more children, we would have to act quickly. Accordingly, I became pregnant right away (Ilene was born in 1952) and conceived again six months after Ilene was born. When I was three months

I was a happy mother with a sleepy baby in this 1950 picture with Steven.

along with this third pregnancy, one of my ovaries became so enlarged and painful that it had to be removed. Once again, we faced a frightening situation, but Dr. Wharton was confident that the surgery would not disturb the baby, and he was right. Our daughter, Nina, was born without incident in 1953. After that, the doctors decided I would not have further difficulties with pregnancies, so we felt we could take our time before having another child. Our youngest son, Sanford, was born in 1957. Then my other ovary became painfully cystic, and that put an end to pregnancies. At one time, Jerry and I had contemplated having six children, but with two boys and two girls, we were content to consider our family complete.

I was a typically anxious mother at first, made more so by Steven's early physical problems. Although we worried and saw the doctor frequently, his health caused us nowhere near the strain my parents felt over my brother Zvi's early difficulties. Then Ilene had digestive distress that was finally diagnosed as an allergy to milk; once we had her happily eating something called Mull Soy she was a placid, easy baby. By the time Nina was born, I was well settled into my role as a mother, comfortable taking care of three small children twenty-four hours a day. I was even able to take it in stride when, as a newborn, Sandy was diagnosed with pyloric stenosis. This potentially dangerous condition of the digestive tract was relieved by surgery when he was one month old, after which he thrived.

We lived on Auchentoroly Terrace when Steven was born, but the apartment was not big enough for two children, so we bought a house on Carlisle Avenue before Ilene and Nina came along. We finished the attic and basement of that house and enjoyed doing lots of entertaining there. There were many young children in the neighborhood with whom our kids played easily, and I enjoyed getting to know the other young mothers. Then, a year or two before Sandy was born, the City condemned our block to make way for a new school. We were given a year to move out, enough time to build a house. We bought a lot in Baltimore County, off Stevenson Road, and carefully planned a house that would nurture the family life we envisioned.

Jerry's primary business at that time was real estate and homebuilding, so we were comfortable designing the house ourselves. My husband traveled around to see the latest architectural plans being used in tract housing. I enjoyed going along with him, and I often helped him design the kitchens for his houses. (I sometimes even demonstrated those kitchens for customers when the models were built.) With all of this looking and comparing, we became very familiar with the house styles and products that were available to homebuyers at the time. The subdivision was restricted to houses of one story, posing a challenge for our family of almost four children—by the end of this process, I was pregnant with Sandy. Fortunately, we

(l–r) Ilene, Nina, me and Steven on the swing set in our Carlisle Avenue backyard, 1953.

were inspired by a front-to-back split-level model we saw in California, and decided that was the design that would work for us. We spent months drawing and refining it, and had a lot of fun. Then, since neither Jerry nor I knew anything about structural engineering, we hired an architect to draw up plans our contractor could actually build.

When we moved to Baltimore County on August 1, 1957, ours was only the fifth or sixth house to be completed on this tract. The area was quite rural then. We had no public transportation or even home-delivered mail service; we went to the Stevenson Post Office to pick up our mail. There were no supermarkets, just a tiny grocery store at the bottom of the hill. And while the postman did not come to our subdivision, the produce man did, every Thursday. He would pull his truck, loaded with wonderfully fresh fruit and vegetables and eggs, into our driveway and I would come out and buy whatever we needed for the week.

The area was something of a paradise for our kids. We were delighted when two other families from the Carlisle Avenue neighborhood, with children around the same ages as ours, also bought in the area, so they all had a large and growing group of playmates. They had plenty of space to run outdoors, with an old orchard and Fort Garrison to explore. And there was wildlife to watch—foxes and deer and loads of rabbits.

In 1957, *Ladies Home Journal* did a spread on our house, my new kitchen with its innovative use of the color lilac, and our family life. This photograph of (l-r) Ilene, Nina, and Steven was taken for the article but never published.

The rustic nature of the area was brought home to us rather dramatically one of the first winters we lived in the county. It snowed twenty-six inches during a single storm, and it happened when Jerry and I were out of town. The children were being cared for in our absence by a couple we had living-in at the time.

Planes were grounded by the weather, so Jerry and I took a train to Baltimore and then a cab from the train station, but we couldn't get past Clarks Lane because Park Heights Avenue —a major thoroughfare—hadn't been plowed. We managed to make it to Jerry's parents' home, which was located on one of the last plowed streets, and stayed there for the night. In the morning, with road-clearing beginning, we borrowed my in-laws' car and drove partway up Stevenson Road. But our street had not been plowed, and Raz, who lived with us—fortunately a very large and strong man—broke a path from our house out to the main road. We abandoned the car and walked the rest of the way home. Drifts of snow, piled to five feet high by the wind, blocked our front door. The electricity was out, so we had no light and no heat, and because we had well water pumped into the house, there was no running water either. Luckily, the refrigerator was well-stocked, and we put the food in the snow to keep it cold. Of course, the children had a ball. We lit fires in all the fireplaces and camped out in front of them. We melted snow for water, and boiled it for drinking. We cooked over the fires, and we slept there under piles of blankets. One neighboring couple decided to walk to "civilization" but their young son wanted to stay and continue the adventure, so he moved in with us. We went on this way for five days until we were able to get an electrician to come out and hook up a small generator that produced just enough electricity to run the stove and a few lights.

For one neighboring family, this storm was an ominous indication of what life would be like outside the reach of city services—"What if we need an ambulance?" they asked—and they moved away as soon as they could. We enjoyed "pioneering" our subdivision, even with what proved to be regular power outages, and never regretted staying put.

Another factor that made our neighborhood attractive was its proximity to Chizuk Amuno Congregation. The synagogue on Stevenson Road had not yet been built when we moved in, but the land had been purchased and it was common knowledge that construction would begin soon. We were a fairly traditional family in terms of Jewish observance, and we liked the idea of being able to walk to *shul*. Equally important was that this would be a generally Jewish area—we did not want to live in an area where we might experience anti-Semitism. When we bought the land, we had many friends who already lived in the neighborhood around Stevenson and Old Court Roads, and we knew that our subdivision a couple miles farther up Stevenson was going to become an extension of the Jewish community.

Judaism was important in our house, and it was a joy. The kids could invite anyone they wanted to join them on Friday nights, so with our kids and their friends, my parents, Jerry's parents (who ate with us every Friday night without fail), and other guests we regularly had anywhere from sixteen to twenty-six people for *Shabbat* dinner. The conversation was always lively, and the children were always part of it. They would participate in discussions of world events, or tell stories; often, there was something the children had been thinking about and wanted to explain to the rest of us. My rule was that a child could be excused from the table for only one reason: to look up a word in a dictionary or an issue in the encyclopedia. I had both the *Encyclopedia Britannica* and the dictionary on my kitchen bookshelves, within easy reach.

On the Jewish holidays, we all went to *shul* together. I was president of the Chizuk Amuno Religious School PTA, and I worked to make the High Holiday services enjoyable for children. I felt strongly that if we didn't take care to show them the joy of the festivals, the observances would only be a burden or a bore. My parents usually stayed with us to celebrate the holidays. The children adored their grandparents, so their presence added to everyone's enjoyment. Though my father was not a traditionally religious man, he loved Jewish culture. He knew so many songs and melodies, and so many stories. He could quote from any of the texts of our tradition, and he used to somehow make them part of every conversation. The children sat at his knee and soaked it up.

Jerry and I were very involved in fund-raising for the Jewish community, for Democratic politicians, and for other charitable organizations. It was important to us that the children understand the enjoyment and satisfaction we gained from these activities, and since we hosted many events at our home, our volunteer work frequently provided a source of family excitement. Israeli generals visited us; we hosted dinners for United States Senators Henry Jackson, Abraham Ribicoff, Jacob Javits, Charles Mac Mathias, and Daniel Brewster; we entertained Vice President Hubert Humphrey. We held major events for Israel Bonds and Jewish National Fund, and for the Retinitis Pigmentosa Foundation, now known as the Foundation Fighting Blindness, for which Jerry served as founding chairman.

Our house had been designed for this kind of entertaining. We even planned the garden to accommodate a tent that would hold 150 people if necessary. And as part of all of our entertaining, we wanted our guests to know right away that this was a Jewish home. To that end, we displayed Jewish art on the walls, and Judaica that we used for holiday celebrations decorated the shelves.

Family organization became more complex as the children began to go to school. At one point, my four children were attending three different schools. Steven went to McDonogh, which was then a private military academy for boys. This came about in a rather odd way. Jerry's sister's son applied for admission to McDonogh when he was in the third grade. The McDonogh admissions officer suggested that if our nephew repeated the third grade he was more likely to be successful at McDonogh. My brother-in-law was convinced that this suggestion was motivated by anti-Semitism, but we had Jewish friends whose children attended McDonogh and Jerry just couldn't believe that was the case. Jerry decided to prove that it was not anti-Semitism by having Steven, who was entering the first grade, take the admissions test. I was not happy with the idea, because the boys at McDonogh wore heavy woolen uniforms; they drilled with toy rifles, and, as they grew older, they were given real rifles and took target practice. The school was academically challenging, which Steven needed—he had been in kindergarten for only three months when the teacher called me up to tell me what an impossible child he was, because he had already read all the stories she was reading to the class—but I wasn't certain the rigidity and the discipline that went along with the academy would be good for him.

It was August when we took Steven in for an interview with the dean of the lower school. By late summer, as a rule, private schools have concluded their recruitment for the upcoming year. We were told at the outset that there was no room on the

Our family in 1963, when we celebrated Steven's bar mitzvah.

bus for him, and at McDonogh that meant that you could not attend the school—it was their philosophy that the cohesiveness of the group began with the bus ride to and from school. I was hoping that they wouldn't find room on the bus, but Jerry had attended a military high school and didn't have the reservations I had. So Steven took the test, and the following week we received a phone call saying, "Hello there, we found a seat on the bus for your son." He had done exceptionally well, and they really wanted him as a student. We hadn't hidden the fact that we were Jewish, and they didn't deny Steven a space.

In the early years, Steven did well there. The school's academic program was strong and his teachers excellent. So we had no reason to select a different school seven years later when Sandy was ready for first grade. Steven graduated from McDonogh in 1968, but Sandy switched in the eighth grade to Milton Academy, which his brother had identified for him as a feeder school for Harvard. Sandy graduated from Milton in 1975.

Ilene and Nina went to public school through sixth grade, and then, since I was not terribly pleased with the public school, they both went to the Park School, a private nonsectarian school dedicated to progressive education. It turned out that the seventh grade was a difficult time to make the transition to a small school like Park—the friendship cliques were already set. The experience was particularly uncomfortable for Nina, so at her insistence, at the age of fifteen, she spent a year at Kfar Silver, a Zionist Organization of America school in Israel. That experience was quite an eye-opener for her. Many of the children in the program were troubled, and Nina found herself dealing with a suicidal roommate. She stayed the year, coming home a wiser, more mature young woman.

Steven went to Clark University, and then earned master's degrees in Philosophy and Economics from Columbia University. Ilene went to Elmira College for one year and then came home to attend Notre Dame, because she was engaged to a young medical student in Baltimore. She earned a master's in Speech Therapy and Deaf Education, returning later to earn a master's degree in Organizational Development. Nina went to Connecticut College, and then to the Jewish Theological Seminary, where she received a master's in Talmud and was one of the first women to be ordained as a rabbi. Sandy went to Harvard as he had hoped, then to law school.

I had very definite ideas about raising children. I believe in boundaries; I believe in expectations. I became known to the kids and their friends as "the Warden" because I did not have any difficulty saying to the girls, "This is the time that you will come in." The boys were told, "If it's after midnight, you are to call me every hour until you're home. I will be concerned, and I want to know where you are." My children seemed to appreciate their limits, and other parents respected my judgment. They often would call me to find out what I thought about this party or that activity. If I allowed my children to participate, they knew I had determined it would be supervised and safe.

I also felt it was important to regard each of my children as an individual, to help each one to be comfortable in his or her own skin. I always encouraged them to do the best they could, but never compete with one another. I worked very hard to make sure no one felt they were not as good as another and to convey the message, "Do the best that you can—whatever that best happens to be." As a result, my children have developed their intellectual capabilities to the fullest, and maintain a wide range of interests.

Even though I expected a certain discipline in their behavior, I believed strongly in free play. The children's birthday parties were a whirl of fun and games of their own choosing; they and their friends were seated only for the requisite serving of cake and ice cream. We also had a lot of fun together as a family. We always went out on Sunday evenings, often to go bowling. We visited with other families that had children, because I wanted our kids to develop friendships outside of school. Almost every Christmas vacation, we took the children on a trip. Frequently, we drove to Florida—twice including my parents in the trip, so there were eight of us in a station wagon! We also traveled overseas with our children, especially to Israel.

I tried taking them to museums and to the symphony, but they were not very interested in those kinds of activities. That is one area where my practical experience as a mother failed to live up to my theories about what was good for children. However, I was able to instill in all of them a love of reading. They always enjoyed visits to the library, and when Chizuk Amuno would hold its annual Book Month sale, each child would eagerly pick out the books that he or she wanted. I would buy them up to three books each, but they almost always wanted more and would use their own spending money to buy them.

Running the house and organizing the family were my responsibilities, a somewhat formidable charge given our large home, and energetic and distinctly individual children. People ask me how I balanced the childrearing with the weekly entertaining and my growing volunteer commitments, but looking back, it didn't seem so difficult. The key was in knowing what result I wanted to achieve—that is, to be clear about what was important to me, and what behavior and values I expected the children to live up to—and to run an orderly and disciplined household. And I had one unbreakable rule that kept my priorities clear: family always comes first.

I also had plenty of help. Around 1955, I began hiring college students to come in on weekends to help with the children. Later, during our first nine years in Baltimore County, we had staff who lived in. I hired and fired our staff, and there was a time when we seemed to have installed a revolving door. I was very exacting and was not willing to put up with employees who could not meet my standards.

Jerry was out with work or volunteer activities many evenings, but the children and I ate dinner together each night on a regular schedule. Then it was bath and bedtime, beginning with the youngest and working up to the oldest. Clothes and toys were all put away so they could be easily retrieved when wanted. I kept lists of everything that needed to be done and stuck with them religiously, so much so that the children later swore they'd never make a list of their own.

I planned my work around the needs of my family. On Mondays I took care of household errands, and on Fridays I shopped and cooked for *Shabbat* dinner. On Tuesdays, Wednesdays, and Thursdays, I was available for volunteer work. When the children were young, I worked only for organizations that met during the evenings after the babies were asleep and secure with a sitter. As they grew older, I sought out volunteer opportunities with groups that met during the day so I could be home when the kids arrived after school.

After the children were in bed, I had the house to myself for several hours. This was the time when I would bake or take care of organizational work that needed my attention. When Jerry finally came home around eleven o'clock, I would stay up with him, often until two in the morning, discussing the issues and concerns of our days. Jerry was a true night owl. Luckily, I only need a few hours of sleep each night so I could be up with him at night and still be ready to start my day with breakfast and children at six the next morning. I looked forward to those late-night hours with him; we exchanged information, shared our problems, and planned for the future. I also valued this time together as a way to maintain the health of our marriage.

Through it all, my volunteer responsibilities expanded, satisfying work made possible by peace of mind brought about by the order that reigned at home. I moved through the chairs and became Worthy Matron of Beacon Chapter in 1959, when Sandy was only two. That same year, I co-chaired, with Lou Sagner, the Israel Bonds High Holiday campaign. I was involved with the Parent-Teacher Associations and other activities at the older children's schools, and in 1960 I joined the board of the Federation of Jewish Women's Organizations of Maryland. By the mid-sixties, with our family well-launched, I was poised to engage in some unique leadership opportunities.

Above: I am sitting among the delegates at the convening session of the 1967 Constitutional Convention of Maryland, in Annapolis. This is a detail of the official photograph of the convention delegates in assembly, which was presented to all of us. Opposite page: Discussing the credit rights of women with Jane Pauley on the *Today Show*, March 23, 1977. The other guest was a vice president of Diner's Club. Reprinted with permission of Wagner International Photos, New York.

VI
Fixing a Corner of the World

I was raised in a family where volunteerism wasn't discussed: it was done. The adults I knew assumed that each of us had a responsibility to the community, however one defined it. In those days, we didn't use the phrase *tikkun olam* to describe what we did, but we were motivated by Jewish thought and Jewish law in our attempts to "repair the world," the literal meaning of the phrase. I never felt I could choose whether or not to be involved in the community—my only choice was where in the community I would work.

In many ways, I began to fulfill that responsibility when I became involved with Beacon Chapter. Granted, it was primarily a social group, but our charitable component was strong and our communal ethic vital, and it was my first formal leadership role. When I completed my term as Worthy Matron of Beacon Chapter in 1960, I was asked to join the board of the Federation of Jewish Women's Organizations of Maryland.[1] I knew nothing about this group, so I investigated and learned that, as the name suggests, it was an umbrella group of Jewish women's philanthropic, social, and political organizations. The Federation was a platform for discussion of local and national social issues affecting women, and for legislative action that would have an impact on women's lives. A second and very important part of its mission was to teach women about parliamentary procedure, and to help them develop leadership and speaking skills. I found that the group had an impressive record of leadership among women since 1916, and I happily accepted the nomination.

The board of the Federation was made up of sitting and past presidents of the member organizations. For the most part, these women had long been active in the Baltimore community—women like Irene Soboloff, Marie Hammerman, E. B. Hirsh, Hilda Blaustein, Helen Dalsheimer, and others. I, on the other hand, was as unknown to them as the organization had been to me. I was nominated by a Federation board member I did not know, someone who was a guest at a Beacon Chapter meeting while I was presiding. I was such an outsider among the Federation women that I once overheard one of the officer matriarchs say of me in a loud whisper, "Who is that? I've never seen her at the club" (meaning Baltimore's mostly German Jewish Suburban Club). In spite of that, the group wasn't stand-offish and they welcomed me. The whisperer became my warm friend.

The Maryland chapter of the Federation of Jewish Women's Organizations has played a very important role in the Jewish community. At one time, there were twelve related Federation chapters nationwide, and the national group was accorded representation at the United Nations as a nongovernmental organization.[2] Today, the Maryland chapter is the only one still active. The Federation monitors issues of social justice in general and Maryland legislation on women's issues in particular. Our representatives study bills pending before the legislature and report on their effect on women's lives. The group makes recommendations about which legislation should be supported and which should be opposed. The Federation board members then take these recommendations to the membership of their own organizations— some of which have thousands of members—powerfully multiplying the impact of this process.

When I was on the board in the 1960s, it cost $25 for an organization to join. For that fee, we held three or four educational workshops a year. We offered a small book, *Leadership Logic: A Manual of Organization Know-How*, written by the very able E. B. Hirsh and myself in 1974, explaining basic parliamentary rules and procedures such as how to establish an agenda, how to take minutes, and more. The Federation recently published the third edition of that book. We also staged an annual convention that usually dealt with a significant social issue.

At one annual convention, we joined the movement to integrate the motels and restaurants along Route 40. In 1962, no establishment on Route 40, a major thoroughfare between Baltimore and Washington, D.C., would accept an African-American patron. They literally said, "Sorry, we don't serve your kind." It was clear that individuals had no recourse to combat this discrimination: there had to be a collective will to put an end to it. Marie Hammerman—a wonderfully bright and competent woman—was president of the Federation then. She felt strongly that, as Jews, we had personal knowledge of the pain and isolation of segregation. I was in complete agreement with her, as was the rest of the group. Marie asked me to see if I could secure a speaker for our annual meeting who could discuss the ills of segregation. I contacted Pedro Sanjuan, then deputy chief of protocol in the State Department, and he agreed to speak. "We cannot preach the values of democracy if we ignore the struggle for human dignity in our own country," he told us. After his speech, our organization passed a resolution against segregation.[3]

We weren't alone. Rabbis and other Baltimore clergy were speaking out against segregation and calling for legislation to make the practice illegal. Our resolution was covered by the newspapers and garnered added publicity for the anti-discrimination effort.

At the same time, I was becoming more involved in the Women's Division of the Associated Jewish Charities & Welfare Fund. I had been supporting the Women's Division as a donor and a fund-raiser since the early days of my marriage. Back then, Baltimore women participated annually in something known as "G-Day," for Giving Day. On G-Day, as many as fifteen hundred men and women canvassed Jewish neighborhoods to solicit funds for the Associated. It was a massive undertaking.

Everyone would assemble at the Pikesville Armory, which was the only place in the area large enough to hold so many people. We were accompanied by men who had volunteered to carpool teams of

Martin K. Miller drove a team of women to canvas their assigned territory for G-Day, in 1957. It was a day of high community spirit for many years. JMM 1995.142.F22. Papers of the Associated.

women to their assigned blocks. Our drivers would drop us off on designated street corners, and we would spend the morning ringing doorbells and talking to the women who answered. It was, for many years, a day of high spirits and positive energy, but by the early 1960s, the social landscape that made the program work was changing. More people had moved to the outer suburbs, where neighborhoods were not solidly Jewish, houses were farther apart, and more ground had to be covered by our volunteers. Also, more women were driving their own cars, which meant we were less likely to find them home during the day.

In 1963, Geetze Myerberg was chairman of G-Day and I was vice chairman. We concluded our responsibilities with a strong feeling that G-Day had lost its effectiveness, and afterward we wrote a long memo to the Associated leadership explaining our thinking. An effort involving twelve hundred women and as many as three hundred men, times three hours per person, divided into the amount of money raised, we wrote, was netting too few dollars per man-hour. Many more donors could be reached in far less time via telephone, we went on, and we advocated ending G-Day. We were persuasive, because 1963 was the last G-Day the Associated ever ran. But our position was not popular with everyone, and Geetze and I became known as the women who "killed" G-Day.

In 1965, I became president of the Federation of Jewish Women's Organizations, and my two organizations collided. Back then, federations of Jewish communal organizations around the country were pushing to consolidate local Jewish organizations and eliminate duplicate services and fund-raising efforts. On the whole, it was a necessary effort with a laudable goal, one I supported. But when the Associated Jewish Charities approached the Maryland chapter of the Federation of Jewish Women's Organizations about merging with the Associated Women's Division, I turned it down.

It was my opinion, and the Federation board concurred, that the Associated and the Federation, while both serving as umbrella groups, were very different in mission and style. The Federation was primarily an educational resource and advocacy organization; the Associated, while sponsoring some educational ventures, was mainly concerned with fund-raising and the financial support of communal needs. Leadership in the Associated Women's Division usually came by way of financial gifts to the organization; in the Federation, monetary gifts had no role to play at all. Related to this, the Federation of Jewish Women's Organizations was fundamentally a democratic organization, while the Associated Women's Division was not—there, some votes would always count more than others. And in what was then perhaps the key difference between the two organizations, the Women's

Division of the Associated was an auxiliary branch of a larger organization then dominated by men, while the Federation worked to help women hone their leadership skills and gain power without competition from men. Accordingly, we in the Federation believed that there was room in Baltimore for both the Associated Women's Division and the Federation of Jewish Women's Organizations, and that women would be best served if the groups remained independent of one another. Robert Hiller, executive director of the Associated Jewish Charities, invited me to a meeting to discuss our position. When I outlined for him our vision of separate roles for the two organizations, he accepted that the Federation was declining the merger.

In 1963, I helped "kill" G-Day; in 1965, I withstood an incursion by the Associated Jewish Charities; and in 1966, I received another lesson in brokering power, when Jerry became really serious about local politics. That fall, it appeared there was a chance to elect Melvin "Mickey" Steinberg to the Maryland Senate; he would be the first Jew from Baltimore County to win that seat.[4] Jerry played an instrumental role in the campaign—using his contacts and raising money—and I was right there beside him. In an important strategic move, Jerry convinced several disparate Jewish groups to unite under one banner so that Steinberg could be elected. And in a flash of marketing creativity, Jerry also produced an innovative sample ballot to be mailed to every registered voter, with the names of our slate of candidates circled in red. From the state senator right down to the clerk of the Orphans Court, almost every circled name on that ballot was Jewish, all hoping to ride the coattails of the popular Steinberg.

With so many Jews living in Baltimore County today, the excitement of that campaign may be difficult to understand. At that time, however, Jews were not a known quantity among the old-guard leadership of the county Democratic machine. We were not considered to be partners in political endeavors. In fact, Jerry knew one fellow who amiably explained to him how Jews were becoming part of the "white race," by which he meant, becoming acceptable. In 1966, it was long past time for us to flex a little political muscle.

Our house became a second Steinberg campaign headquarters, filled with the cacophony of electoral politics—phones ringing, voices raised excitedly in incessant debates on strategy, and the chatter of perhaps a dozen volunteers who were stuffing tens of thousands of envelopes with those sample ballots. Our basement was set up for months for the campaign. Mickey and his wife, Anita, filled with contagious energy, regularly dropped in at our home office, and the noise level would jump. We were all optimistic about the outcome—we knew that Mickey was going to win the election. Of course, he did win, and later went on to become the state's lieutenant governor. As a community, we felt a sense of real triumph, having proven that Baltimore County Jews had a role to play in public service in the state.

The following year, with our political machine already revved-up, I ran in an election for delegates to the Maryland Constitutional Convention of 1967. Maryland's constitution had last been redrawn in 1867. Many laws on the books were no longer enforced, and many more had been written which were not reflected in the constitution. Rather than amending each section piece by piece, the General Assembly decided to authorize a state-wide convention to draft a new constitution.

Lorraine Weinstein and I were working on a political campaign in Jerry's and my home, 1963. Our basement looked pretty much the same just a few years later when it became Steinberg campaign headquarters.

It was Jerry's idea that I enter the crowded field of candidates from Baltimore County. This was a surprising departure from his usual reluctance to part with me for such a time-consuming project, and I have always believed that he saw my candidacy as a statement of his own political power. I, on the other hand, was dubious about the whole enterprise. I didn't know the Maryland Constitution well, so I'd have to do some studying. The convention would last several months and was to be held in the state capital, Annapolis, about an hour's drive from our house. In 1967, three of my four children needed special attention: Sandy was only ten years old, Nina was fourteen and unhappy at Park School, and Steven was working through difficulties at McDonogh. I had to ask myself, "Is this the time to do this?" I knew that I wouldn't be home with the children at least a couple of evenings during the week. I told Jerry that if my absence from the dinner table was okay with our children I'd run. We put it to a family vote, and the children returned an enthusiastic "yea."

I anticipated running independently, but, as I realized later, Jerry was not completely confident that I would win, so he joined a group called the Council of Independent Voters for an Improved Constitution (CIVIC) and negotiated for me to be part of a slate with two other Jewish candidates from Baltimore County. Jerry must have applied some political pressure to get me named to the slate, for the group subjected me to a rather hostile interview to determine whether I would be an asset to their ticket. I had the feeling that my being a woman was not a positive factor in their eyes, but in the end, they accepted me.

This time, we didn't need so much manpower to get the job done. I was one of three delegates elected to represent District 2 in Baltimore County, including one other member of the CIVIC slate. In total, 142 delegates participated in the Maryland Constitutional Convention. Nineteen were women, and I'm proud to say that I was one of them.[5]

The delegates to the Constitutional Convention operated in much the same way as the Maryland General Assembly. There were the same number of seats; we had a chairman, H. Vernon Eney, who presided over the group; we had pages and secretaries. We divided into committees, and I was appointed to the Suffrage and Elections Committee, an interesting assignment. This was a time when young people were protesting the war in Vietnam, and the age at which a citizen becomes eligible to vote (at that time, twenty-one) was a hot issue. Regardless of committee, however, all delegates participated in the formal plenary discussions that ran the gamut of social rules and norms as the group worked to reinvent the state constitution. I found myself keenly interested in those issues dealing with legal equality between the sexes. Another issue very dear to my heart was the funding of public education.

Chairman Eney asked me to play a key role during the debate on education. The question under discussion was the distribution of state tax dollars for education: should the state taxes raised for education be apportioned equally among all the counties, or should they be disbursed according to need? I was asked to take the position that state tax dollars for education should be granted according to local needs, an unequal apportionment that was a decidedly unpopular view. I did some research and found out how much money Montgomery County had in its education budget, from all sources, what Baltimore County's budget was for its system, and how much money was available to the city of Baltimore. I then argued that Baltimore City—with its significant problems and relatively low tax revenues— should receive a larger allocation than Montgomery County. Given the inequities, I argued, it was a disservice to spend the same amount of money in both locales. My side won the debate.

When I began my presentation on the issue before the assembly, I introduced myself as "just a homemaker." When I finished speaking, Congressman Carlton Sickles stood up and said, "I wish to take exception to what the delegate has just said. Mrs. Cardin is definitely not 'just a homemaker.'" That's when I realized I had passed a very important test: it didn't matter that I was a woman, and it didn't matter that I was a Jew. I was able to meet and hold my own with anyone on that floor—a very diverse group that included professors, attorneys, physicians, a university president, and well-known political leaders with divergent views on many issues. I soon found that my role in the convention was to work out compromises. I helped people to feel comfortable. When they relaxed, a meeting of minds could be reached. I was able to associate with every faction there, and I was regarded as an ally, even when I disagreed with someone's opinions.

After we drew up the new constitution in Annapolis, I traveled around Maryland to try to convince citizens to vote for it. Unfortunately, the proposed constitution was doomed the day it was signed. It was too progressive and too comprehensive, which quickly became apparent to me as I talked to people throughout the state. So I wasn't surprised that it was not approved. Yet I am pleased to report that as the years went by, much of what we included in that constitution was transformed into legislation and finally voted into law.

The defeat of the proposed constitution hurt, but my efforts to develop support for it had been good for me. For one thing, I learned to listen very carefully to those with opposing opinions. In addition, I became a public figure. While trying to explain to the public what proposals the new draft constitution offered, I was interviewed repeatedly for newspaper, radio, and television. A direct result of my role in the convention debates and this public exposure—and a recommendation from Anne Hopkins, another female delegate to the convention—was an invitation from the office of Governor Spiro T. Agnew in 1968 to join the newly revitalized Maryland Commission on the Status of Women (later, the Maryland Commission for Women). Already cognizant of the problematic legal status of women (and with a nod from Jerry, who was friendly with Agnew), I eagerly accepted the position. Later, from 1974 to 1979, I served as the commission's chairman.[6]

The commission was basically an advocacy group that lobbied state legislators to alter outdated and unfair laws and initiate new ones. It successfully pushed for higher penalties for rapists, the establishment of shelters for battered women, and fairer distribution of property in divorce settlements. Our group also championed legislation that enabled women to get credit cards without a husband's or father's signature.

This last project was extremely important to me, because I had witnessed the financial difficulties of some of the women of Beacon Chapter, and of other friends and neighbors, after they divorced or became widows. Watching these women, I began to understand the personal meaning of the statistic that the average American woman was going to outlive her mate. I saw that when this happened, women would have to function independently, and, typically, would not be prepared to do that. One particular problem for women was that very few had credit in their own names. That meant they could not qualify for a mortgage or finance the purchase of a car, circumstances that severely constrained a responsible adult lifestyle.

I was quite vocal about the issue. I even testified before Congress at one point. Then, in 1975, I had a chance to buttonhole Brenda Shelley, associate for women's accounts at Commercial Credit Corporation, the venerable Baltimore financial institution then a division of Control Data Corporation. Brenda was impressed with what I was saying about women's rights, and she asked me to meet with her boss, Robert Irvine, director of public relations, to discuss what their institution could do to encourage women to get credit. At the meeting, I suggested to them that we needed a hotline women could call for help in negotiating the credit system; we needed printed materials explaining the rights of women regarding credit and borrowing; we needed to be certain these materials were put in women's hands; and we needed a way to spread the word throughout the country. At that time, no other organization was addressing the issue from a national perspective.[7]

WOMEN'S RIGHTS TO CREDIT
Maryland Commission For Women

Commercial Credit responded to my suggestions. Sensing an opportunity to tap into a large potential market, they helped the Maryland Commission For Women publish a small booklet called *Women: Where Credit is Due*. The commission began to distribute the brochure, and soon after, we set up a toll-free hotline where women could find further answers to their questions. Then, because the credit rights of women were still not well known, Mr. Irvine asked me if I would consider going on the *Today Show* to discuss them. On the show I would be debating a representative of Diner's Club, which had refused to issue cards in women's names.

In February 1977, the producers of the *Today Show* flew me to New York, where I met with two women for about an hour and answered their

Undated (c. 1976) booklet published for the Maryland Commission for Women by Commercial Credit Corporation.

questions about credit rights, the law, what was happening in Maryland, and what was going on at the federal level. As the discussion came to a close, they said, "We'll let you know," and I suddenly realized that I had been auditioned! A month later, I was called back to do the show.

I always thought it was a very interesting episode of the *Today Show*. Jane Pauley deftly played her guests against each other. The gentleman from Diner's Club insisted that if they wanted credit cards, women would have to acquire them in their husband's names. I told him his company's policy was unconscionable and irresponsible in an age when women were working, managing their incomes, and expecting to meet men as equals in any arena. He left the show licking his wounds, and we never heard from Diner's Club again, but the following month American Express hired a woman to promote women's credit rights.

Commercial Credit was way ahead of the curve. The national platform I had suggested they develop was forming, and they asked me if I would continue speaking for them on the issue. I was on television in Boston and I traveled to Atlanta. But when they asked me to go to Denver, Jerry finally decided that even though the children were pretty much grown and on their own, this was not what he envisioned his wife doing. When he voiced his discomfort, I told Commercial Credit, "No, thank you very much."

In retrospect, I feel as though we were trying to drag Maryland out of the Dark Ages. Given present realities and the ubiquity of dual-earner couples, it seems surreal that such discriminatory practices existed, but I'm here to say that indeed they did. The Commission accomplished many of its goals, and effective legislation which protected women's rights was enacted. I count that experience as one of the three most important contributions I have made in my life towards improving the world.

Now that I was known as an activist in Maryland, I was invited to run for lieutenant governor and for the United States Senate. I was immensely flattered by the requests, but I turned them down. I discussed the offers with Jerry, but he didn't like the idea of my pursuing such visible public positions. Nor was he willing to talk about the reasons for his objection, but I understood: he never would have been comfortable being "Mr. Shoshana Cardin." I wasn't pained by Jerry's objections; I had long ago promised to respect his wishes with regard to my work, and he had been very patient and supportive. Besides, there were other important tasks at hand that were absorbing my energy.

Above: I was completing my chairmanship of CJF when I shared this dais with Vice President George H. W. Bush and Natan Sharansky in Jerusalem (on the video monitor), at the UN General Assembly in 1987. Opposite page: Here I am, in a group of past chairmen of the Council of Jewish Federations, the only woman in the room, 1988. Both photos by Robert A. Cumins. Reprinted with permission.

VII
Acharai: After Me

I n the 1960s and 1970s, I believed that organizations ought to maintain auxiliaries for women, and I still do. Special divisions within primarily male organizations afford women an opportunity to develop leadership skills and hone a distinctly female leadership style that might be crowded out in a co-ed group. I benefited from an education at an all-girls high school, and I support single-sex education in colleges. I learned a lot working in women's organizations prior to coming to the Associated Women's Division, and I continued to gain valuable experience once there.

"Killing off" G-Day could have ended my career at the Associated, but it didn't. We replaced door-to-door solicitations with a much more efficient phonathon. At first it was difficult to reproduce the excitement of G-Day in a room with a bank of telephones, but we soon learned how to get the electricity going: lots of people talking at once, the Associated president scoring a big donation as everyone listened in, and all the top community leaders working side-by-side and cheering on the rest of us. In the beginning, it was a woman's day, as G-Day had been, but soon everyone became involved. Over a period of time, we refined the conversation and provided a script so people knew exactly what to say, and the whole undertaking became very sophisticated—United Way came to study us and see how they could copy the setup. Shortly thereafter, the phonathon became as much a community tradition as G-Day had been.

With a successful phonathon in place, I was asked to chair several committees in the Women's Division, including chairing the major fund-raising campaign for two years, from 1973 through 1975. Interestingly, because I was not among the wealthier members of the community, and didn't belong to either Woodholme or Suburban country clubs, I was not permitted to chair the campaign alone. As a rule, the Women's Division did not operate with co-chairmen in the campaign position; however, I was asked if I would object to working with Louise Gomprecht, who was in that social set. We divided our responsibilities so that she planned activities for and solicited the women who were expected to give more than $3,600, while I worked with those who gave smaller gifts. We had a strong first year, but by the end of it, Louise was ready to retire and I continued on alone, permitted to solicit women whose gifts were greater than mine. After I successfully completed that responsibility, I became president of the Women's Division.

At that time, the Women's Division was branching out into the broader Jewish community and expanding its horizons. As campaign chairman I had initiated a higher category of giving, raising expectations for women. Then, as Women's

Division president, I began to introduce a series of educational programs aimed at broadening our mission beyond fund-raising. One program, on women and money, was called "Dollars and Sense," which

Making plans for the Women's Division of the Associated Jewish Charities and Welfare Fund, 1976, with (l–r) Ellen Miller, Mary Greenblatt, Ferne Walpert, Myra Schaftel, me, Naomi Levin, and Joan Askin. JMM1995.142.F17. Photo by Jerome F. Esterson.

dovetailed with my experiences at the Maryland Commission for Women. We also began training for board and leadership skills, building on what we were doing at the Federation of Jewish Women's Organizations. These skills are portable, and our women became effective board members of community organizations as well as Jewish agencies. I encouraged women not to limit their horizons to women's issues and to see themselves as major players in the general community.

I also encouraged the group to use and make reference to Hebrew text and literature when we discussed Jewish issues of interest at the time. I believe it was during my second year as president of the Women's Division that we held a city-wide education day during the holiday of *Sukkot*. We presented workshops and seminars with Rabbi Irving (Yitz) Greenberg, of the National Jewish Center for Learning and Leadership (CLAL), as the keynote speaker. That event, chaired by Grace Abramowitz, was designed to raise Jewish awareness as well as community awareness.

Grace Abramowitz was the first Orthodox woman to serve as vice chair of the Women's Division. I persuaded her to take the chair after she had originally turned me down by telling her that her visibility would help to bring the non-Orthodox community together with the Orthodox. People would be able to ask her how she did things and they would understand how similar we all are. She did a superb job, and we both felt then and still feel to this day (for we remain close friends even though she and Irving, her husband, moved to Israel many years ago), that we had initiated a rapprochement for the various segments of our community.

The mid- to late-seventies was a period of consciousness-raising for women, a time of nascent awareness that women had a role to play beyond the Women's Division. During my administration, we encouraged women to understand that they were responsible for the future of the Jewish and general community, whether local or international, so they had an obligation to speak in their own names for their own interests. The Women's Division was no longer just an auxiliary to the main organization; we were there to help define the social issues of the day. We could participate in identifying needs in the community, and we could help make decisions about communal priorities.

As my presidency of the Women's Division was coming to a close, the male leadership of the Baltimore Jewish community was beginning to recognize our significant contributions. We were still housed in the basement of the Associated Jewish Charities' building—in itself a statement about the step-child status of the Women's Division—but women were being invited to serve on the Associated board of directors. Jess Friedman had served as vice president of administration a few years earlier, and in 1977 I was offered a vice president's seat on the board.

Bob Hiller had been quietly acting as my mentor at the Associated ever since I had turned down the proposed Federation of Jewish Women's Organizations/Associated merger. Now, he and Associated President Calman "Buddy" Zamoiski approached me about taking the position of vice president of planning and budgeting. I have always imagined that I was recruited for the "Big Board," as we call it in Baltimore, not because of my Women's Division service, but as a result of the numerous community leadership positions I had held.

Bob and Buddy met with me at my home to discuss the position, and to secure Jerry's approval. Normally, a position at the vice president level on the Big Board carries with it the assumption that if the leader ably carries out the attendant responsibilities and is willing, he will eventually be considered for the presidency of the Associated. Buddy assured me at that meeting, however, that I should not consider this position as an automatic step to the presidency. The times being what they were, I understood that I was being provisionally admitted into the boardroom and could expect to be tested. I assumed the responsibility knowing that it was for two years, and there was no certainty of either a promotion or an opportunity to serve again.

Serving as vice president of planning and budgeting was a new challenge for me because although I had been responsible at the Maryland Commission for Women for a budget of somewhere around $100,000, the Associated's budget was at the time at least $20

As vice president for planning and budgeting for the Associated Jewish Charities, c. 1978. Photo by Carl D. Harris Photography. Reprinted with permission

million. I was then just completing a two-year master's degree program through Antioch College (which maintained a campus in Baltimore and offered one of the few programs in the country on management of nonprofit organizations) in organizational management, a curriculum I had helped devise with a colleague, Betsy Morrison. I registered for a course in financial management that would give me the background to understand those large figures. Bob and Buddy were impressed that I would bother to make the effort; given the increased level of responsibility I've taken on since then, I've always been extremely glad I did.

When I completed my two-year term as vice president of planning and budgeting, I became vice president of administration and then returned to the planning and budgeting position to complete someone else's term, through 1981. During that time I had a close-up view of how the needs of the community were being served by sitting on the boards of some of our constituent agencies, including the Jewish Community Center, Baltimore Hebrew College (now Baltimore Hebrew University), and the Baltimore Jewish Council. And somewhere along the line, I was asked, after all, to consider the position of president of the Associated. Once again, I consulted my husband, and when he agreed, I accepted the offer.[1]

Normally, succession to the presidency from that point would take about six years. It was traditional in Baltimore to serve a long apprenticeship of about twenty years from first steps in the Associated system to election as president, granting the system unusual stability and continuity. Considering that I fulfilled my first leadership responsibilities in 1963, it was my twenty-year anniversary with the organization when I was elected president in 1983, two years earlier than anticipated (earlier because the man in the rotation ahead of me declined the presidency).

I was the first woman elected to head the Associated, a historic, trail-blazing event, to be sure, but at the time I didn't see myself as a pioneer. I had been an activist, breaking barriers and changing the roles of women in our community for fifteen years. Nevertheless, I did not think of myself as a woman president; I simply felt that my experience and track record had proven I was up to the responsibility. I never felt that the community's expectations of me were either greater or lower than if I were a man, nor was I taken less seriously than a male president would have been.

There was only one time when I was treated differently because of my gender, and that came about when I tried to offer a toast to the King of Morocco. I led an Associated mission to Morocco, and the Casablanca Jewish community gave a reception to honor us. The mayor of Casablanca gave a toast to the king, and out of respect I also picked up my glass and prepared to rise to offer a toast. I never made it to my feet. The leader of the Jewish community, seated to one side of me, leaned over and whispered that a woman could not toast the king in public, even though the king was not in attendance. Feeling insulted, not just personally, but on behalf of all women, I turned to Alvin Katz, chairman of the campaign and the next ranking Associated officer on the trip, and said, "Alvin, would you please make the toast? Because women in this country are chattel and don't count!"

I had some interesting challenges ahead of me as I assumed the presidency. The Associated had come through a difficult period during which we had suffered a fiscal deficit. The annual campaign could no longer be counted on to provide

Touring Casablanca with an Associated mission in 1983.

contributions for local, national, or international emergencies, or even for the kind of growth our local agencies anticipated. We needed to change the way we operated the agency; we needed to change our annual campaign methods; and we needed to reactivate our endowment effort. At the urging of Louis Fox, a visionary Baltimore leader and past president of the Council of Jewish Federations (CJF), a $100 million endowment campaign had been in the planning for some years. I am proud to say that we initiated it in 1984, at the beginning of my administration, with Buddy Zamoiski as chairman and Lou Fox as honorary chairman. Nationwide, endowments were then just beginning to emerge as a powerful federation tool. Lou, known around the country as the godfather of Jewish federation endowment programs, was visiting communities all over North America to promote the idea. In 1984, the Associated endowment was worth only one million dollars, and many federations had none at all. Since then, the idea has caught on widely. Today, the United Jewish Communities reports that a total of about 12.5 billion dollars is held in endowments by the 150 federations throughout North America.[2]

It was clear to me that to lead our organization into the endowment campaign I would have to take seriously the Jewish concept of *acharai*—after me. Therefore, with Jerry's help, I made a major financial commitment to the campaign to get it off the ground. The campaign was successful, continuing well past my administration. In the years following the establishment of the endowment fund, it has contributed to the growth of the Jewish Community Centers in Park Heights and Owings Mills, the expansion of the Jewish Museum of Maryland, and new facilities at Levindale Hebrew Geriatric Center, to name just a few.

We also embarked on a program to stabilize the declining neighborhood surrounding our lower Park Heights Avenue campus, which had fallen victim to deteriorating older buildings and "white flight." The aging Jewish population that lived around our rather extensive campus—which included synagogues, Baltimore Hebrew University, the JCC, and a social services building—was not able to maintain the properties as well as it should have. We developed what we thought would be a temporary community program called Comprehensive Housing Assistance, Inc. (CHAI; also "life" in Hebrew). It has since become a full-fledged agency, ably led by Kenneth Gelula, which has served to stabilize the entire area around the Park Heights campus, as well as contributing to the ability of seniors to stay in their own homes.

Open communication and an emphasis on community accord were the hallmarks of my administration. I worked hard to reduce tensions between the member organizations and the Associated by managing in an inclusive style. I believe that I was probably among the first Associated presidents to announce publicly that I would meet with all segments of the community in an effort to seek greater unity with all area Jewish agencies, whether or not they participated in the Associated campaign. We also offered a board development program to synagogue leaders to assist in strengthening synagogue management and emphasize mutual goals.

I always sought to reinforce the Jewish foundations of our work, as I had done in Women's Division. There were times when one could attend an Associated meeting and not know that it was a group of Jews meeting to accomplish Jewish purposes. Therefore, I incorporated references to Jewish tradition and texts whenever possible. For example, if I were to give a report on the elderly, I might use the phrase, "Cast me not out in my old age," saying it first in Hebrew and then translating it into English. This effort was formally recognized in the Orthodox community when I was invited to be a speaker at the Ner Israel Rabbinical College annual banquet. Less formally, when a successor as chairman of the Associated asked me to give him a list of the ten most popular Hebrew phrases that he might use comfortably at meetings and in speeches, I thought with some satisfaction that it must have had an impact.

While I began my term of office as "president" of the Associated, I finished it as "chairman of the board." That change in title didn't matter, really; the duties and responsibilities of the office remained the same. The alteration simply reflected the times, when the professionals within the federation movement were assuming titles equivalent to those that were conferred upon their peers in other charitable institutions, where the chief professional was the president, and the chief volunteer officer was the chairman of the board.

My various positions at the Associated had long involved me in the workings of the national governing body of federations, the Council of Jewish Federations. Years back, while president of Women's Division, I raised funds throughout the country through the CJF Speakers' Bureau. I also participated in a trial cooperative project between the Women's Divisions of CJF and the Jewish community's national fund-raising organization, the United Jewish Appeal (UJA), which sent thirty women leaders to the Wharton Center in Philadelphia to learn marketing and management skills and to learn how to train others to be more effective solicitors. Later, while Associated president, I chaired the CJF Personnel Committee, and then-CJF president Morton Mandel asked me to help establish a new Human Resources Development department. HRD, as we called it, considered issues relating to professional personnel, but it also helped volunteers improve the skills they needed to help federations grow. I was invited to serve on the CJF Budget Committee at that time. I attended, as I had for some years, all of the CJF gatherings of professional and lay leaders, known as "Quarterlies" and the annual General Assembly, or GA.

Of course, CJF had long been an important resource for our work at the Associated. We called upon CJF professionals to assist us in sorting through local

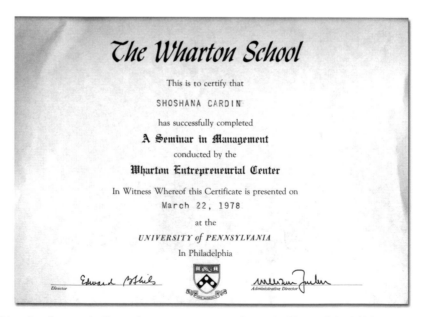

Lifelong learning opportunities such as a management seminar at the Wharton School, University of Pennsylvania, have been very helpful to me over the years. Certificate of completion, 1978.

concerns, and benefited from their knowledge of the national community. Remarkably, four CJF presidents had come from our Associated system: Louis Fox, Chuck Hoffberger, Sidney Hollander, and Irving Blum. All in all, by this time I was quite familiar with CJF.

In January 1984, just one year and three months into my term as president of the Associated, I heard from Bob Hiller, my mentor at the Associated who had by that time retired as interim executive director of CJF. He called to ask me if I would consider becoming president of the Council of Jewish Federations.

I said to him, "I don't understand. I've never been an officer of CJF, and besides, I am in the middle of my term as president of the Associated!" I was thinking, "I'm a local leader; I have no national profile. How can he imagine I'm qualified for this?" Quite frankly, I was a bit intimidated by the idea.

"Well," he explained, "I've been looking at the field of presidential candidates and I think you should be among them."

"If this is a serious offer, we can't discuss it further until you speak to Jerry. And by the way, don't tell him you've already spoken to me about it!" I was dubious about Jerry's reaction. I knew the presidency of CJF would entail an enormous amount of travel, to CJF headquarters in Manhattan, throughout North America to numerous local federations, to Israel and other Jewish communities all over the world that federations assist. Increased responsibilities and travel would mean I would not be able to accompany Jerry on his business trips, and would not be able to spend the winter months in Florida, as we had planned.

And, no small consideration, I knew the position would be expensive. Not that our donations would have to increase—we were already at our personal maximum—but all of that travel would come out of our pockets: plane tickets, hotels, meals, and cabs can add up to a staggering sum.

Bob must have been very persuasive, because after he and Jerry talked, Jerry said to me, "You should take the position if it's offered. I think this is your destiny." With this blessing, I told Bob I was in the running, and Bob passed the information to the CJF Nominating Committee. Of course, there was no guarantee that I would be selected. There were three capable and experienced men ahead of me—people who were well known to the national Jewish community—and as there had never been a woman president of CJF, I was a long shot. I pushed the offer to the back of my mind and returned to my life.

In April, the CJF Nominating Committee evidently encountered a problem with the previously identified top candidate. I was asked a little more seriously if I would consider the presidency if it were to become available. I said I would consider it but I would not leave the Associated before my term was completed. I wanted the second year to complete initiatives I had started, including the endowment fund, CHAI, and breaking ground on a building for the Maryland Jewish Historical Society (later the Jewish Museum of Maryland).

In September 1984, I led a combined UJA/Baltimore Associated mission to Czechoslovakia. I was anxious for our leadership to see for themselves the extent to which the Jews in Eastern Europe needed our assistance. It was Friday evening and we were just sitting down to dinner at the Jewish Community Center in Prague when I was informed that I had a phone call. It was CJF President Martin Citrin, telling me that the Nominating Committee had reached a decision: Would I accept the presidency of CJF?

I had known of this possibility for months, of course, but when the formal offer finally came, I was surprised at how mixed my emotions were. I was excited and moved to be asked. In many ways it was also a humbling moment: I had not aspired to this and I knew I had not been the committee's first choice, but I thought I could make a difference, so I accepted with delight and trepidation. And I remember feeling fortunate my parents were alive to share this honor. My election to lead CJF was proof of something my father had told me long ago: to make a contribution to a community what you needed most was commitment—not the ability to give away money. If you worked hard, those around you would appreciate it.

I now found myself in an odd and somewhat amusing position. I had been working all year as program chairman for the CJF General Assembly to be held that November in Toronto, Canada. Now I would be the president who would be installed at that meeting. As it turned out, the program did not go exactly as planned.

The day before the meeting began, Marty Citrin, outgoing CJF president, Carmi Schwartz, CJF executive director, and I were told that a Canadian group was threatening to disrupt our opening session. They were demanding a platform to protest CJF inaction on the plight of the Jews of Ethiopia, many of whom had fled a famine in their home region of Gondar and were then gathered in refugee villages in Sudan. At that time, there were many who were criticizing American and Israeli authorities for not intervening to save these people. A conversation was taking place in the media in which Israel was condemned for what was seen as racial discrimination, while others wrote to defend her.[3] The Canadian protest group was an ad hoc part of the effort to generate action on this terrible crisis.

We met several times with the young man who was the leader of the group, trying to convince him that a demonstration and disruption of our meeting would do nothing for our common cause. We explained that CJF was indeed concerned about the Ethiopian Jews (although we could not tell him specifically what we were doing because that would have jeopardized the international plans underway, which were secret), and told him that while we could not give him a place on the agenda of the opening session, we would be happy to schedule a separate session on this issue alone, at 10 p.m., just after the opening plenary. He rejected our suggestion, bent on disrupting our meeting—the better, in my opinion, to gain publicity for himself.

We called the police, but learned that in Toronto if someone were to be barred from entering a public hall and attempted to do so anyway, he would be arrested. We certainly didn't want this young man arrested; we didn't want to do anything that would give him the attention he was seeking.

The plenary began at 7:45 p.m. The dignitaries were all at the table on the dais, including the mayor of Toronto and a representative of the Canadian government. The hall was full, with more than two thousand people present, including my husband, my sons, Steven and Sandy, and my parents. As program chairman for the General Assembly, I was at the microphone to thank our dignitaries and introduce Marty Citrin, who was to give a summation of his term of office. True to his threat, in walked the young man with his group of fifteen or twenty people—including some crying infants—all shouting, chanting, and demanding to speak.

During the first minutes of havoc the group created, I managed to let the audience know the protesters had rejected the offer to speak at a special session to be held after the plenary, and I told the protesters that while I would not give the microphone to their leader, I would permit someone else to speak, if they wished. They consulted, but the leader would not allow anyone in the group to speak for him. That confirmed for me that he was more interested in his own fifteen minutes of fame than in the cause, and I was more determined than ever not to give in. (When we later found out that he had invited the media to our conference hoping to capitalize on the disruption—reporters were barred from the ballroom but waited outside to interview him—I was very glad I had remained firm.)

The group kept stomping through the aisles while shouting slogans, and the audience was growing restless. It could not have been comfortable to sit and watch the unfolding scene. Someone told Bob Hiller, "You should go up there and rescue her!" To which he replied, "Rescue her? Look at her—she's having the time of her life!" I don't know that I was having fun, precisely, but I held my ground and did not become visibly angry or upset.

Finally, at 8:45 p.m., Marty Citrin gave up trying to make his speech and gaveled the meeting to a close. We did hold the 10 o'clock session that night, as promised, but the young protester, who came alone, had nothing to say.

What was ironic was that this protest was taking place just one week prior to the onset of Operation Moses, the historic airlift that rescued nearly eight thousand Ethiopian Jews from the Sudan. CJF was a partner in this enterprise, having helped to negotiate key aspects of the operation, but we were committed to silence due to the sensitive international politics that surrounded the mission. However, the protest at the plenary and subsequent questions raised by delegates at the special session so disturbed Jewish Agency for Israel (JAFI) and World Zionist Organization Chairman Leon Dulzin, that he tipped his hand, strongly hinting to the special session participants that rescue was impending. Unfortunately, instead of satisfying the federation leaders who attended the meeting, Dulzin's statements caused concern that the secrecy surrounding the mission had been compromised.[4]

I served as president of the Council of Jewish Federations from 1984 until 1987. For the first five months of that term, I also served as chairman of the board of the Associated. In the history of CJF, it had never before happened that a sitting national president was at the same time a sitting local federation president; it has never happened again. I was able to carry out my duties for both positions because I had excellent professional and lay leadership teams in both places. We understood each other, we respected each other, and we were in constant communication. My successor in Baltimore was Jonathan Kolker, with whom I met frequently to share agendas and to plan for a smooth transition. He was prepared for the situation and was ready to step into the breach as needed. As it happened, my term at the Associated was shortened when it was decided to hold elections in May rather than September, to conform to the fiscal year.

As president of CJF, I was nominated to serve on the boards of the three national partners of CJF, United Jewish Appeal, United Israel Appeal, and the American Jewish Joint Distribution Committee. I also became a member of the Jewish Agency for Israel Executive, necessitating five to six trips to Israel each year. JAFI is a quasi-governmental Israeli organization that provides services or grants for rural settlement, immigration and absorption, youth education and training, urban rehabilitation, housing, and other activities. Working with JAFI broadened my views and underscored my commitment to addressing the needs of Jews in the United States, Israel, and around the globe.

A national platform is an interesting opportunity. Sometimes I was able to spearhead a new initiative. For example, we convened the first National Conference on Disabled Jews, hoping to raise sensitivity to issues important to that segment of our community. I also initiated the use of newer technologies such as teleconferencing within the United States and between Israel and the United States, and secured a grant from Mandell (Bill) Berman, who succeeded me as president of CJF, to underwrite the costs. When we held the National Conference on Disabled Jews, we planned it as a teleconference in order to enable representatives of the agencies that serve those with disabilities to join in, as specialists sharing their expertise.

At other times, I found myself dealing with familiar issues that had a new, national twist. When I began my term, campaigns were not keeping up with the rising costs of serving community needs. At our January retreat, we convened focus groups to help us understand the apparent listlessness settling over our volunteers. To my surprise, I learned that even some of our most involved volunteers didn't understand the roles and responsibilities of the CJF officers. One gentleman asked me, "Who gave you the authority to speak for the CJF?" I said, "If you voted for me, you did! That's what the president is for!" That exchange led me to realize how disconnected CJF was from the federations in the field. Local federations had lost their sense of partnership with the larger collective, so I made a commitment to visit eighty of our communities during my three-year tenure. My aim was to make the rank and file more aware of the services available to them through CJF, and to connect one federation to another as they wrestled with similar challenges.

Those visits also enabled me to hear criticisms that I could carry back to the office and begin to address. In general, the concerns I heard were institutional. It became clear to me that CJF needed to enhance its human resources department to help our corps of volunteer leaders implement the programs that were going to be coming our way.

We learned that if the individual federations felt disconnected from the whole, we needed to make a great effort to promote our concept of collective responsibility. This concept was Sidney Hollander's vision. He believed that unless we worked cooperatively—establishing an agenda that affected the totality of our community, and then sharing the work and expense of achieving it—we would not have the cohesiveness that would be needed to address the future. On a practical level, this meant that if, for example, a community suffered a devastating flood and needed an influx of volunteers and financial assistance, then all of the federations would pitch in. We held the Hollander Colloquium in 1987 to establish collective responsibility as a guiding principle of the CJF, and I promoted it at every turn, with the support of our executive, Carmi Schwartz.

We faced another challenge that had the ring of the familiar to me. A complaint I heard across the country was that CJF was not providing the services that were needed by the federations, and that the United Jewish Appeal—the community's fund-raising agent—was also ineffective. It was suggested that if the two merged, one large organization could be more efficient than two separate entities. This made some sense to me, and when UJA approached us with the idea, I said that if they would be the campaign arm of CJF—a structure parallel to that of local federations where the campaign is one facet of the whole organization—we would be interested. However, UJA wanted to subsume CJF under its organization, a proposal that was rejected by our board. Instead, our two organizations agreed to work more closely together, which worked well for a time because UJA Chairman Martin Stein and I had a productive, collegial relationship. The subject of a merger was not raised again during my administration.

We weren't always good at this business of collaboration, but I particularly remember one challenge the two organizations faced together. The San Francisco federation, under their executive director, Rabbi Brian Lurie, decided to withhold a portion of its campaign-collected funds that would normally have gone to the United Israel Appeal to be distributed in Israel through JAFI, and to use those funds to establish a program that the Jewish Agency was not ready to undertake.

This was a dangerous precedent. First of all, the Jewish Agency was under contract as the sole entity in Israel to receive UJA funds. In addition, collective responsibility suggested that all federations pool a percentage of their campaign funds to be allocated in Israel by JAFI. So when the San Francisco leadership disagreed with the priorities of the JAFI directors and attempted to head in a new direction, it threatened the foundation of the entire federation system, as well as the funds distributed to Israel.

At my suggestion, UJA and CJF issued a joint resolution condemning San Francisco's action. Then, I asked the San Francisco board to receive me so that we could discuss the downside of what they were doing. When I heard what their concerns with JAFI were, and how they proposed to use their funds, I had to concede the worthiness of their goals. They wanted to use some of their funds to resettle Soviet Jews in Israel and another portion to initiate programs for Israeli Arabs, something that was outside of JAFI's mission. So, in order to avoid dismantling the concept of collective responsibility, we negotiated a compromise in which San Francisco would direct their funds through the Jewish Agency to a foundation in Israel whose by-laws met the requirements of JAFI, but whose mission accomplished San Francisco's goals.

This was the earliest expression of what eventually became a movement within federations. Slowly, American communities began to recognize that they could raise more money by developing personal relationships between their donors and communities in Israel, eventually resulting in the formal "adoption" of Israeli communities now known as "Partnership 2000." This has proven to be a very effective concept for the Israeli communities, but for good or for ill, this bypassing of the national system has sent us sliding a little farther down that slippery slope towards a more fragmented system.

I was proud to hang the mezuzah on the doorpost of the CJF office in Israel, in 1986, even though it created some controversy at the time.

I agreed completely with Rabbi Lurie about our need to engage more fully with Israelis. During his term as president, Marty Citrin had set the stage for CJF to establish an office in Israel—with a mandate to focus on American-Israeli relations—and we opened and staffed it during my administration. Our directive to Martin Kraar, the executive, and his staff was to help members of the Knesset (Israel's parliament) and other decision-makers in Israel better understand the concept of American federations and the diversity of American Jews, and, in turn, to convey the concerns of Israelis to Americans.

I felt strongly that the opening of this office was a great step forward, and I convinced our board to hold the first CJF board of directors meeting in Jerusalem as a show of support. We invited Israelis from across the political and religious spectrum to attend the meeting, hoping that as they witnessed our procedures and discussions, they would come to better understand our concerns. This meeting, held in February 1987, was among the highlights of my administration. It sent a strong signal to the Israeli leadership that we considered ourselves partners in this enterprise called *Medinat Yisrael* (State of Israel).

Another result of the meeting was that I gained both personal credibility and institutional visibility for CJF in Israel. This turned out to be very propitious, because not long afterward we were confronted with an issue that promised to be one of the most divisive ever to arise between American Jews and the Israeli leadership.

Above: The question of a possible change in the Law of Return—and the American Jewish community's response—became an overwhelming concern to the delegates at the 1988 General Assembly in New Orleans. Here, I outline a strategy for action. Photo by Robert A. Cumins. Reprinted with permission. Opposite page: This editorial cartoon, drawn by Noah Bee in 1984, depicts the attitude of many American Jews towards the determination of the Israeli rabbinate to examine the Jewish credentials of American couples. Courtesy of the National Museum of American Jewish History.

VIII
Who is a Jew?

WHO IS A JEW?

AMERICAN JEWISH COUPLE

he issue of "Who is a Jew" seemed to explode all at once in the American consciousness. In reality, it did not develop overnight; it was discussed repeatedly by the American Jewish leadership from the time that the Knesset amended the Law of Return in 1970. And I had a lot to say about the issue.

According to the Law of Return as originally enacted in 1950, Israeli citizenship is automatically granted to any Jew, from anywhere in the world, seeking to live permanently in Israel. This principle has all the consequence that an article of the American Constitution has in the United States. And although it begs the question of just who, exactly, is considered to be a Jew, that question was not debated by the Knesset until the law was amended in 1970. While defining a Jew as anyone "born of a Jewish mother" or one who has "become converted to Judaism," the amendment also extended the same benefits of automatic Israeli citizenship to anyone who had at least one Jewish grandparent. In many ways, this "definition" of who is a Jew raised more questions than it answered.[1]

For most Israelis, one's official identity as a Jew becomes significant only occasionally, primarily at the time of marriage. However, one's status as a Jew is quite important to new immigrants to Israel, because Jews are accorded immediate citizenship and sizeable financial benefits at the time of *aliyah* (immigration). The question of how the state defines a Jew is also important to Israel's Orthodox rabbis. The Knesset's interpretation of Jewishness is far broader than the traditional legal (*halachic*) definition. According to Orthodox interpretation of the law, to be considered Jewish one's mother—not a grandparent—must be demonstrably Jewish, or one must be converted to Judaism by an Orthodox authority. Orthodox rabbis in Israel argue that in this matter, as for other questions, Israeli secular law should conform to Jewish religious law, or *halacha*.

For years, Israeli religious parties have introduced into the Knesset amendments to the Law of Return that would restrict those who would be accepted as Jews. And for years, there have been those in Diaspora Jewry—particularly in North America, where we live in a pluralistic Jewish community—who have watched with concern successive attempts to amend the Law. They have long understood that changing the Law of Return to bring it into conformity with Orthodoxy would also constitute a repudiation of all the non-Orthodox movements to which the majority of American Jews belong. Other voices in our community, however, have insisted that the question is a matter of Israeli internal politics, and world Jewry should not interfere. In the 1970s, the issue did not fully engage the American Jewish community because it didn't seem to be critical. The religious parties, who represent a minority in Israeli society, seemed unlikely to achieve the power needed to push their agenda through the Knesset.

Students demonstrated at the Knesset against proposed changes in the Law of Return, November 21, 1988. Agence France Presse photo, published in the *Jerusalem Post*.

By the early 1980s, however, the issue was picking up steam in Israel, and that meant more leaders here were paying attention. The question was, how should the American Jewish community respond? Four long and difficult deliberative sessions by the CJF leadership in 1981 culminated in a resolution passed at the 1982

General Assembly in San Francisco. There, our organization decided to take no position because, to quote from the resolution itself, "it is inappropriate for CJF to deal with religious issues in Israel." But there was a second part to the resolution that recognized that the level of concern over the issue was growing in communities throughout North America, and delegated to the president of CJF the responsibility for communicating this concern to "the appropriate bodies" in Israel.[2] This schizophrenic language reflected unresolved divisions among the federation leadership. What it meant was that no public statements could be made, no debate held in the General Assembly, and no resolutions issued from the floor of a CJF meeting, but it was all right for the president of CJF to convey private concern about the issue to Israel's prime minister or others in the Israeli government.

I disagreed with the first part of the resolution. In my opinion, Israel belongs to all Jews, and we have a responsibility to take a position on Israeli affairs (with the exception of security matters, which are the concern only of those whose lives are on the line). The position I take on this matter is that to define who is a Jew by a strict standard that recognizes only the authority of the Orthodox Israeli rabbinate is extremely divisive and dangerous to world Jewry. Since the second part of the resolution allowed me to convey my concerns, I found myself right in the center of the controversy.

Shortly after I assumed the CJF presidency in 1984, the issue took on greater urgency because of the political situation in Israel. Neither the Labor Party nor the Likud Party had won a clear majority in the July elections. Yitzhak Shamir, head of Likud, and Shimon Peres, head of Labor, agreed to a coalition government in which they took turns as prime minister. Every unaligned seat in the Knesset gained importance as the two men continued to jockey for power for their parties. The religious parties told both leaders they would support the party that agreed to amend the Law of Return. Shamir and Peres did not particularly want to change the law, but the offer to put together a governing coalition was tempting.

I saw what was going on, and I told our executive, Carmi Schwartz—who felt as I did on the issue—that it was time to invoke my responsibility to communicate our concerns about the proposed amendment to the Israeli leaders, and to report their responses to the membership. I wrote to Shamir and Peres in 1985. While we were unofficially given to understand that neither man wanted to bring the amendment to the floor, that letter, like all previous communications to Israeli leaders on the issue, went essentially unanswered while the religious parties continued to make slow headway.

At the 1986 GA in Chicago, our language became stronger. While noting that the 1982 "hands off Israel" resolution had served federations well, CJF officially supported the Jewish Agency's position "guaranteeing respect for religious pluralism in all funded programs and activities," and added, "To the extent that actions on religious issues might impact the North American Jewish community by being discriminatory, CJF opposes them....We call on all Jews everywhere to respect all streams of Judaism."[3]

In the summer of 1987, one of Israel's largest religious parties, Shas, which was spearheading the effort to change the Law of Return, tried a new strategy. Their proposed amendment, which would have denied Reform and Conservative converts and allowed only Orthodox converts to Judaism to immigrate to Israel as Jews, had been defeated in the Knesset. Now, Shas introduced a separate piece of legislation dealing with rabbinical courts, which stated that "no conversion to Judaism shall be recognized in Israel, and shall not be valid in Israel for any intent or purpose unless it has been approved by the [Rabbinical] Court." Shas leadership imposed a deadline for passage of this bill, timed so that its passage would bring them into the governing coalition, and the Knesset appeared to be seriously considering it.[4]

Finally, American Jews awoke to the notion that while the proposed law would directly impinge on only a few of the Americans who made *aliyah* to Israel, it also, in effect, invalidated the conversion of any Jew in the world who was not converted by an Orthodox religious court. Furthermore, the legislation threatened to delegitimize every non-Orthodox rabbi and, ultimately, the congregations and movements they led. That affected millions of American Jews, including the families of some very powerful supporters of federations across the country. With the deadline looming, I pulled together a committee, including representatives from national and interna-tional organizations including the American-Israel Political Action Committee (AIPAC), the Jewish Agency, UJA, CJF, United Israel Appeal (UIA) and UIA Canada, the National Jewish Community Relations Advisory Council (NJCRAC), and from federations in New York, Los Angeles, and Philadelphia, to prepare a strategy to deal with the threat. I had invited still more federation leaders and non-federated Jewish organizations, but many could not or chose not to attend. Even with the general alarm over this law, there was still some reluctance to take a public stance on Israeli politics. No one wanted to chair this committee, so I decided to assume that responsibility myself.

The strategy we developed at the meeting called for educating the Israeli public to better understand our stance, a key approach for the long-term. As American Jews began to voice outrage at the proposed amendment, their sentiments were

Martin Stein, Donald Carr, Walter Hess, Carmi Schwartz, and I signed a petition protesting the proposed change in the law, July 29, 1987. From *Ma'ariv*; Kodak photo.

widely reported in Israel. The Israeli newspaper *Yediot Ahronot* stated that Steven Hirsch, president of the Los Angeles federation, had told the Israeli consulate general that passing the amendment would severely restrict his federation's donations to Israel. The Anti-Defamation League of B'nai B'rith sent a message to Israeli leaders, saying that the government should in no way underestimate how profoundly American Jewry opposed amending the Law of Return, adding that doing so could have a deleterious impact on American efforts to aid Israel. CJF and the Jewish Agency reiterated previous statements in support of pluralism and warned of the divisiveness of the issue.[5] We decided that these messages should be repeated with every leadership mission to Israel.

In the short-term, we decided it was time for a group of lay leaders to go to Israel to lobby in person against the bill. Carmi Schwartz and I were accompanied by Marty Stein of UJA and Walter Hess and Donald Carr of UIA Canada. Bob Asher of AIPAC also offered assistance during our mission.

Prior to leaving, I received two phone calls from the prime minister's office asking us not to come, suggesting that our action could disrupt Israeli-American Jewish relations, and warning me that the responsibility would be mine since I was clearly leading the charge. I had expected this kind of pressure, and I had consulted beforehand with our leadership and received their support. So I calmly replied that we were arriving on Monday; our mission had reached the point of no return.

Although we had been told that no one would see us, we were indeed received by the coalition leaders. We met first with Shimon Peres, who would not publicly oppose the change in law; nor could I convince him to do so. I then spoke with Yitzhak Shamir, telling him what I believed with every fiber of my being—that the fates of Israel and world Jewry are inextricably bound together, and it was a grievous error in judgment to do anything that might sever that tie.

Prime Minister Shamir listened. When I was finished, he leaned forward and patted my knee. "Don't exaggerate the issue," he said. "If the Knesset passes the amendment, American Jews will learn to live with it."

"Mr. Prime Minister, not this time!" I told him, surprised by my own vehemence.

We left without the commitment we had sought, but in the end Shas withdrew the legislation after losing the support of the National Religious Party. In November 1987, Prime Minister Shamir stated publicly at the CJF General Assembly that he had formed a committee to study the issue and was seeking a negotiated solution outside the framework of the Knesset. Since committees can "study" a problem and officials can negotiate a solution for an indefinite amount of time, this development could have taken the matter off our agenda for quite some time. This is not what happened, however. One year later, when the elections of November 1, 1988, were once again inconclusive and both Likud and Labor were courting the votes of the religious parties, the "Who is a Jew" amendment was back on the table.

Everything came to a head in late November, at the GA in New Orleans, which happened to be scheduled just as another deadline was looming to form a government in Israel. Likud had thirty days to assemble a coalition, and it was evident they would recruit their allies wherever they were to be found. Suddenly, there was only one subject of conversation at the GA and that was the specter of a change in the definition of "Who is a Jew." It made no difference what topics were planned for the 360 scheduled sessions; this issue overwhelmed the delegates. The air was charged with pain, and also with dissension. Some delegates, primarily those from various Orthodox groups, said that this was an internal religious issue—the old argument. The opposite opinion was represented by a former president of CJF—a man who had given his life to Jewish causes—who stood up in the plenary session and introduced a resolution stating that if Israel were to amend the Law of Return, they should not receive another penny of philanthropy. I spoke against such an action and it failed, but his motion illustrated how high passions were running.

The GA was permeated by a sense of crisis. Grandparents realized that some of their grandchildren would not be accepted as Jewish; husbands recognized that their wives would not be part of the Jewish family. Speaking for the group, I used the word "disenfranchised"—we felt that such a change would disenfranchise many thousands in our community. Put simply, the American Jewish community felt it had been attacked, and something had to be done.

Surprisingly, we were not fully prepared to deal with all of this controversy at the GA. The issue had not been included in the conference agenda (although I had requested it be), so delegates arrived with no instruction from their federations on how to vote. A challenge to the Israeli government was not to be taken lightly: it would be an act bordering on heresy. Although we had not planned to, we convened a task force at the GA and began a round of emergency sessions. We had late-night meetings; we had early-morning meetings. We worked on strategy around the clock. The leadership moved from group to group of caucusing delegates to assure everyone that this time CJF would take strong action. Finally, on Friday morning we used a quickly restructured plenary session to permit final discussion and to outline our plan of action. A special mission was scheduled to leave on Sunday, directly from New Orleans to Israel, to explain our perspective and our concerns to Shamir and Peres one more time, in the hope of having an impact before the new government could be formed. And we would expand our efforts to state our position not just to members of the government, but to the average Israeli. CJF was going to go public in the Israeli press. Our group would be followed within a few days by a staged series of missions sent out from several communities, representing not just federations but other Jewish communal groups as well. These staggered arrivals would continue to focus media attention on the issue and keep up the pressure for several weeks.

We flew to Israel. As before, Prime Minister Shamir didn't want to meet with us, and we were not sure if we would be able to see him at all. But on Monday evening, the day before our press conference was to be held, we received word that the prime minister would give us an hour of his time. Once again, we explained to him how serious this issue had become. We told him of our strategic plan—that he could expect to hear from a series of delegations, which we named—and let him know that we had urged the Jewish Agency to use all means at its disposal (a reference to JAFI's role in distributing the considerable funds collected by UJA for Israel) to impede all attempts to divide the Jewish people. I then tried to exact a promise from the prime minister.

"Make a public statement that you will not make or break a government on this particular issue of the Law of Return and the definition of 'Who Is a Jew.' Use another issue, but not this," I begged him. "You and Minister Peres can issue the statement simultaneously—we will have people in both offices. The two of you must say that there will be no deal with any religious parties or anyone else on this issue."

He said, "Get that commitment from Peres and then let me know."

We shuttled to Peres, who, as the head of Labor, would become prime minister if Shamir failed to put together a coalition government. Perhaps we were unrealistic in hoping for a sympathetic answer from him; he was unable to make the commitment we requested, and there ended our attempt at shuttle diplomacy.

When our talks with Shamir and Peres collapsed, we had to maintain pressure elsewhere. We met with several Knesset members. We held a series of press conferences and did numerous television interviews. We even met with the two chief rabbis of Israel (one, the head of the Sephardic community; the other, leader of the Ashkenazi Jews). We asked only that they listen as we explained our position, and expected no statement of any kind from them. Then, following our agreed-upon strategy, just as we were to leave Israel, representatives of the sixteen major federations began arriving. Our delegation returned home on Wednesday, after three days in Israel, and four days later, on Sunday, I again flew to Israel to meet the second wave of delegations.

The average Israeli did not understand what all the furor was about, which is why we needed the press conferences and television interviews. Until it was pointed out to them, many Israelis did not see how their country's internal action could cause an identity crisis among Jews in the rest of the world. Peres and Shamir also did not realize the danger, in spite of their more sophisticated awareness of the American Jewish community. They were certain the storm would blow over, thinking that it was American organizations, particularly the Reform and Conservative movements, who were driving the crisis their way. But with wave after wave of delegations arriving, each one larger in number and garnering more media attention than the previous ones, they recognized that for American Jewry this issue had become a matter of passionate, personal concern.

Finally, Prime Minister Shamir told me, "I will see to it that this will not be an issue in my administration."[6] He did not promise he would not introduce the "Who is a Jew" legislation. He simply said, "It will not be an issue during my administration," and, although there were those who advised me not to, I trusted him. History has proven me right: the amendment was not then enacted, and to this day has not been enacted.

Our group met with Ashkenazi Chief Rabbi Avraham Shapiro (seated) and Sephardi Chief Rabbi Mordechai Eliahu (in robes) to explain our concerns, November 1988. Photo by Andre Brutmann. Reprinted with permission.

Life doesn't comprise only serious matters; there was one aspect of my 1988 travel marathon that I look back on with laughter. The decision to go to Jerusalem directly from the GA was intended to send a message about the severity, the magnitude, the explosiveness of the situation. That decision was made late that weekend and none of us was prepared to go. I left New Orleans on Sunday at 6:30 a.m. for Baltimore, picked up my passport and packed the appropriate clothing for Israeli weather. I then flew on to New York to meet the others. When I arrived in New York, I realized that my suitcase hadn't made it there from Baltimore. So what does a woman do, particularly when her first stop after landing is a television interview?

There were no clothing stores at Kennedy Airport. Luckily, the plane stopped in Paris on that trip. In the thirty-five minutes it took for the plane to pick up additional passengers, I rushed down the corridors of the Paris airport, found a women's clothing store, and bought the first jacket and skirt in my size I could put my hands on. I arrived in Israel with these clothes rolled up in a plastic bag, and nothing else—no cosmetics, no toiletries—literally nothing! While in Paris, I also called to tell the person who was picking us up to bring me a change of hosiery so I could feel as if I were dressed. I then spent the next seventy-two hours wearing the same outfit in which I had traveled, alternating with this one change of jacket and skirt.

Some things are just unimportant. I appeared on television and met with heads of state three days in a row, dressed in the same two outfits, without giving it more than a passing thought. One of my colleagues said, "I don't know many women who could do what you're doing. You have no time to buy, no opportunity to change, and you're not even bothered by it!" And truly, I wasn't bothered by it at all. I said, "They will have to get accustomed to how I look. The issue is far too serious to be concerned about appearance."

My luggage never caught up with me. I realized pretty quickly that our stay in Israel was not long enough to try to get it sent to me, so I didn't waste time trying to retrieve it. It just stayed in Baltimore until I returned, and I picked it up at the airport on my way home. When I left for Israel again the following Sunday, I took the suitcase with me on the plane. I had learned something: use carry-on luggage whenever possible!

Looking back, leading the American Jewish community through this difficult crisis to a satisfactory resolution was one of the most gratifying episodes of my career. Any feelings of triumph I might have had at the time were tempered, however, by terrible events at home. Jerry was in trouble and together we were struggling through an unexpected ordeal—a nightmare that would haunt him and our family for years to come.

Above: Jerry was a respected and successful businessman. Here, in his office, with partner Morton Macks pictured in the portrait hanging behind him, in the 1960s. Opposite page: Jerry on a mission to Israel, c. 1976.

IX
Heartbreak

I t should never have happened. Never. I blame my husband, not for the alleged crimes that were trotted out in court, in the newspapers, or on television. I blame Jerry for the qualities I had always loved about him, the qualities that made him a first-rate husband and father and friend: an irrepressible, boyish enthusiasm for new ideas and ventures that was undimmed by middle age; his generosity toward others with his time and money; and his willingness to lend a hand whenever anyone called requesting assistance, an almost constitutional inability to say no if he felt that someone needed him.

His desire to throw himself into a fray on behalf of others sprang from a sincerely caring nature, complete confidence in his ability to make a difference, and a constant search for approval and love. It was this quest, combined with his penchant for uncritical trust, that plunged us and our children into what has evolved into one of the ugliest rituals of American life, the destruction of an individual's reputation in the full, cruel glare of the media. If this sounds like the defensiveness of a loving wife, then so be it—I am guilty as charged. Still, I have my story to tell; I have been to places others have not been. I occupied a ringside seat at the destruction of my husband and find it difficult to feel charitable toward those I hold responsible.

Jerry's long, successful track record in development and banking had earned him a reputation as a straight shooter. In the 1940s, his father and uncles had served as lawyers for savings and loan associations, earning steady, if not spectacular fees doing title searches, handling closings, and negotiating investment contracts—the meat and potatoes work of real estate transactions. They, and everyone else who worked in real estate, knew that the way to make real money in this business was to invest in land and develop it.

Enjoying a family moment in 1963.

When Jerry became a lawyer, he joined his family law firm and took over the day-to-day real estate work. But even before we married, he was also buying land in Maryland, planning to build houses in places that were then quite rural, such as near Salisbury, on the Eastern Shore, and in Belvedere Beach in Anne Arundel County. In fact, he started with a piece of property near Annapolis that J. L., his father, had bought for back taxes early in the 1930s. J. L. had subdivided it and sold off some lots, but around the time of our marriage it was still largely unimproved. Jerry decided this was the place to build after the war. He went into partnership with a young Hopkins-educated engineer named Morton Macks, who could plan and oversee the development, and in a matter of a few short years their company, Admiral Construction, became the largest pre-fab builder in the state. J. L. had a lot of land down in Belvedere Beach, but they didn't build only there. It turned out that Jerry had a genius for picking out property that would offer a substantial return on investment, and he was able to find choice parcels around Glen Burnie and a huge tract of land out toward Reisterstown. In the early 1950s, he was developing the Reisterstown Shopping Center.

By the time he was thirty-two years old, around when we moved to Baltimore County, the foundation of Jerry's assets was laid. As Jerry expanded his operations as a developer, he founded Admiral Savings & Loan Association, later Old Court

Savings & Loan, with William Weinstein, also an attorney, and other investors. I was the first depositor—I opened an account with ten dollars. It was common at that time for a developer to found an S&L as a private company to aid in financing his projects. "Insider loans," as loans to the principals of the bank were known, were considered risky but were perfectly legal. In this way, it was possible for a careful, skillful, and lucky real estate investor to do quite well for himself and for partners or stockholders of the bank this way. Over time, Jerry became trusted as a prudent manager of the bank's money.

He also became quite knowledgeable about the S&L industry. In 1967, Governor Spiro Agnew appointed him to the board of directors of the Maryland Savings-Share Insurance Corporation (MSSIC), the state agency that oversaw the S&L industry.

Jerry became president of MSSIC in 1976. Three years later, he was part of a seventeen-member task force that recommended modernizing the state's savings and loan laws. At one point, he was a dollar-a-year consultant to the federal government on S&L policy and operations. In this capacity, he met with chief federal economic advisers in Washington, and in the 1970s the government sent him to Las Vegas, Nevada, to help bail out a failing S&L. From 1982 to 1985, he was also a director at the Harbor Bank of Maryland, one of the top-ranked, minority-owned financial institutions in the nation. His was a highly respected name in the banking field.

When it began to experience solvency problems in 1981, Old Court was in company with other thrifts throughout the country. Interest rates had soared in the late 1970s but state laws capped the rates that S&Ls could pay depositors. Customers were withdrawing their funds from the S&Ls to take advantage of higher interest money market funds and certificates of deposit offered elsewhere. At the same time, most of the long-term mortgages that S&Ls held were made years earlier, at a time when interest rates were much lower, reducing the current value of the banks' assets. Finally, high interest rates depressed the real estate market. Loans made to builders were not being repaid as houses remained unsold and apartment and office buildings unleased. In other words, lots of money was going out of the bank, and not enough was coming in.[1] Even Jerry, with all his experience in suburban Baltimore real estate, couldn't solve the cash-flow problems at Old Court in such an adverse business climate.

The Maryland Savings-Share Insurance Corporation was always reluctant to make such cash-flow problems public, for fear of creating a run on the challenged bank. Instead, they commonly sought investors willing to pump new funds into the bank. MSSIC urged Jerry to merge Old Court with First Progressive Savings and Loan, another S&L that was seeking a cash infusion. Accordingly, Jerry sold 41% of the shares of Old Court's stock—the controlling interest—to each of First Progressive's two owners, Jeffrey A. Levitt and Allan H. Pearlstein, in 1982. I felt uneasy about this move. I later found out that Pearlstein was a shoe manufacturer, without a great deal of experience in the banking business, and Levitt was downright unsavory. A lawyer and owner of inner-city rental properties, Levitt was cited for housing code violations so frequently his appearances in court became known as "Levitt days." He sold off most of his run-down buildings after a great deal of bad publicity in 1975, but in 1979, just a few years before approaching MSSIC about buying a bank, his license to practice law in Maryland was suspended when he lied to a Baltimore judge about a lawsuit filed against another property he owned.[2]

Jerry placed his confidence in MSSIC's recommendation of Levitt and Pearlstein, and didn't go through due diligence procedures that would have uncovered Levitt's record or First Progressive's questionable position. Why not? Jerry was uninterested in discussing my misgivings, so I must make some guesses about this. For one thing, he was hard at work pursuing an exciting new venture he called Medi-spa, a Canyon Ranch-like concept that turned out to be a decade ahead of its time. (He poured quite a bit of effort and money into this idea, but was ultimately stymied by a lack of funding.) Too, the glamour of the banking industry—if there ever was any glamour—had worn off, particularly given the economic climate of the early 1980s. Having retained less than twenty percent of Old Court, Jerry no longer qualified as a principal, and he felt able to relinquish the attendant responsibilities and headaches. This proved to be a tragic mistake.

Old Court had such presence in the market that the two new partners retained the name. However, as soon as Levitt became president of Old Court, he and Pearlstein shifted the nature of the bank's investments. They began investing in downtown real estate and in an oil-and-gas exploration company. They also bankrolled an enormous housing development near Orlando, Florida. The partners even paid $1 million for a corporate jet. These moves were unusual, but Jerry pushed aside my growing concern, and enjoyed his share of the jet.

The bank also raised the rate of interest it paid on deposits until it offered about two percentage points higher than any Maryland competitor. New deposits poured in and Old Court doubled in size. Unfortunately, the partners' high risk investments were not generating enough cash to pay the high interest rates offered. In the summer of 1984, MSSIC directors began sending letters warning of violations of the standards of practice, all of which the partners ignored. In February 1985, the MSSIC board voted to issue a cease and desist order to Old Court, and Jerry, who was finally paying full attention, convinced Levitt to resign as president.

This is what a "run on the bank" looks like: depositors lined up outside Old Court after it was reported the bank was in trouble, in May 1985. Photo by Lucian Perkins. © 1985, the *Washington Post*. Reprinted with permission.

He brought in a new man to run the operation and thought the bank would survive if he could just avert a run by depositors while selling off some assets in an orderly and advantageous way. I suspect he still thought it was possible to succeed right up until the time Old Court collapsed.

He never got the chance to set things right. MSSIC took over Old Court in April, the story broke in the press with all the fanfare of fireworks on the Fourth of July, and as feared, there was a run on the bank. Jeffrey Levitt was accused of using bank funds for personal gain. People clamored for their money and the state stepped in and closed the bank.

The failure of the state's largest savings and loan caused a political as well as a financial tidal wave. Fingers were pointed at the state-appointed MSSIC directors, and at everyone involved in state banking regulation all the way up the line to the governor. At the time, Jerry's cousin, Ben Cardin, was running for governor against Maryland Attorney General Stephen Sachs. Jerry was actively supporting Ben, and the Sachs campaign made some political hay by wedding the two names in the press while the attorney general's office pursued the case. The federal government offered to step in and take over the case. State officials, more concerned about gathering votes than sorting out the depositors' dilemma, rebuffed their offer. This was the final nail in Old Court's coffin. Maryland politicians refused to listen to Jerry and sold off the bank's assets—some very good investments—in a fire sale.

The regulators found deals at the bank with Jerry's name on them that Jerry knew nothing about. Not for a minute did Jerry think he was in trouble, believing his reputation as a man of integrity would carry him through. He was angry that he was not given a chance to prove the bank owned enough good assets to balance the books. I felt that Jerry was being unrealistic about his situation. I don't recall feeling frightened, but I knew what was going to happen, knew that Jerry's life, and my life, would soon be changed forever.

On Friday, July 11, 1986, a Baltimore grand jury indicted Jerry. The indictment claimed that he had stolen $385,000 from Old Court by billing for services he did not perform. The Baltimore *Sun* had a field day with the indictment, referring to Jerry as a "Baltimore County political power broker," which I suppose was true, but the implication in their reporting was that the government was going after a fat cat.[3]

Jerry appeared in court on July 17 and pleaded not guilty. He claimed that the $385,000 he'd been accused of stealing represented about one-third of fees that were owed to him under the partnership agreement made with Levitt and Pearlstein, but he immediately paid that money to the state. He continued to be optimistic that he would be vindicated.

That same month, Jeffrey Levitt was sentenced to a thirty-year prison term after pleading guilty to stealing $14.6 million from Old Court. Once Levitt entered a guilty plea, he never answered any questions, which made it nearly impossible to corroborate Jerry's claim that his name was signed to deals he'd never heard about.[4]

Jerry's trial began in Baltimore Circuit Court on Monday morning, November 3, 1986. I attended every day of the trial. At one point, I was shuttling, after court, between Baltimore and Chicago, where I was presiding over the CJF General Assembly. Jerry told me to go, saying, "If you don't continue, I will have ruined your life." The trial was terribly traumatic. Judge Edward J. Angeletti presided. He was from the opposite side of the political spectrum from Jerry, and he was quite harsh. Jerry's attorney, Aubrey M. Daniel III, a well-known lawyer with the prestigious firm of Williams and Connolly, tarnished his summation with a flawed chart of the evidence. The most effective lawyer in court was the prosecutor, who was young and aggressive.

As the trial wore on, I watched Jerry disintegrate before my eyes. His three-pack-a-day cigarette habit had caught up with him a couple years earlier, and he was suffering from advanced emphysema. During the trial, the disease progressed from an occasional need for oxygen to requiring access to a tank twenty-four hours a day. In addition, he struggled with depression and disillusionment as years-long friendships vanished into thin air when he most needed support. People who had once relied on him for favors now failed him. He received no calls, no letters, no visits.

Although I attended every day of the month-long trial and was constantly by his side, I was not called to testify for Jerry. Our lawyers determined that I did not know enough about the savings and loan business to be helpful in any way; however, if I expressed my reservations about Mr. Levitt's character on the stand, it would probably be detrimental to Jerry's cause. On December 3, after a trial during which reams of financial documents were submitted to the court, the jury deliberated for less than two hours before returning a verdict of guilty on all charges.[5] I took that as evidence not of their certitude of Jerry's guilt, but of their inability to carefully consider the complexities of the evidence. I also saw in his conviction a reflection of the public's desire to make Jerry the emblem of the national savings and loan scandal. It was at this point that I asked to say a word on Jerry's behalf, hoping, I suppose, to soften the sentence. Our lawyers permitted this, since at that point I could no longer hurt him. I told the court that Jerry was fundamentally a decent human being who had done much good for his fellow man. "Do his good deeds weigh less than a feather on the scales of justice?" I asked.

Observers in the courtroom later told me my impassioned remarks did more for Jerry than his lawyer's summation, but they weren't very effective with Judge Angeletti. On December 3, without allowing Jerry's attorneys to argue for an appeal bond, the judge sentenced Jerry to fifteen years in prison and ordered him to begin serving his sentence immediately, claiming that a doctor had told him Jerry was suicidal. Jerry was handcuffed by the sheriff's deputies and taken to a maximum-security reception center for Maryland prisons. Family members were not permitted to visit him in this facility, but because our youngest son, Sandy, was an attorney, he was allowed into the reception center. Sandy called me from there, and it was the only time I ever heard him so emotional. Sandy screamed at me on the phone, "If we don't get Dad out of here he'll die." Jerry, a person who needed assistance breathing and enjoyed people around him at all times, spent the night in solitary confinement without his oxygen.

In the morning, with his ankles chained together—as if a man in his sixties who has trouble breathing might make a dash for it—Jerry was brought before a different judge, Clifton J. Gordy. Looking for a new ruling, Jerry's lawyers had first approached two other judges who recused themselves, afraid to touch this political hot potato. Judge Gordy ruled that Judge Angeletti had made a mistake not setting bail. The prosecutor requested a $5 million bond. (Accused murderers were bailed out for $200,000 that same week—I checked at the time because I was so outraged by the amount of this bail.) The judge finally set bail at $3 million. I cleaned out my accounts and went to Jerry's father to borrow money, and a bail agency posted bond the next day. Judge Gordy also ruled that Jerry could remain free until all his appeals were exhausted, since he was not a danger to the public.

We appealed the conviction on several grounds. One was that the sentence was unusually harsh. His cousin Howard Cardin, representing him, stated in pleadings submitted to the court, "For someone of Mr. Cardin's age and health, it is tanta-mount to life imprisonment."[6] Other grounds included mistakes by his lawyer, and that two jurors turned out to have relatives with savings in Old Court, a fact the defense had been prevented from discovering by a ruling of Judge Angeletti.

By the fall of 1988, Jerry had exhausted his appeals and on Thursday, October 13, he was sent to a medium-security prison in Hagerstown, Maryland. There was little I could do for Jerry while he was in jail. I visited as frequently as allowed— weekly—and brought food once a month, also according to regulations. Fortunately, as an attorney, Sandy was allowed to see his father more often. Jerry's health was deteriorating rapidly, and we were frightened that he wouldn't survive his incarceration.

I am not ashamed to say that I tried to call in any favor I thought I was owed by my many political acquaintances in the state. Finally, Judge Angeletti initiated a release request and Governor William Donald Schaefer expedited matters to secure the release on medical grounds, partly as a favor to me. His comments, as reported in the newspapers, indicated the extent to which the deck had been stacked against Jerry: "Treat him the same as everybody else….We shouldn't keep him in jail just because he's Cardin."[7] After a little more than thirteen months in jail, Jerry was released on November 30, 1989.

The ordeal had taken its toll on all of the family. It was terribly hard to see our children's pain as they agonized over their inability to help a father they loved and who had supported them materially and emotionally through their young adulthood. Jerry came home a sick and broken man. He stayed in our home in Maryland for one week, and then we packed up and left for our apartment in Florida. He simply could not look at the people in our community who, from his perspective, had at the least let him down, and at worst, had helped to destroy him. Not even the three politicians who initiated and pursued Jerry's incarceration gained anything but notoriety from the entire episode. All either failed in their next political attempt or left politics.

The emotional devastation I felt defies description. I didn't believe Jerry belonged in a cell then, nor has the passage of time done anything to change my mind. My husband was a good man who had done so much for people during his life, and I reflect with some bitterness that he lost his good name in part through his own carelessness, but also as a result of the machinations of politicos seeking their own aggrandizement. Still, with a prayer for strength, I resolved to get through it all for the sake of my family. My work was a great distraction and consolation. I was president of the Council of Jewish Federations at that time, speaking for federations all over the country. Never was I made to feel, "You don't belong on that podium, as a leader of our people."

While Jerry's appeals ground on, my term at CJF was coming to a close, and I did not move on to another national position until his case was resolved.

Jerry's illness was quite advanced by the time he was released from prison in 1989. He was using his oxygen tank when daughter Ilene and granddaughter Ahava greeted him in front of the prison. Photo by McCardell. Courtesy of the Baltimore *Sun* Company, Inc. All rights reserved.

Jerry fretted that his difficulties would disrupt my work, so he was encouraging when I was offered the chairmanship of the National Conference on Soviet Jewry. I accepted the task at a time when I needed a project to absorb my energies; it would become a consuming passion.

Above: It was an honor to lead the 1987 march to the Capitol along with (left to right) Anatoly Sharansky, Vladimir Slepak, Elie Wiesel, me, and Jacqueline Levin of the American Jewish Congress. Robert Loup was also with us, on the right, out of the frame. Opposite page: I don't know if what I told those gathered at the Washington, D.C. rally in 1987 was inspiring, but I was very moved and inspired by the size and emotional strength of the crowd. Both photos by Robert A. Cumins. Reprinted with permission.

X
Marching for Soviet Jewry

*F*rom the beginning, my interest in the problems of Soviet Jews was personal: members of my father's family still lived there, and I was concerned about them. So I had put my hand in communal efforts to help Jews in the Soviet Union, joining a Baltimore delegation at a Washington, D.C. demonstration outside the Soviet embassy in the 1970s. The issue surfaced repeatedly during my years in Women's Division, on the Associated Board, and as president of the Council of Jewish Federations. Through the years, I worked on two dimensions of the problem: overcoming the Soviet Union's barriers to Jewish emigration and resettling those Jews who were able to come to the United States from the Soviet Union.

In the 1970s, a period when the Cold War eased a bit and Jews were given a slightly better chance to leave the country, just under 2,000 Soviet Jews arrived in Baltimore, a small percentage of the nearly 225,000 who escaped during those years.[1] The numbers were not enormous, but the Baltimore Jewish community—together with the rest of the organized American Jewish community—was unprepared for them. As a result, we helped them assimilate successfully into the fabric of

I met with "refuseniks" in the Soviet Union whenever possible. Here, in 1989, with Yuli Kosharovsky, the "father of the Refusenik Movement" who first applied for an exit visa in 1971.

American life, but we did not engage them in Jewish life. We met their basic needs for survival—housing, language skills, and jobs—but we did not give them enough time and attention to make them part of the Baltimore Jewish community. They remained on the margins, a community of their own, helping one another. They didn't seek access to Jewish resources, or perhaps we didn't invite them to join us. Then, too, many of the Americans who were attempting to help the newcomers had unrealistic expectations and became offended that recent immigrants seemed to be so materialistic—owning cars, for example. In Baltimore and across the country, we lacked the personnel to study the situation, and ended up making many wrong assumptions and establishing an unrealistic resettlement timetable. In other words, we didn't really know what our newest community members wanted and needed to re-start their lives in a new place, nor did we realize how long it would take.

In 1981, the Soviet Union once again all but closed the doors to emigration by Jews, but those of us involved in resettlement promised ourselves that we would be prepared for the next wave of immigrants should the gates ever reopen.[2] We learned to exercise patience and to extend and re-extend our invitation to the Russians to become part of the Jewish community. We learned that if we provided the right kind of framework—a congenial social setting—we would get to know one another. And with the help of those Soviet Jews already here, we began to develop programs that would assist the next wave. As vice president of planning and budgeting for the Associated in the early 1980s, it was part of my job to know how much money was needed for classes in English as a second language, how much for job training, and how much for social programs—and if those monies were being spent effectively. Together with other Baltimore leaders, I debated policy and priorities and gained insight that would prove very useful to me in future years.

In 1982, I decided to visit the Soviet Union for the first time, to see for myself what conditions for Jews were like there. My son Sandy had just graduated from college and was making an extended trip around the world. I was in Helsinki, attending an international conference for the Retinitis Pigmentosa Foundation, a research foundation for which my husband, Jerry, served as international chairman. Sandy and I decided to meet in what was then Leningrad (now St. Petersburg). Not unexpectedly, each of us was interrogated upon arrival. I was carrying a coded list of "refuseniks"—Jews whose applications for emigration had been refused by the Soviet authorities—whom I had hoped to visit. The authorities did not recognize the list for what it was, and it was not confiscated. Sandy and I were allowed to enter the country, but we were marked as travelers to be closely watched.

Those assigned to watch us were not subtle. Every time we sat down at a table in a restaurant, someone would sit down with us, even if every other table in the restaurant was empty. On one occasion, a couple seated at our table struck up a conversation with us. The man told us he was a reporter for the *Red Star*, and the woman said she was an English teacher who wanted to marry an American so she could leave the Soviet Union. Sandy and I acted as if we didn't understand a thing they were saying. Finally she mentioned that her father was in Ukraine and that he was Jewish. It was clear to us they were baiting a trap, but we refused to be caught. When we didn't respond, they got up and left us.

Being followed in this way was wearying, reducing the pleasure we might have taken in our sightseeing and our enjoyment of being together as mother and son. While our accommodations at the National Hotel were outstanding—we had a lovely suite overlooking Red Square and magnificent antiques furnished our living and dining rooms—knowing that eavesdropping was standard practice kept our conversation dull. For the whole trip, Sandy and I barely spoke with each other unless we were outside and there were no other people within ten feet of us.

Although we behaved ourselves and were the perfect tourists, we had trouble again when we left the country. Our departure appeared unusual to customs officials because we were not continuing to travel together. Sandy was going on to Amsterdam, while I was flying to Israel by way of Frankfurt. Without taking me out of the customs line, the inspectors tore apart my suitcase, opening everything including the paper covers on Band-Aids. They took away some cassette tapes I had brought with me, copied them, and returned them, and questioned me with supervisors standing by. Finally, when two women behind me began screaming, "We're going to miss our plane!" the officials got to the key question: "Are you traveling alone?"

I said, "Yes, my ticket is to Frankfurt and I'm traveling alone."

"But you have a son with you," said the supervisor, and my heart skipped a beat. I explained that Sandy was going to Amsterdam and they said, "We know."

I was now certain that even though they had not wanted to risk a diplomatic incident by detaining an American woman, they'd had no such reservations with Sandy. When I arrived at my hotel in Israel, my son called me from Amsterdam. "I thought you loved me!" he half-teased, half-accused me, implying that I'd left him to the wolves as we went our separate ways. I was relieved to know he was all right. He'd been given a shock and I had been anxious for him. Now that we'd had a taste of Soviet repression, I began to understand what conditions were like for those who wished to behave in unauthorized ways, such as worshiping according to their religion. I returned from the trip more determined than ever to get as many Jews as possible out of the USSR.

When I began my CJF presidency in 1984, Jews in the Soviet Union were being jailed for attempting to teach Hebrew, preparing a bar mitzvah, or carrying out any Jewish religious or cultural activities. The flow of those allowed to emigrate had slowed to a trickle—only 896 souls managed to leave that year.[3] Still, CJF continued to help federations in their work with existing refugee populations, and we tried to prepare for the future. We had a system for placing refugees in communities, and we allocated money from the Refugee Resettlement Fund to those communities. We also coordinated federal government grants for health benefits and English classes for the refugees. We knew that when the floodgates finally opened, the social service needs and the sums of money required for resettlement of immigrants both here and in Israel would be mind-boggling. Experts argued over just how many Jews were trapped in the Soviet Union. Estimates ranged from four hundred thousand to as many as one million, far more than the number who had already applied to leave.

It was at this low point that the movement to pressure the Soviet Union to release the Jews, led by the National Conference on Soviet Jewry (NCSJ), was shifting into higher gear. Encouraged by former refusenik Natan (Anatoly) Sharansky, whose arrest by the Soviets, harsh treatment in prison, and subsequent release had been a *cause célèbre* around which the entire movement had united, NCSJ began to plan a massive demonstration of support for Soviet Jews in Washington, D.C.

When they turned to the major national Jewish communal organizations for help, a committee was formed to plan the event, including NCSJ Chairman Morris Abram, Robert Loup, then chairman of United Jewish Appeal, and me, representing CJF.

Sharansky's idea was to attract 400,000 people to the rally, one for each Jew who had tried to leave the U.S.S.R. and been refused an exit visa. To his shock and disappointment, many communal leaders were pessimistic about our chances of bringing that number of people to a demonstration in D.C. I was among the few who thought something in the neighborhood of a quarter of a million was possible, a target others disparaged as wildly ambitious. We optimists, who included Peggy Tishman of the New York federation and UJA Chairman Bob Loup, were certain we would find an untapped emotional reserve among American Jews in support of this cause.

The rally was years in planning. Bureaucratic infighting between NCSJ and the National Jewish Community Relations Advisory Council (NJCRAC) was particularly debilitating. The relationship of these two organizations was complex and competitive, and they had been vying for years to head the American Jewish community's efforts to help Soviet Jews. This competition led to duplication of services, wasted funds, and conflicting proposals which, when presented to federations and government agencies, resulted in unnecessary debates and decision deadlock. As both were CJF-funded agencies, I found myself in the position of brokering an agreement between them, an effort that was not resolved until long after the march had taken place.[4]

Planning for the rally was also hampered at first by lack of funding and the length of time it took for a sense of excitement and anticipation to build within the community. These considerations led us to scrap the date we had originally set and instead select a date of some significance: Sunday, December 6, 1987, the day before USSR President Mikhail Gorbachev was scheduled to arrive in Washington to begin summit talks with President Ronald Reagan.

Representing UJA and CJF, Bob Loup and I traveled the country and worked the phones for months, convincing people it was crucial that they come to Washington to show their solidarity with Soviet Jewry. CJF contributed financial support so that federations around the country could mobilize their membership to attend the rally. Three accomplished professionals in organized American Jewry, Rabbi David Saperstein, David Harris, and Carmi Schwartz, planned the logistics of the march, putting together transportation and housing and drawing up the list of speakers and the agenda of the day.

Excitement built slowly but steadily. As community after community made a commitment to attend, we began to realize that this would be the largest single rally American Jewry had ever mounted, and more importantly, that the demonstration could truly be effective in changing Soviet policy. Federations around the country began chartering buses and planes, synagogues mobilized their congregants, and day schools planned to travel with students and their parents.

December 6 was a bitterly cold day, appropriately so, I thought, because it brought to mind the countless Soviet prisoners who had died in Siberia. The newspapers and U.S. Park Police estimated that approximately 200,000 demonstrators joined the rally. They came from across the country, by the bus-, train-, and plane-load, carrying banners that identified their home communities. The Washington Metro was packed with people overflowing the platforms and the subway cars.

I was with those at the head of the march, linking arms with Nobel Laureate Elie Wiesel and Morris Abram, who was walking next to Natan Sharansky. We led the group up Constitution Avenue from the Ellipse, past the IRS building and the Department of Justice to Capitol Hill, carrying placards and chanting, "Let our people go!" We sang "God Bless America" and "Hatikva," the Israeli national anthem. It was unprecedented and thoroughly exhilarating, an experience accurately described in newspaper reports as "an emotional collage of religion and politics."[5]

As we reached Capitol Hill, the marchers stopped and gathered at the foot of the Mall. Mary Travers and Peter Yarrow sang to the crowd. So did Pearl Bailey. And there must have been at least twelve speeches. Natan Sharansky spoke, as did Vice President George Bush, Senator Bob Dole, and Congressmen Jack Kemp, Jim Wright, and John Lewis. Reverend Arie Brouwer from the National Council of Churches and Bishop William Keeler from the National Conference of Catholic Bishops also made remarks, showing that this was not merely a Jewish matter, but a concern that encompassed the larger issue of religious freedom. In the midst of the American press, a Soviet TV crew covered it all.

Elie Wiesel, survivor of the Nazi concentration camps, looked out over the demonstrators and tied the past to the present, observing that if there had been such a protest in support of European Jewry in the 1940s, millions might have been saved. "Too many of us were silent then," said Wiesel. "We are not silent today."

After Morris Abram read a letter of support from President Reagan, I got up to speak. I'll never forget approaching the microphone and facing that sea of humanity in front of the Capitol. Since Chanukah was approaching, I used the meaning of the holiday in my remarks, telling the crowd that every generation, without exception, must wage its struggle with oppressors; that the Soviet Union should understand that Jews had gathered in larger numbers than ever before to rededicate themselves to that struggle for freedom. I left the podium that day absolutely convinced that Soviet Jews would soon be freed.

Although I was representing CJF that day, I had completed my term of office the month before. Earlier that year, Morris Abram had called to ask me if I would consider taking on the chairmanship of NCSJ. At the time, Jerry was enmeshed in his legal troubles. His case was on appeal, and we still had some hope that he would not have to go to jail. I told Morris that I would be very interested in accepting the challenge, but that Jerry needed my support just then. Would it be possible, I asked, to defer taking the helm of NCSJ until I knew what was going to happen to my husband? Morris stayed on until I took over in October 1988.

It had been an auspicious moment for the Jewish community to make our grand statement of solidarity, and it was an interesting time to be leading NCSJ. Gorbachev's *perestroika*—his plan to rebuild his society with a new openness (*glasnost*) and democratization—was not proceeding smoothly, but he had raised the Iron Curtain. Jewish emigration numbers that year had jumped to 8,155. Then in 1988, the year following our demonstration, Jewish emigration reached 18,965. In 1989, emigration rocketed to 71,217, a record number under Soviet rule.[6]

I do not wish to give the impression that our march on Washington was the sole reason for this turn of events. The Soviet Union was in economic disarray and Gorbachev urgently required the assistance of the United States to improve conditions at home and retain his hold on power. President Reagan and Secretary of State George Shultz detested Soviet repression, and had already demonstrated that they recognized this was the time to push for concessions at the bargaining table. Secretary of State Shultz, who was a reliable friend of American Jewry and of Israel and an effective partner on this issue, was particularly forceful in asserting that its record on human rights was the standard by which a nation asking for U.S. assistance would be judged. He was aided in playing this critical role by Assistant Secretary of State for Human Rights and Humanitarian Affairs Richard Schifter, who regularly updated the State Department's lists of refuseniks and provided them to Shultz whenever he met with Soviet officials. Schifter also provided those lists to NCSJ, so that our members could visit with refuseniks whenever possible.

An equally important, yet far less noticed factor contributing to these new freedoms for Soviet Jews was the sudden thaw in the relationship between Moscow and Jerusalem. The Soviet Union had broken off diplomatic relations with Israel in 1967 over the Six-Day War, allying themselves with the Arab countries and against the interests of the United States. And the Arabs—who were quite astute about the

As emigration restrictions eased, Jews waited in line for hours at the Dutch embassy in Moscow to apply for a visa to Israel. This picture, taken in 1990, gives just a hint of how many people were there each day. Photo by Doron Bacher. Courtesy of Beth Hatefutsoth, Photo Archive.

importance of the Soviet Jews to the long-term survival of Israel—wanted more than logistical and financial support from the Kremlin: they wanted the Soviets to hold on to their Jews. As far back as 1953, a high-ranking member of the Egyptian government remarked that the anti-Semitism then sweeping the Soviet Union and its Eastern European satellites was a threat because, like the Nazi persecution, it could increase Jewish immigration to Israel "with a concomitant resurgence of Zionist pressure against the Arabs." Between 1968 and 1971, the majority of Jews who trickled out of the U.S.S.R. came to the United States, but in 1971 the Lebanese premier told a group of visiting Soviet politicians that "every new Jew who arrives in Israel is more dangerous than a tank, cannon or fighter plane." The delegation leader replied that "the number of Soviet Jews who had expressed their wish to go to Israel was not large."[7]

The Arabs weren't fooled. An organization calling itself the Eagles of the Palestinian Revolution published a statement in a Beirut newspaper threatening that if the Kremlin didn't stop issuing exit visas to Jews, Soviet embassies and interests would be attacked throughout the Middle East. In 1973, under pressure from the White House and Congress, the Kremlin allowed more than thirty thousand Jews to leave. The Palestinians struck back: a Palestinian-led terror incident resulted in the closing of an Austrian transit camp where the émigrés were housed.[8] When Gorbachev came to power after a long period of very cold relations with the West, the Arab world again pleaded with the Kremlin not to let the Soviet Jews go. But with the end of the Cold War, the U.S.S.R. no longer needed its former allies. While we were marching, Gorbachev was hoping to find new friends.

In 1988, with Soviet-Jewish immigration to Israel and the U.S. resuming in earnest, there was more than enough work to be done—work that, for me, was a continuation of what I had begun at CJF. By now I was convinced that the largest projected emigration figures were correct. Each time we reached a conclusion about the number of people in the Soviet Union who identified as Jews, another large group would come forward and identify themselves. We were facing a rapidly changing emigration figure: it would be an exodus of hundreds of thousands of people—so many that I sometimes wondered whether the American Jewish community and Israel would be up to the task. Furthermore, after speaking with Russian ethnographer Mikhail Chlenov who told me, "I'm not leaving, and my family is not leaving, and my associates and friends are not leaving," I began to see that almost as many would remain in the Soviet Union. When Chlenov went on to say, "We are going to re-create the Jewish community throughout the Soviet Union," I foresaw the shape and scope of a different challenge that would soon be facing the American Jewish community.

Another major point of ongoing discussion—in fact, the subject of multi-agency meetings I convened in 1985 and 1986 while at CJF—was our policy regarding where Soviet Jews should go once they left the USSR. Our community had long taken the position that immigration to Israel was the fastest and surest way to rescue a threatened population and ensure their physical and cultural survival. However, not all Soviet Jews wanted to go to Israel, and many who already had family in the United States urgently wanted to be reunited with their loved ones.

In an immigration situation complicated by global politics, this kind of personal choice initially was not an option. Strained diplomatic relations between the USSR and the United States meant that all of the more than 8,000 Jews who left the Soviet Union in 1987 did so with visas for Israel. Lack of diplomatic ties between the Soviet Union and Israel also meant that the immigrants could not fly there directly. When the immigrants disembarked at transit points in Vienna or in Ladispoli, Italy, many would then attempt to alter their destination to the United States. In 1987, 4,500 Soviet Jews found their way here in this manner. They were called "dropouts" because they left on Israeli visas (supplied through the Dutch embassy), but dropped out of the *aliyah* process to come to the United States.[9] As the number of Jews leaving the Soviet Union grew exponentially, the number of dropouts applying for United States visas while in Europe soon outstripped the ability of the U.S. Immigration Service to approve their refugee status and process their applications. Still, people continued to drop out, demonstrating their determination to stay in Europe until they could acquire sought-after American visas. The number of dropouts in Ladispoli grew to huge proportions.

Whether these new immigrants should settle in Israel or America was a debate that deeply divided the American Jewish community and its leading philanthropic institutions. On one side of the question were those who maintained that the Soviet Jews should go to Israel. Israel had clandestinely nurtured and supported refuseniks since 1967. After many years, Russian Jews were getting out of the Soviet Union because Israel invited them, and Israel needed and expected to benefit from these highly skilled, highly educated people. Now that they had their freedom, was it fair that they should come to America on Jewish community-raised money and Israeli visas? Morris Abram and I were of the opinion that the emigrants should honor their Israeli visas. An additional consideration, in my opinion, was that the Russians might become assimilated Americans and cease to identify as Jews if they came here, but in Israel they would be returned to the Jewish people.

The other side, represented by the Hebrew Immigrant Aid Society (HIAS) and others, also argued a valid point: the Soviet Jews themselves should decide in which country they wanted to live. After all, how could Americans rescue people from a

The Jewish community of Moscow enjoyed a rebirth of cultural activities in 1989, with the opening of the Solomon Mikhoels International Cultural Center, named for the last director of the Moscow State Jewish Theater. Naomi Liebler, Sara Frankel (a member of Israel's Prime Minister's Liason Bureau for Soviet Jewry), and I attended the opening of the Center's first theater production, December 1989.

American leaders often greeted the new *olim* (immigrants) as they arrived in Israel. I am on the left, applauding the arrivals, February 1990.

totalitarian society and then proceed to make such an elemental choice for them? It was not only hypocritical, that side asserted, it was profoundly un-American.

Regardless of my personal opinion, it was necessary to work out a compromise position for NCSJ, given the divisions among us. First and foremost, we supported the idea that all who wished to should be allowed to leave the Soviet Union. Once free, we felt they should honor the commitment they made when they accepted the Israeli visas. However, we also believed strongly in family reunification and, with CJF at our side, we supported both philosophically and financially the refugees who could demonstrate family claims. In addition, we committed to helping those who decided to remain in the USSR to rebuild the Jewish community there.

While the debate raged on, the costs to the American Jewish community tripled. The average dropout's stay in Europe stretched to 100 days; maintaining the entire group was costing Jewish philanthropies nearly $80,000 a day.[10] Pressure was also being exerted by the rather primitive accommodations that were available in Ladispoli, originally meant to be temporary and now overloaded and rapidly deteriorating. There seemed to be no solution to this growing logjam of refugees, and then, in the summer of 1989, Max M. Fisher called a meeting.

Max had held nearly every notable position in organized American Jewish life, but at that moment he was not representing a particular organization; he was simply a concerned communal leader with connections at the highest levels in the

Operation Exodus was a record-breaking fund-raising effort in which the American Jewish community kept our promise to the Jews of the Soviet Union. Photo by Robert A. Cumins. Reprinted with permission.

Republican administration. As a leader, Max was widely known as a consensus builder, but consensus was not what he had in mind. It had become obvious that American Jewry was emotionally incapable of reaching an agreement on where the Soviet Jews should go to live. Perhaps, Max suggested, a solution could be worked out with the United States government in the form of an immigration policy decision. If the U.S. would accept and process a much greater number of refugees— enough to take care of those with legitimate claims to family reunification—that would unclog the transit system.

Max's meeting was small, attended only by myself, representing NCSJ, CJF President Mandell (Bill) L. Berman, Mark Talisman, director of CJF's Washington Action Office, and a group of officials from the State Department, including Deputy Secretary of State Lawrence Eagleburger, Undersecretary of State Ivan Sellin, Dennis Ross, an assistant secretary, and Priscilla Clapp from the Office of Policy Planning. To avoid the appearance that we were a clique of leaders imposing a solution to this dilemma on our community (which, of course, was exactly what we were doing), we kept the meeting a secret and dubbed ourselves the "No Name Committee." It was years before anyone spoke about the No Name Committee, and in the end, the silence was broken by the initiator, Max Fisher.[11]

Negotiations were arduous. We didn't come to an agreement at first, and so we met a second time. When we began, the government wanted to reduce the number of Russian refugees allowed each year; finally, they suggested raising the number to 25,000 but we held out for a much higher figure. We ended by agreeing that the United States would accept 40,000 per year, a number we thought was fair and equitable, as a percentage of all those who were going to emigrate. Furthermore, we felt we could commit the Jewish community to paying a share of the costs for resettling that number of people, guaranteeing the immigrants would not become wards of the state. The deal was sealed.

This agreement made it possible for us to unclog the pipeline, but it was a temporary fix to the back-up at the European transit centers. We needed a more permanent arrangement, so we asked the State Department to convince the Kremlin to permit Soviet Jews to apply for exit visas either to America or Israel while they were in the Soviet Union. Then, these new immigrants would ideally leave Moscow on direct flights—and with the correct visas—to the United States or to Israel. Since the United States would be limiting the number of immigrants from the USSR to 40,000 per year, once those spaces were filled, those Jews wishing to leave would either have to wait another year in the Soviet Union or go to Israel.

The option to validate Israeli visas and stop the "dropouts" became public knowledge when Abe Foxman, executive director of the Anti-Defamation League (ADL), invited me to address his board on the subject. After my presentation, the ADL board passed a resolution to promote the integrity of Israel's visa and the two-destination option, becoming the first national organization to take that position. I was then very optimistic that the rest of the community would come along.

Israel and Moscow agreed to exchange consulates in 1990, and a year after that, direct flights between the countries commenced.[12] Emigration soared to almost 200,000 in each of those years, and U.S. immigration restrictions being what they were, the large majority of Soviet Jews chose to fly to Tel Aviv. The debate over freedom of choice that had divided American Jewry was no longer relevant, and while some of the Soviet Jews grumbled about not being able to come to the States, they still left the USSR at an astounding rate—over a half a million during the next five years.[13]

Soon the American Jewish community was making good on our promise to pay for the resettlement. Our first attempt, the "Passage to Freedom Special Campaign," was kicked off with a "Passage Seder" in April 1989. I threw myself and the resources of NCSJ into the project, along with Bill Berman of CJF and a host of other agency leaders, but we fell short of our goal of $75 million. "Operation Exodus," spearheaded by UJA Chairman Marvin Lender, picked up where "Passage to Freedom" left off. It was launched in 1990 with the goal of raising $420 million for transportation, absorption in Israel and the United States, and advocacy in the Soviet Union.[14] We soon raised this goal to an unprecedented $1 billion as estimates of the number of Soviet Jews who would emigrate kept rising. All over America, Jews came forward with more than money, welcoming refugees into their own communities. Collective responsibility was reinforced in spirit and practice as cities and towns with fewer refugees to resettle assisted those who had accepted greater numbers.

The American Jewish community could be proud. We had faced down Soviet oppression and had succeeded in rescuing an endangered Jewish community of historic size. We would soon learn, however, that rescue brought with it new challenges and new costs.

George P. Shultz and the American Jewish Community

Sometimes a single individual, in the right place at the right time, can change the world. Secretary of State George P. Shultz, in the administration of President Ronald Reagan, did just that as our vital ally in the campaign to free the Jews of the Soviet Union. He had a deep personal understanding of the repression under which the Soviet Jews lived, and he found many opportunities to put their case before the Kremlin. He urged Reagan to remain tough in enforcing the Jackson-Vanik amendment's prescribed trade restrictions until the Jews were allowed to emigrate. He also directed his undersecretaries to continually press the point. And, in a highly symbolic and ultimately influential move, he hosted a Passover seder for refuseniks at the United States embassy in Moscow on April 13, 1987.

After Secretary Shultz completed his Cabinet appointment, the leadership of the Jewish community decided to convey our gratitude to him at a dinner during the CJF General Assembly in his hometown of San

George Shultz accepted a well-deserved award from the Council of Jewish Federations in 1990. Photo by Robert A. Cumins. Reprinted with permission.

Francisco, November 17, 1990. To commemorate the 1987 seder, we presented him with a seder plate, tucked under his arm in this photograph. Afterwards, in a heartfelt declaration, Secretary Shultz expressed his sense of kinship with the Soviet Jewry movement and his satisfaction at what, by that time, was a clearly successful outcome, telling us, "Fellows, I miss you!"

Above: Gas masks were standard issue for our 1991 mission to Israel at the outbreak of the Gulf War. Photo by Robert A. Cumins. Reprinted with permission. Opposite page: The Conference of Presidents of Major American Jewish Organizations met regularly with President George H. W. Bush during my tenure as chairman. This photo was taken at the White House in 1990. George Bush Presidential Library. Reprinted with permission.

XI
Guaranteeing Turmoil

*I*n October 1990, I became the first woman to be elected chairman of the Conference of Presidents of Major American Jewish Organizations. I faced some extraordinary challenges during my term, and I needed to draw from every resource at my disposal to deal with them. Luckily for me, my long association with the Soviet Jewry movement, my decades-long experience working with local and national officials and politicians, and my bone-deep conviction about the centrality of Israel to Jews combined to provide the perspectives and skills I needed to cope with breaking events.

As the name implies, the Conference of Presidents draws its members from the key leadership of national American Jewish organizations. At the start of my term on January 1, 1991, forty-eight communal leaders constituted this important group. The Conference of Presidents (also referred to as the Presidents Conference) was founded in 1956, during the Eisenhower administration. A member of the State Department, exhausted from his frequent meetings with a variety of American Jewish leaders expressing similar views and objections to U.S. foreign policy, requested that these representatives visit the White House or State Department as a single group.[1] Over time the Conference of Presidents evolved into an attempt—often effective, sometimes not—for a diverse and opinionated Jewish community to speak to the administration with a more unified voice regarding issues that specifically affected world Jewry.

Note that I said "administration"—the executive branch of the government, including the president and his cabinet secretaries—not Congress. The work of lobbying Congress is normally left to the advocacy arm of the organized Jewish community, as exemplified by the American Israel Public Affairs Committee (AIPAC). I underscore the difference here between the Presidents Conference and AIPAC, for I believe confusion on this point helped to feed the disagreement that erupted between the George H. W. Bush administration and the American Jewish community in 1991.

Once again, my selection as chairman of the Conference—which comes by a vote of the membership—was an unlikely circumstance. It might have been more likely had CJF been a member of the Presidents Conference during my tenure, but CJF had declined to join. Although I had not been a member of the Conference, I was well known on the national and international Jewish communal scene. I had been in the White House during the Reagan administration, I had traveled to the Soviet Union and Eastern Europe many times, and I had been practically commuting to Israel. My reputation for dealing with heads of state was by that time established— I had a track record. However, the chairmanship had been held as recently as 1988 by Morris Abram when he was president of the National Conference on Soviet Jewry, as I then was. The selection of two leaders from the same organization in such close succession to one another seemed unlikely because the Conference deliberately sought to spread the power and the responsibility of leadership across its membership.

My role in the "Who is a Jew" campaign in Israel also worked against my selection. When I was interviewed for the Presidents Conference chairmanship, the first question I was asked by the Orthodox representatives on the nominating committee was whether I would introduce the issue of "Who Is a Jew" again. I answered that I didn't think it was relevant in that political climate. As everyone knew, when I was president of CJF I had taken a public position on that issue; if the Conference of Presidents deemed it best to take no position, I would abide by that policy during my chairmanship. I recognized this was an important condition for them. The Conference is a much more diverse group than CJF, including the full spectrum of the American Jewish religious movements. Given their widely differing perspectives, it would not be possible for members of the group to come to a consensus on such an issue. Then too, I was certain that if amendments to the

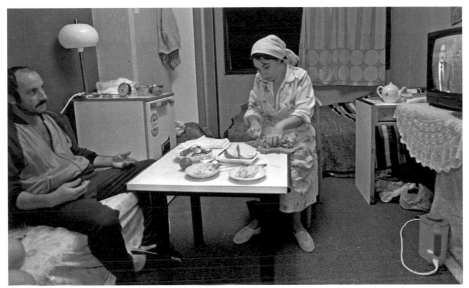

Soviet Jews Yusseff and Soya Pinhasow in temporary living quarters in Jerusalem assigned to new refugees, September 1991. Associated Press photo. Reprinted with permission.

Law of Return were once again proposed, CJF would persist in leading the fight against them.

What probably weighed most in my favor was that in 1990 we had just experienced the highest-ever rate of Soviet Jewish emigration, and the eyes of the world Jewish community were focused on this effort, one in which I had already played an integral part. Because issues involving Soviet Jewry were pending, my selection could be viewed as appropriate. As events unfolded, it was indeed the knowledge I had of the issues facing Soviet Jewish immigrants that led to my stance in one of the biggest political fights of my career.

In 1990, just before I assumed the Presidents Conference chair, Israel was suffering through the social and economic dislocation of absorbing the massive influx of Soviet Jews. One of the major hurdles to effective absorption was a housing shortage that could only be addressed with additional economic aid. The United States had recognized that fact the year before by increasing its refugee resettlement grant to Israel from $25 million to $80 million. Then, in October 1990, after long and complicated discussions between Israeli Foreign Minister David Levy and Secretary of State James A. Baker III, it appeared that the two men had agreed to a measure that would provide some temporary relief to Israel: the United States would grant Israel $400 million in loan guarantees and Israel would use the guarantees for additional borrowing at advantageous interest rates to build new houses. That initial agreement on loan guarantees with the State Department lasted a matter of days. It fell apart because Israel would not accept the American condition for the guarantee, which was that the borrowed funds should not be spent to build housing in the West Bank.[2]

These negotiations were hardly in the foreground of the world's field of attention. In August 1990, Iraq had invaded Kuwait and the threat of war dramatically overshadowed the question of the loan guarantees. By the start of 1991, it was clear that Saddam Hussein would have been content to trade insults with the White House indefinitely, but his troops were not going to withdraw from Kuwait without a fight. The United States, seeing an opportunity to spread its influence in the Middle East, sought to assemble a coalition of Arab countries to oppose Iraq. A key element of this plan was to keep Israel out of the fighting even if Iraq attacked her, so as not to alienate the Arab members of the emerging coalition.

The Israeli government, headed by the conservative Yitzhak Shamir, was understandably reluctant to go along with the idea. Even though America promised to protect Israel with U.S.-operated batteries of Patriot missiles, it would be the first time in their history that Israelis wouldn't defend themselves. Dependence on a foreign power for protection is an unusual circumstance for any nation. In Israel, which was founded in large measure to counteract Diaspora Jewry's inability to protect itself, the decision to go along with the American request was charged with emotion. However, Shamir agreed, and Israelis prepared to sit out this war with gas masks in sealed rooms.

On the night of January 17, 1991, a large gathering of volunteer and professional leaders of the American Jewish community was having dinner at the New York City apartment of Uri Savir, the Israeli consul-general. It was a social occasion, but many conversations in the room were about the escalating situation in the Persian Gulf. Suddenly, we all became acutely aware of a news broadcast on the television somewhere in the room: American fighter jets had just led a devastating air strike against the Iraqi positions in Kuwait. The Conference of Presidents had been among the first groups to support President Bush's promise to oppose Iraq militarily, and now it was time for us to show support for Israel. The dinner lasted until after midnight, and by the time it ended we had planned a mission to Israel. A group of about thirty leaders and their spouses departed shortly thereafter, on January 26.

During the six weeks that it took for the U.S.-led coalition to defeat Saddam Hussein's forces and liberate Kuwait, I visited Israel three times. Iraq launched forty Scud missile attacks against Israeli civilians during the war, and I became quite adept at donning a gas mask and rushing to the designated safe room. I got a first-hand look at the destructive power of a Scud in Tel Aviv. I also had the opportunity to visit one of the American-staffed Patriot missile sites, where the soldiers were friendly but the much-heralded Patriots proved ineffective when it came to blowing the Scuds out of the sky. Still, the Israeli government complied with the Bush administration's request not to retaliate against Iraq.

After the Gulf War, the Bush administration went seeking what has long been considered the greatest accomplishment the president of the United States could add to his record—a solution that would bring about a lasting peace in the Middle East. While I applauded the goal, I was concerned. Past experience had taught me that when an American administration in pursuit of this elusive objective was confronted with recalcitrant Arab leaders, it would try to force unacceptable concessions on Israel—which would lead to a clash between the White House and American Jewry.

In a speech on March 6, 1991, President Bush declared his intentions: "In the conflict just concluded, Israel and many of the Arab States have for the first time found themselves confronting the same aggressor. By now, it should be plain to all parties that peacemaking in the Middle East requires compromise....We must do all that we can to close the gap between Israel and the Arab States—and between Israelis and Palestinians.... A comprehensive peace must...provide for Israel's security and recognition and at the same time for legitimate Palestinian political rights....The time has come to put an end to Arab-Israeli conflict."[3] Soon, the Bush administration began talking about a peace conference with face-to-face meetings between Israeli and Arab heads of state, and a group representing the Palestinians.

By early summer, though, Arab leaders, including nominees to the Palestinian delegation, claimed that they would not attend the peace conference unless Israel stopped building settlements in the West Bank. The Bush administration asked Israeli Prime Minister Shamir if he would consider freezing the settlement program, and Shamir refused. The Arabs and Palestinians then changed their position, saying that they would, in fact, attend without the freeze.[4] Unfortunately, the Americans could not then reverse their position on settlements without losing the appearance of neutrality. Besides, the administration knew the question of settlements would certainly have to be resolved if progress were to be made once the conference got underway.

In the midst of these negotiations, Israel renewed its request for American loan guarantees, but this time on a much larger scale. The Israelis now hoped to secure $10 billion in U.S. guarantees for the money that they planned and needed to borrow over the next five years in order to resettle the Soviet Jews who were flooding into the country. A good deal of this money would be spent to build housing for the refugees, some of it in cities in Israel, but much would also be spent in building homes, roads, schools, and other infrastructure located in new towns springing up in disputed territories.

I thought Israel was entitled to the additional help. First of all, the need for immediate assistance on humanitarian grounds was enormous given the startling jump in population, and those needs increased every time a refugee stepped off a plane. Moreover, the Shamir government had taken a major political risk by not retaliating against the Iraqi Scud attacks. Prime Minister Shamir had not restrained the Israeli military because of his government's strategic calculations, or by popular demand of the Israeli electorate—quite the opposite, since the customary course of action from the moment the state was founded has been to let no attack go unanswered. The

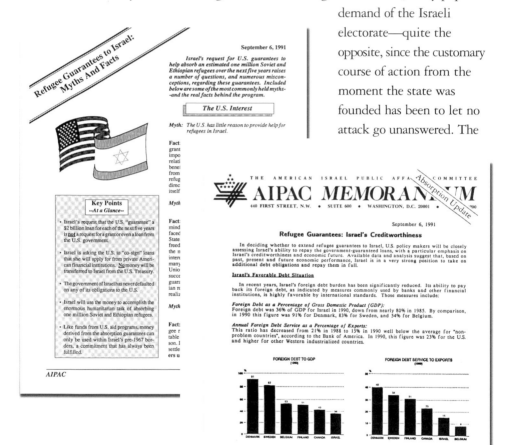

AIPAC pamphlets explain the facts concerning the loan guarantees to Israel, September 1991.

Israelis had not responded to the Scuds for only one reason: President Bush had asked them to hold back. Wasn't there supposed to be some *quid pro quo* for Israel? Apparently not in the minds of President Bush and Secretary of State Baker.

Some months earlier, when the first agreement on loan guarantees failed, it became evident to me and other members of the Presidents Conference that the average American was naïve and misinformed about the guarantees, believing that U.S. taxpayers were being asked to fork over $10 billion to Israel. In truth, what Israel wanted was for the United States to, in effect, co-sign their loans, since banks offer lower interest rates and longer repayment plans for loans guaranteed by the U.S. government. A percentage of the money would have to be set aside—reserved, not spent—and those funds would be drawn from the foreign aid budget. Israel would pay the millions of dollars of administrative fees. But since the Israelis had never defaulted on a loan, the possibility that the U.S. Treasury would be on the hook for any of the $10 billion was remote. So in the spring of 1991, in an effort to get this point across, the Presidents Conference convened a strategic-planning committee to devise a campaign to educate Americans on the subject of loan guarantees.[5] With the help of the AIPAC research staff, we wrote and printed pamphlets in which we dubbed them "Refugee Guarantees" to emphasize their purpose as relief for refugees to Israel. These materials also included charts and graphs detailing Israel's creditworthiness, aimed at reassuring the public that the guarantees would not cost the taxpayers anything. The pamphlets and accompanying press releases also projected benefits to U.S. companies as the Israelis increased purchases of building supplies and other materials in order to carry out their large-scale projects.[6] By June, we were releasing a new document for national distribution each week.

As negotiations for a peace conference continued, opponents of the loan guarantees became more vocal. As expected, they seized on the fact that Israel, along with Egypt, received the largest sum of all U.S. foreign aid grants. Although this fact was irrelevant to the issue itself (since the requested United States loan guarantees did not entail sending the Israelis more money), this objection never failed to disturb me because it obscured the truth about Israel's foreign aid assistance. In 1990, the United States granted Israel $3 billion in aid. However, most of this aid was for defense— $1.8 billion for the purchase of weapons systems, at least 75 percent of which are manufactured by U.S. companies and thus directly benefit American workers. The lion's share of the remaining $1.2 billion was designated by Israel for the repayment of its military debt to the United States, leaving a small percentage to be used for direct aid. In my opinion, it was an excellent deal for American taxpayers.[7]

Of course, the real objection was that President Bush and Secretary of State Baker were worried that Israel's plan to spend $560 million on new West Bank settlements—a plan that would be facilitated by the massive loans Israel sought—would undermine their October peace conference initiative. The State Department had figures showing that construction had jumped from 200 to 750 housing starts a month, and this increase had come on the heels of millions borrowed on the world market. What would happen when the Israelis received $10 billion in low-cost loans?[28]

As we pressed on with our plans for a national campaign to educate Americans on loan guarantees, we scheduled a large meeting to be held at the Mayflower Hotel in Washington, D.C., on September 12. We chose a September date because we fervently hoped to get the set-asides for the loans incorporated into the fiscal year that would begin in October, thus avoiding a full year's delay. The last thing we wanted was to further politicize humanitarian aid; unfortunately, our schedule clashed with the Bush administration's.

We expected about three hundred people to attend our meeting where, once again, we would explain our talking points on the guarantees. The plan was that after receiving their instructions, the attendees would leave the Mayflower Hotel and make visits to members of Congress to spread our message: Israel was being inundated with refugees, many of whom were suffering from poverty and lack of housing, schooling, and social programs, because the country lacked the money to absorb them. How could America, with her honorable tradition of compassion, refuse to cosign a note that would enable the Israeli government to care for her most vulnerable citizens?

It wasn't a moral issue solely for Jews. A number of Christian leaders agreed with our position and joined us in Washington: Sister Marjorie Boyle, of the Sisters of Our Lady of Sion; Rev. Dr. Christopher Leighton, chairman of the Religion Commission of the American Center for International Leadership; Bishop John Burt, president of the National Christian Leadership Conference for Israel; and two other notable members of that organization, the Rev. Dr. William H. Harter and the Rev. Dr. Robert Everett.[9]

Meanwhile, since it now appeared quite likely that the Bush administration would delay the guarantees, I decided the Israeli government needed to be convinced the White House wasn't just posturing. In the last week of August, I flew to Israel and met with Prime Minister Shamir at his office in Jerusalem. I explained to Shamir that he should in no way consider the loan guarantees a done deal and suggested that it would be wise not to include those monies secured by the guarantees in his budget. With this in mind, I urged him to consider drawing

Secretary of State James Baker makes a point to Prime Minister Yitzhak Shamir at a news conference in Jerusalem, September 1991. Baker was very unhappy that the Israelis had pressed their request for the loan guarantees against his express request that they hold off. Associated Press photo by Jerome Daley. Reprinted with permission.

up some contingency plans for financing the absorption with Israel's currently available resources. Our meeting was cordial, but the prime minister was famously stubborn, and I didn't convince him to hold off on the Israeli request.

After I returned to the States, a group of us, including Tom Dine from AIPAC, Malcolm Hoenlein, executive director of the Presidents Conference, and Abe Foxman, executive director of the Anti-Defamation League, heard from Gordon Zacks, a Jewish leader and personal friend of George Bush who had visited with the president over Labor Day weekend at his home in Kennebunkport, Maine. The president told Gordy that as long as Israel stepped up settlement growth while the administration was working on a Middle East peace plan, the administration was inclined to oppose loan guarantees—the president's most definitive statement on that point to date. Briefly, we discussed canceling the upcoming Education Day, but I strenuously objected since the whole purpose of the day was to de-politicize loan guarantees and position them where they belonged—under the heading of humanitarian aid.

Prompt passage of the guarantees appeared even less likely after Secretary of State Baker phoned Shamir and asked him to postpone his request for four months, or at least to hold off for ten days, when Baker was scheduled to visit Jerusalem. The prime minister was no more accommodating with Secretary Baker than he had been

I had a particularly warm relationship with Deputy Secretary of State Lawrence Eagleburger, with whom I worked closely on issues relating to Israel, Soviet Jewry, and the recision of the anti-Zionist United Nations Resolution 3379. On occasion, I would bring him quarts of my homemade chicken soup to soothe his smoker's cough. Even in those days it was quite unusual to carry jars of soup to the White House or to the State Department, and my friendly gesture caused quite a stir with the security detail!

with me. He told the secretary that he would call him back with his decision. When Shamir phoned Baker, he told him the needs of the new immigrants were too pressing. Shamir felt he had no choice but to submit a formal request for the loan guarantees. Furthermore, contrary to the advice that he'd been given by me and other American Jewish leaders, he was counting on $2 billion that year and had included that sum in his budget. Later, a source close to the administration who spoke to Shamir after this conversation claimed that the prime minister never even considered deferring his request. He felt it would have been perceived by the Arabs as a sign of weakness and would send a dangerous signal to them that suggested an unfavorable turn in U.S. foreign policy toward Israel. Moreover, Prime Minister Shamir was determined to prove to Israelis that only his right-wing Likud Party could bring in aid without relinquishing even an inch of land to the Arabs.[10]

On September 6, the Israeli government submitted a written application for the loan guarantees. Within an hour, Secretary of State Baker summoned leaders of AIPAC and pleaded with them not to lobby for the loan guarantees, while President Bush urged Congress to ignore the Israeli request for 120 days, so that peace negotiations could get under way.[11] AIPAC didn't listen. They went to work lining up enough support in the Senate to override a veto of the loan guarantees by the White House.

I still didn't feel that our purpose in Washington on September 12 would be to lobby members of the House, or anyone else for that matter, but the administration didn't regard our Education Day as anything but a method for pressuring Congress, and they wanted to stop it. On a Friday afternoon, the week before we were to gather at the Mayflower Hotel, I received a phone call from Deputy Secretary of State Lawrence S. Eagleburger. I had known the deputy secretary for a number of years and attended numerous meetings with him dating back to the early years of my work with Soviet Jewry. He is a brilliant, compassionate man, and I considered him a friend of Israel. But he was working for the Bush administration, and in the gentlest of diplomatic language, he asked me to cancel the meeting.

I explained to the deputy secretary that since it was just before the start of the Sabbath, I had no one to consult with about his request, so I was forced to consult with myself. I told him that for the hundreds of thousands of Soviet Jews who were waiting to be free, for the millions of Israelis who were already taxed to the gills and yet willing to assume an extra 5 percent tax to absorb these refugees, the message that would be sent by canceling Education Day would be disastrous.

"Shoshana," he said. "I understand what you are saying. But the president is very concerned about the upcoming peace conference, and he is only requesting a hundred-and-twenty day delay."

"I would like to do what the president is asking, but I can't do it because it would be interpreted as a lack of support for both Soviet Jewry and the Israelis on the part of American Jewry. And the truth is we are already late in providing the assistance that Israel needs."

Our conversation ended on a friendly note. Fifteen minutes later, he called back and said: "Secretary Baker has asked me if he should call you because my persuasive powers were not eloquent enough."

This call was not as strange as it sounds. Actually, this kind of "feeling out" is often done in national politics. A cabinet secretary has his or her deputy test the waters before jumping in. Secretary of State Baker wouldn't want to contact me if he knew that I would say no to his request. So he had Lawrence Eagleburger make the call. If I had been receptive to his request, then I would have heard from Secretary Baker. He would've gotten the answer he wanted, and the credit for assisting the president.

I said, "Please tell Secretary Baker that I thought your language was most eloquent, but the cause is more persuasive."

I imagine Deputy Secretary Eagleburger reported this to Secretary of State Baker. Still, the administration kept trying. The morning of the conference, President Bush invited Mayer Mitchell, president of AIPAC, to the White House and asked him to call it off.[12] Mayer Mitchell had been a vocal supporter of loan guarantees from the beginning. In fact, just the day before his meeting with the president, I received a letter from Mayer, written from his home in Mobile, Alabama. Mayer described the three days in August he had spent in Washington meeting "personally with over 70 U.S. Senators" to urge them to support the Israeli request. Not only did Mayer discuss his meetings regarding this "great humanitarian effort," he added a paragraph in which his passion for his and AIPAC's work was clear: "In my grandfather's day," wrote Mayer, "he could never have imagined that so many officials would listen to American Jews make the case for their brethren. Because tragically in his lifetime,

President Bush gestures during his September 12, 1991 news conference, threatening to veto loan guarantees to Israel to maintain his "principles." Associated Press photo by Greg Gibson. Reprinted with permission.

so many didn't listen."[13] Mayer told President Bush that Israel both deserved and urgently required the humanitarian financial assistance it requested, and that the "day of action for loan guarantees had been planned long before and could not now be stopped."[14]

We convened our Education Day meeting as planned at the Mayflower Hotel. Due to the publicity about the administration's postponement of the guarantees, however, instead of the three hundred people we expected that day, one thousand people showed up at the hotel.

After a few short speeches, some of us were scheduled to go to Capitol Hill to try and educate the legislators. Concurrently, President Bush made his own bid to win support for delaying the guarantees by holding a press conference at the White House. The president opened with a short statement, reiterating that he felt there were "new and exciting possibilities for peace" in the region, and that the United States was "close to being able to convene a peace conference that...would launch direct peace negotiations between Israel and the Arab states."[15]

This, the president explained, was his reason for asking Congress to defer consideration of Israel's request for $10 billion in loan guarantees for 120 days. Not to delay the consideration, said Bush, "would raise a host of...issues so sensitive that a debate now could well destroy our ability to bring one or more of the parties to the peace table." Then the president said that his request for a delay had created "a good deal of confusion," which he hoped to clear up by talking to the press.

That was far from what happened. Venerable White House correspondent Helen Thomas asked the first question, wondering whether the money used for Israel would be better spent on poverty-stricken Americans. Had President Bush truly been interested in explaining away the confusion surrounding loan guarantees, here was his chance. He could have presented the plain truth in facts and figures, using a chart or a handout or both, and it would've shown the negligible cost of the guarantees to U.S. taxpayers. Instead, he simply replied that indicators showed that the American economy appeared to be moving again, and the private sector should create the jobs, not the government. The press conference then moved on to other topics of the day.

A bit later, a journalist brought the conference back to the question of the loan guarantees by observing that even the president's "Republican supporters on the Hill say that Israel should have had this money a long time ago and they don't support [the delay] you're asking for....You sound very tough today on wanting to hold to that 120 days."

"I just sound principled," President Bush replied. "I'm convinced that this debate would be counterproductive to peace...and we've worked too hard to have that request of mine denied....I'm up against some powerful political forces, but I owe it to the American people to tell them how strongly I feel about deferral."

For the president, it was a remarkably poor choice of words. The reference to "powerful political forces" suggested that President Bush felt the American Jewish community was attempting to pressure Congress to pass legislation that ran contrary to the interests of the United States, whose interests only the president could interpret and represent. That would've been bad enough. But a reporter picked up on the president's phrasing and used it in the next question, saying, "Are those powerful political forces ungrateful for what you've done so far in the peace process and why doesn't the peace argument sell with them?"

"I think it will sell," said the president. "But it's taking a little time."

The reason for the delay? That, said President Bush, was due to the fact that he was "up against very strong and effective groups that go up to the Hill. I heard today there were something like a thousand lobbyists on the Hill working the other side of the question. We've got one lonely little guy down here doing it." The journalists laughed. All those Jewish lobbyists, and one little president.

Regrettably for President Bush, millions of American Jews didn't think it was funny. I later heard that the White House switchboard was flooded with phone calls from white supremacist groups supporting the statement. President Bush's comment sounded like a politely restated anti-Semitic characterization to much of American Jewry as well. Suddenly, the statement became a far bigger story than the issue of loan guarantees, and the anger his remark created was immediate and loud. President Bush's comment sounded like a euphemism for a manipulative, power-mad Jewish lobby. With a few poorly chosen words the president of the United States made the Jewish community feel they were deemed to have fewer political rights than a group of retired persons or gun owners or any other group who felt strongly enough about an issue to call on their senators and congressmen. Perhaps American Jews were not as equal as they thought they were.

I didn't believe then—nor do I believe now—that President Bush was aware that his comment would wound millions of American Jews. I had met him and spoken with him briefly on several occasions when he was vice president, and he had always been a supporter of Israel and especially interested in helping oppressed Jews make *aliyah*. Without him, it would have been far more difficult to rescue Ethiopian Jewry. In fact, one month before the press conference, President Bush addressed the Supreme Soviet of the Republic of the Ukraine, saying that

> Freedom requires tolerance, a concept embedded in openness, in glasnost, and in our first amendment protections for the freedoms of speech, association, and religion—all religions. But freedom cannot survive if we let despots flourish or permit seemingly minor restrictions to multiply until they form chains, until they form shackles. Later today, I'll visit the monument at Babi Yar—a somber reminder, a solemn reminder of what happens when people fail to hold back the horrible tide of intolerance and tyranny.[16]

These are not the statements of an anti-Semite.

Furthermore, I doubted the president had ad-libbed his statement; off-the-cuff comments were not his style. Indeed, I later learned that the comment was actually scripted by National Security Council staffer Richard Haas, the highest-ranking Jew working on Middle Eastern affairs in the White House. Furthermore, three of the other top advisers on the Middle East to President Bush and Secretary Baker were Jewish—Dennis Ross and Aaron Miller on the Policy Planning staff and Daniel Kurtzer in the Near East Bureau—enough to make the Arabs suspicious of "Jewish influence" on American policy. Whatever one might say about the current United States position on Israel, it surely was not being guided on the staff level by anti-Semites, a charge that may well have been true in other administrations.[17]

I knew that I would have to respond to the president. After the Bush press conference, I hurriedly convened a press conference and followed up by sitting for a round of interviews with print, radio, and television reporters. I kept my comments low key, telling the media the plain truth: I was not a lobbyist, nor were the other people visiting their representatives on the Hill, and I was dismayed by the president characterizing us as such. We were there to inform Congress why we, as private citizens speaking for ourselves and other like-minded private citizens, felt that Israel should be granted the loan guarantees without further delay.

My explanations in the media did little to relieve the tension generated by the president's remarks. Also, talking to journalists was certainly not the best way to communicate with President Bush, since one could never know which reports he read or heard. A formal and focused reply to his remarks was in order, so, after consulting with past chairmen of the Conference of Presidents who assured me this step was correct, I wrote to the White House in my official capacity.

I worked late into the night on Thursday and for hours more on Friday morning, drafting and redrafting my letter. I was careful not to offend President Bush. For better or for worse, George H. W. Bush was president of the United States, and the Presidents Conference would be dealing with him and his administration again in the near future. Further tempering my response was my realization that the president hadn't said he didn't support loan guarantees; he just didn't support their passage at that moment. Loan guarantees were on the table; Congress supported them, and I knew with complete certainty that they would pass. I did want the president to realize, however, that he had caused a good deal of pain in the community.

I faxed a draft of my letter to New York so Malcolm Hoenlein could review it. We made a few additions and deletions, had it typed up on Presidents Conference stationery, and faxed it to the White House.

Here is what I wrote:

> Dear Mr. President:
> We recognize and appreciate your past and continuing support for the State of Israel and the successful absorption of Soviet Jewish and Ethiopian refugees. We also share your aspirations for the proposed Middle East peace conference and direct negotiations between Israel and her Arab neighbors.
>
> Because of our commitment to the hundreds of thousands of Soviet Jews who have arrived in Israel and the countless others who have yet to emigrate, we support Israel's request for loan guarantees to enable

these new immigrants to become productive and self-supporting citizens in their new homeland. For that reason more than 1,200 Americans representing Jewish communities in 40 states, and numerous Christian leaders came to Washington to meet with their senators and congressmen. They came out of personal conviction to participate in a day of education and dialogue on a matter of great concern —a matter which has often been misconstrued. They were exercising their right—even obligation— as American citizens, consistent with the democratic process, to advocate their position on this vital humanitarian issue. A position we believe to be consistent with the efforts for peace in the Middle East, with United States national interests, with the needs of our ally Israel and the absorption of Soviet and Ethiopian Jews.

Therefore, I found some of the comments at your press conference on Thursday to be disturbing and subject to misinterpretation. In particular, the references to "1,000 lobbyists on the Hill working the other side of the question" and to the "powerful political forces" trouble me and many others.

Reasonable people can have honest differences on issues. Clearly, we agree on far more than we disagree. We are committed to the same principles, even if we differ on timing or other specific aspects. These differences are best resolved through dialogue and close communication. I am confident that with good will and cooperation on all sides the two goals of achieving a comprehensive Middle East peace and enabling acknowledged pressing human needs to be adequately addressed, can and will be met.[18]

I sent the letter with some anxiety, uncertain how the White House would respond. The administration undoubtedly had the option of raising the stakes by going all out to fight for the delay in Congress. If that happened, what would I do? And then an Israeli cabinet minister labeled George Bush an anti-Semite, and we found ourselves defending our president. The Presidents Conference, along with the American Jewish Congress, the Anti-Defamation League, and the Simon Wiesenthal Center condemned the minister's remarks in statements that were faxed to the press and the White House.[19] All this occurred while I waited for a response to my letter.

Although I let the people calling me know that I had written President Bush about his remarks, the reality was that I had no way of knowing whether he'd actually read my letter. (While writing this memoir, I contacted the George Bush

Library in College Station, Texas, and asked them to send me the paperwork that I knew letters to the White House generated as they made their rounds past presidential assistants. In this way, I discovered that my letter was in fact treated with a fair amount of concern at the White House. The draft of the president's reply to my letter was marked urgent and quickly approved by Chief of Staff John Sununu, who noted on the draft that was forwarded for typing, that it should be sent immediately by Federal Express.)

Finally, my phone rang, and an assistant to President Bush was on the line. She said that the president was in the process of replying to my letter and asked if I would object to the president sending his letter to the member organizations of the Presidents Conference. I replied that I had no objection, but I asked if the White House would be kind enough to enclose a copy of my letter to the president with his reply. I wanted our members to know precisely what I had written, that the official position of the Presidents Conference was quite emphatically that George Bush was not the enemy of American Jews or Israel. Furthermore, this correspondence would demonstrate to the community that we not only had a voice, but an ongoing dialogue with the administration.

The White House assistant told me that the president would be happy to include a copy of my letter with his own. I thanked her, and there the conversation ended.

Several days later, I received an excited phone call from a friend.

"Shoshana," my friend said. "Did you read the president's letter?"

"What letter?" I asked.

"He wrote you a letter," said my friend.

"I haven't gotten a letter from the president," I replied, and knew that if one had arrived at the Presidents Conference headquarters in New York City, Malcolm Hoenlein would have been in touch with me.

"I just read it in the *New York Times*," my friend explained.

I was sure that my hearing was fine, though I must admit that at first the whole thing sounded like a joke. However, after I hung up the phone and walked outside and picked up my subscription copy of the *Times* in the driveway, my political instincts returned. The president writing a public letter to me made sense. In fact, I was impressed with the intelligence of it, since he had initially considered replying to American Jewry through their organizations. Writing me a personal reply instead of addressing members of a group appeared warm and reassuring, which was exactly the way the administration needed to appear at that moment. By publishing that personal letter in a newspaper, his reply was immediately communicated to a large segment of that group and at the same time entered into the public record.

I took the *Times* into my kitchen, unfurled the paper, and began to read President Bush's answer to my letter.

He wrote:

> Dear Shoshana:
>
> I have received your letter of September 13 and appreciate your kind words about my support for the State of Israel and for the successful absorption of Soviet Jewish and Ethiopian refugees. I also appreciate your noting that we share aspirations for a Middle East peace conference and direct negotiations between Israel and her Arab neighbors.
>
> I am concerned that some of my comments at the Thursday press conference caused apprehension within the Jewish community. My references to lobbyists and powerful political forces were never meant to be pejorative in any sense. As a veteran of many years in the governmental and political arena, I have a great respect for the exercise of free expression in the democratic process. It is essential that all our citizens have the right to present and advocate their positions on the issues. Politically organized groups and individuals are a legitimate and valued part of the decision-making process in a democracy.
>
> We obviously disagree on the question of a 120-day delay in the submission of the loan guarantees. I believe, as you do, that we can have honest differences on issues. I also share your belief that we are committed to the same principles and that our areas of agreement far outweigh our areas of disagreement.
>
> I continue to value your thoughtful input and perspective. You are always honest and forthright in your comments to me, and that is invaluable as we move forward in this delicate process for peace. The lines of communication will always be open between us.
>
> Barbara joins me in sending you good wishes for the New Year.[20]

It was a beautiful, thoughtful letter. I believed that the president was sincere when he expressed his concern that his comments had wounded parts of the Jewish community and that he had never meant to denigrate our "exercise of free expression." However, while the president stated the lines of communication would remain open, he had not altered his position on delaying loan guarantees.

As a practical matter, then, the Israelis and the American Jewish community were right back to where we had started. It would be nice to say that the problem ended with the letter, but that is not what happened. The truth is that during the next year the conflicts grew more intense. This leads me to conclude, with the clarity of hindsight, that at bottom the wounds of Jews from New York to Jerusalem had much less to do with the president's careless comments than with his resolve not to permit any distraction from his effort toward peace in the Middle East. And so what I saw as humanitarian aid was buried under the weight of international politics.

On October 31, 1991, Israel finally met face-to-face with its Arab neighbors in Madrid. In an effort to underscore the historic nature of the meeting, President George H. W. Bush and Soviet leader Mikhail Gorbachev were on hand for the opening ceremonies. Prime Minister Yitzhak Shamir had come to represent Israel.[21]

I was in Madrid to put together a report for the Presidents Conference. I observed each day's deliberations and spent much of my time talking to reporters who could tell me, off the record, what was really going on. I understood it was going to be a long, protracted process. Israel and the Palestinians were nowhere near peace, but it was a beginning and I believe in beginnings.

Shamir's presence in Madrid did not represent a shift in his position regarding settlements. Nor did the U.S. administration alter its view on extending Israel loan guarantees. However, President Bush agreed to meet with a delegation of approximately two dozen American Jewish leaders on Tuesday, November 12, at the Waldorf-Astoria Hotel. Before I left for New York City, the White House called me at home, and an aide requested that I speak privately with the president prior to the larger meeting with the delegation.

Malcolm Hoenlein accompanied me to the Waldorf. I was under the impression that he would be joining me at the meeting, since I rarely did official business without my executive. But at the hotel a presidential assistant informed us that I would be speaking privately with the president.

Suddenly, riding on the elevator to the floor of the presidential suite, I was more than a little nervous—a feeling that did not subside when a Secret Service agent ushered me into a huge ornate sitting room and I discovered that speaking privately with a president is not quite the same thing as speaking privately with a friend. There were several other people with him waiting to listen to our conversation, and for an unsettling instant, I glimpsed the fish bowl in which the president went about his job. White House Chief of Staff John Sununu was there, as was National Security Adviser Brent Scowcroft, Richard Haas from the National Security Council, and Bobby Kilberg, a presidential assistant and community liaison.

I shook hands with the president. We said hello and exchanged pleasantries. Then I sat on a sofa, and President Bush sat to my left in a wing chair.

President Bush met at the Waldorf Hotel with the members of the Conference of Presidents and other Jewish leaders, November 12, 1991. George Bush Presidential Library. Reprinted with permission.

"How are you, Shoshana?" he asked.

"Upset," I said.

"Yes?"

"Yes, Mr. President. I think you need to understand how deeply American Jewry was hurt by your statement."

The president seemed to sit up a bit straighter.

I said, "Because of your statement, you drew blood and the sharks came swimming."

The president stood up, moved his chair closer to me, sat down, and said to Brent Scowcroft, "I didn't use the word 'Jews' in my statement, did I?"

"No, Mr. President," Scowcroft said.

I said, "Mr. President, you didn't have to. Everyone understood that the people you were referring to were Jewish. That's why the White House switchboard lit up with so many messages of support from anti-Semites."

"I never intended to hurt anyone," he said. "Or give encouragement to anti-Semitism."

"I know this happened inadvertently, Mr. President. But it did happen."

He nodded, but didn't reply. Briefly, we talked about the loan guarantees, and I saw that he had no intention of changing his mind about linking the guarantees to the Israeli settlement building policy.

Someone announced that it was time to head downstairs. President Bush and I left the suite together. The president was a forthright man, but he had the reputation of being emotionally reserved, so I wasn't surprised that as we walked down the narrow hallway he held my arm and said, "Shoshana, I would prefer if you told your group what we discussed."

I took a deep breath. "No, Mr. President. I believe you have to tell them."

We continued walking; it was a long hallway, perhaps the longest I had ever walked down in my life. As we reached the elevator and the door opened, the president asked me again if I would pass his words along to the other Jewish leaders.

"Mr. President, I can't do that. I really believe it has to come from you."

Downstairs, after some polite hellos, everyone took their seats. The president sat me on his left, and his longtime friend and venerable Jewish Republican, Max M. Fisher, on his right, a photo opportunity for the administration that would be as important to American Jewry as the president's words.

President Bush began by saying, "Shoshana is a very direct and gracious woman, and she told me that I inadvertently made a remark that some in the Jewish community perceived as hurtful. I would never knowingly hurt anyone I understand that I may also have inadvertently resurrected some ugly feelings. I certainly would not want to exacerbate anti-Semitism. And I intend to find the appropriate venues to correct that impression."[22]

The meeting lasted for more than an hour, and by the end I felt certain that the president had redeemed his image among leaders of the American Jewish community (although his dismal performance with Jewish voters in November 1992 later proved me incorrect). I couldn't help but reflect, however, that the entire affair had been an unproductive distraction from our concern for the loan guarantees, a situation that would not be resolved without continued work and attention.

In the meanwhile, I had just returned from the Soviet Union and another historic meeting.

Above: Martin Wenick and I in front of the newly dedicated monument at Babi Yar, October 6, 1991.
Opposite page: Martin Wenik and I met with President Gorbachev in a historic visit at the Kremlin,
October 2, 1991. Reuters/UPI. Photo by Genady Galperin. Reprinted with permission.

XII
Remembering Babi Yar

O n September 19, 1941, the Nazis captured Kiev. A few days later, on the pretext of punishing saboteurs, they rounded up the Jews of the city and marched them to a wide, deep ravine known as Babi Yar, the "grandmother ravine." For the next two days, German soldiers, acting with the Ukrainian auxiliary police, shot 33,771 Jews and dumped their bodies into the *yar*. In the months that followed, more than 100,000 Jews, Gypsies, Turkmen, and Soviet POWs were executed there.[1]

This brutal history is not unique; just a small percentage of those who were murdered in the Holocaust died at Babi Yar. Nor is the involvement of Ukrainians in the shootings of particular note. Violent anti-Semitism in the Ukraine is an old story. Still, this does not excuse the Soviet government for taking decades to acknowledge the crimes that had occurred.

It was the poem, "Babi Yar," by the Ukrainian Yevgeny Yevtushenko, that reminded the Kremlin of the slaughter. Recalling his first encounter with the killing ground in 1961, Yevtushenko said: "When I came to Babi Yar I was sure there would be a monument but I didn't find anything. It was just a dump of garbage. I was so shocked and terribly ashamed that no monument existed to remind us and the world what happened there. I rushed to my hotel, locked myself in my room and wrote the poem that very same day."[2]

The poem was a cry of the heart against Russian and Nazi anti-Semitism. Eventually translated into more than seventy languages and set to music in Dmitri Shostakovich's Thirteenth Symphony, "Babi Yar" brought Yevtushenko international fame as well as the condemnation of the Khrushchev regime. When the music and poetry focused international attention on the event, the Kremlin—always sensitive to embarrassment—finally erected a monument at Babi Yar in 1974.[3] On the memorial, the dead were described as "victims of fascism," a statement that ignored the fact that the overwhelming number of those killed there had been Jews. This omission was in keeping with the long-standing official effort to sever Soviet Jewry's emotional connection to their religion, history, and the community of world Jewry. It also obscured the reality that the Nazis had been primarily interested in eradicating Jewry, a goal that not all Soviet citizens opposed and some actively supported.

Now, a half-century after the atrocities, this official distortion of history was slated to be corrected during a commemoration on October 5, 1991, at Babi Yar. A great change in Soviet policy had occurred under the leadership of President Mikhail Gorbachev, demonstrated most forcefully by the emigration permissions which were now being granted to 10,000 Soviet Jews each month. It appeared, however, that the number of anti-Semitic incidents and publications carrying anti-Semitic invective in the USSR grew as Russian repression lessened. Jewish cemeteries had been desecrated and hate literature distributed on the streets. On the morning before the commemoration, Yevtushenko was jogging through the streets of Kiev when he spotted graffiti scrawled across fences that said, "Yids and Russians, get out of Ukraine."[4]

Martin Wenick, executive director of the National Conference on Soviet Jewry, and I were scheduled to attend the Babi Yar ceremony, but first we had some business in Moscow. The human rights committee of the Conference on Security and Cooperation in Europe (CSCE) was meeting there and as representatives of NCSJ, a non-governmental organization, we were considered part of the American delegation to the meeting. While the primary work of the conference that year centered on the growing conflict in Yugoslavia, Martin and I wanted to make certain that the final document also included language encouraging education to combat anti-Semitism.

We'd had difficulty with a similar resolution the previous year. At the 1990 CSCE conference in Copenhagen, Germany and Canada had proposed including an article denouncing anti-Semitism. Robin Saipe, the National Conference on Soviet Jewry staff member in Copenhagen to observe and represent our interests, called the NCSJ office in New York to say she had a serious problem: the head of the U.S. delegation, Ambassador Max Kampelman, a brilliant lawyer with a long and outstanding record of public service, opposed the written denunciation.

"That doesn't make sense," I told her. I was particularly disturbed that the United States was ignoring the symbolic significance that the proposal had come from Germany.

"That's what I thought," she said. "You've got to come here right away."

Robin arranged for us to meet with Ambassador Kampelman, and I boarded the next flight to Copenhagen.

It was an odd and slightly awkward meeting, over lunch at a restaurant, with Mrs. Kampelman in attendance along with her husband. Still, I raised my concerns asking the ambassador why he hadn't signed the resolution.

"I don't see that we should identify anti-Semitism in particular," he told me. "And our human rights staff isn't really anxious to sign it."

Although I strenuously advised him that specifically naming anti-Semitism as unlawful, antisocial behavior in an international document would be a potent weapon, the ambassador shook his head with finality. Surprised and distressed by his position, I sought out Ambassador Sam Wise, international policy director for the delegation, whom I knew from previous human rights conferences. When I asked him whether it was correct that he was recommending that the U.S. delegation not sign the resolution, he denied it. Why, then, hadn't the United States signed on? "Because Ambassador Kampelman doesn't think we should," he told me.

I don't usually do what I did next, but I couldn't ignore this vital opportunity. I went over the ambassador's head and called Secretary of State James Baker. I told him about the resolution, read him the text, and recommended that our country sign the document. Shortly thereafter, the delegation signed it, and many others of the CSCE member states followed suit.

I can only speculate about why Ambassador Kampelman was at first reluctant to support the resolution. At that time, anti-Semitism was generally on the wane in the world (although more evident in the Soviet Union), and he may have feared that drawing undue attention to the issue would backfire on the Jews. Or perhaps he felt he would appear partisan, since he is Jewish. In the end, however, he was proud of the document and its historic significance.[5]

Having almost missed this important opportunity in Copenhagen in 1990, I was resolved to make sure there would be no problems with the language of a new resolution while I was in Moscow for the 1991 conference. The American delegation spent hours in discussion and debate, writing and rewriting until we drafted a statement all would sign. Although this statement may seem obvious and straightforward, every word was examined and every nuance considered. What is more important and should be mentioned first, we asked ourselves? Would it be religious intolerance, racism, or ethnic prejudice? The final Moscow document affirmed that the member nations would "recognize that effective human rights education contributes to combating intolerance, religious, racial and ethnic prejudice, including...xenophobia and anti-Semitism."[6] Little by little, the world was coming to grips with this special brand of irrational hatred.

While I was gratified at the successful conclusion of the conference, another potentially more difficult challenge awaited me. On the heels of the painful public exchange with President Bush, I was preparing to discuss some hard truths with Soviet President Mikhail S. Gorbachev. The re-emergent anti-Semitism in the Soviet Union needed to be stopped, and I wanted a chance to convince the Soviet leader to make a public statement condemning it.

Before departing the United States for Moscow, I had cleared such a meeting with our State Department and sent a request to the Kremlin. NCSJ Executive Director Martin Wenick, a former Deputy Chief of Mission at the United States embassy in Moscow who is fluent in Russian, had used his contacts to arrange everything. When he and I arrived in the city, however, we hadn't yet received an answer from Gorbachev's aides. Instead, we found at our hotel an invitation from Mrs. Gorbachev, and, to our great surprise, one from Vadim Bakatin, head of the KGB.

In former times, an invitation to meet with the head of the KGB would have been rather alarming, but Bakatin had the reputation of a reformer. He had been named to the position after his predecessor was arrested as one of the leaders of the August 1991 failed coup against Gorbachev. In the weeks before our visit, Bakatin had purged the KGB of its most fearsome, hard-line ideologues—the sort of people who had been especially harsh toward Jewish dissidents and had harassed Sandy and me on our 1982 visit to the Soviet Union. So Martin and I were curious, but not afraid.

We were met at the imposing and surprisingly beautiful entrance to the KGB building by a solemn, uniformed guard, who unlocked the doors to admit us. He escorted us into the inner hall, which was deserted except for us. I had expected a bustling office and was disconcerted to find empty corridors and rooms in which the sound of our footsteps echoed. We saw no one until we arrived at Bakatin's office.

The man who was in charge of the secret police was attractive and very well-dressed, with a tailored suit and a fine watch, definitely not in the communist style. He was open and friendly, and he treated us to a disarmingly honest analysis of the situation in the Soviet Union in those weeks before it imploded. The central authority of Moscow was rapidly slipping away, he gave us to understand, and no plan had yet been agreed upon to replace it. He himself expected that there would be a loose federation of nations, and he wanted to show us on the maps in his office where he thought the new borders would lie. However, his large, wall-mounted maps, which were meant to be lowered from their casing at the touch of a button, would not descend. This was indicative of the state of things in his nation, he laughed. More seriously, he pledged that although the Kremlin no longer had the power to dictate policy to the emerging republics, Jewish emigration would continue. I gave him a list of 355 names of Jews who had been denied visas, and he promised to investigate those cases. It was a promising meeting, and not long afterwards I found myself telling an interviewer that the National Conference on Soviet Jewry had just established a working relationship with the KGB. It sounded so odd when I said it that I couldn't quite believe my own ears.

We had assumed that the invitation to tea with Mrs. Gorbachev was a polite way of brushing us off. We were disappointed by this, but you don't say no to the first lady of the Soviet Union, so we had telephoned our acceptance. Now, when we returned to our hotel from our meeting with Bakatin, we found we had an appointment to meet with President Gorbachev himself. We could only assume that the surprise meeting with Bakatin was a test of some sort, and that we had passed. We straightened out our obligations with a call to Mrs. Gorbachev's secretary, and prepared to meet the president the next afternoon.

The Kremlin has long been the locus of awesome power and, as our taxi approached it, our young Russian driver became so terrified and agitated he pulled over to the curb and refused to go on. Luckily, Martin's Russian language skills were equal to the task of convincing him he would be able to drive into the Kremlin and return to tell his friends about it. As we drove through the gate in the high stone walls and navigated the maze of narrow streets leading to the impressive presidential office building, where our driver would wait for us to reappear, I could better understand his fear. After the attempted coup had failed in August, Gorbachev wasn't taking any chances. Soldiers with AK-47s were everywhere, and I felt as though I were entering a war zone.

Martin and I were escorted upstairs to an enormous anteroom with high ceilings, gorgeous scrollwork, tall windows, and nineteenth-century art on the walls. After a brief wait, the chief of protocol led us into the presidential office, even larger than the anteroom, and filled with reporters and photographers.

President Gorbachev was on the phone at his desk at the far end of the room. He quickly hung up as we entered, and came toward us holding his arms out, a genial, energetic man in a well-cut business suit. I was struck by the warmth and intensity in his eyes and smile. Speaking through his interpreter, he greeted us as though we were old friends bumping into each other on the street.[7]

"I know who you are," he said, meaning that he was aware our visit was a historic occasion—the first time a Soviet head of state had met officially with a leader from an American group that advocated on behalf of Soviet Jewry.[8] "I welcome your mission."

We stood around as photographers and film crews did their job. The fact of our meeting was extraordinary enough, but when I realized that it was being recorded by Tass, the Soviet news agency that during the Cold War had a reputation as a dissembler of epic proportions, I was stunned. Not only had Gorbachev agreed to speak with us, he was going to make certain that the rest of his country knew about it.

Martin and I were seated at the large conference table in the office, and Gorbachev and his interpreter took seats facing us. The president indicated it was time for the journalists to leave, and then he began our conversation. "The old USSR is dead," he told us, "and a new one"—which he referred to as the Union of Sovereign States—"is being born. One of our objectives is to help all of our people, including the Jews. We need good Soviet-Israeli relations. One-third of Israelis have their roots in the Soviet Union. Some say one feels more Russian in Israel than here." Once again, I brought up the problem of unresolved refusenik cases, and I gave Gorbachev our list of names. Like Bakatin, he promised to ask about the situation, adding with a smile that "perhaps the Soviet Union [still] has some secrets."

A discussion of the growing anti-Semitism in his country was very much on my mind, and to my surprise, Gorbachev raised the topic before I did. "It is the work of extremists and not a disease that is deeply rooted in our society," he told us, a phrasing I felt harkened back to the bad old days of Soviet denial. I appreciated, however, that any admission that anti-Semitism existed and was being inflamed

Demonstrator in Moscow displays an anti-Semitic message, 1990. Stephen Ferry/Liason. Reprinted with permission.

by intellectuals represented a significant concession on his part. I replied that I thought it would help matters if he would publicly denounce anti-Semitism.

"It would be a mistake to single out one problem when we have so many," he said, "and in a country with over one hundred nationalities, I don't think it would be fair to mention just one." I then suggested he might speak generally about various anti-social behaviors such as xenophobia, racism, and anti-Semitism similar to the way such a condemnation was styled in the CSCE Copenhagen and brand-new Moscow human rights documents, and similar to what President Bush had said in his 1990 State of the Union address.[9] Still, Gorbachev shook his head no, he couldn't say that.

I let the matter drop for the moment, and we continued to talk. He seemed optimistic about his own future and the future of his country, but conceded that "things here change daily. We need to keep our heads. I understand [our fate] is not an empty question for Americans and Soviet Jews. You want to know what you are dealing with." I asked him if there was any way the National Conference on Soviet Jewry could assist him, and he said, "Perhaps Jewish investors can be encouraged to help stimulate business here and not wait for fair weather." I suggested that he meet with American Jewish leaders the next time he was in the United States, and we

Dignitaries were invited to a state dinner and dedication program at the Ukraine Palace.

discussed the Soviet economic predicament, but only briefly, for without being prodded he returned to the subject of anti-Semitism.

"As a child in my hometown of Stavropol, I witnessed the murder of Jews. Those were terrible times, and that was a terrible tragedy," he told us. He didn't say whether the murderers were Nazis or Russians. There was a pause in the conversation then, and I handed him a stack of anti-Semitic Russian language journals that a Moscow-based associate of ours had collected for us. As Gorbachev leafed through the magazines, obviously acquainted with them, I pressed the point that was the primary object of my visit. "Mr. President, I hope you will take the opportunity of the Babi Yar ceremony to issue a public condemnation of anti-Semitism."

He looked at me intently. "I will. I'm sending one of my closest advisers, Aleksandr Yakovlev, to represent me there." And then he added, "The commemoration is more important for the Soviet people than the victims, because it is time for them to recognize the truth about the mistreatment of the Jews."

Our meeting lasted an hour, and he said good-bye with as much warmth as he had greeted us. "I consider our talk to be a continuation of a process," he said. "And I will do what I can on the issues you have raised."

Outside, we met again with reporters, and I passed along my impressions of our meeting. I had achieved almost everything I had come there for, but I still did not know if Gorbachev himself would make the statement I hoped for. The journalists tried to get me to predict what the president might do, but I couldn't say. My personal impression was that Yakovlev's speech for Babi Yar was still being written, and I could only hope that our discussion would have some effect on its final form. We would have to wait, I thought, until the commemoration the next day to find out.

And then it happened. As we rode back to the hotel, our taxi's radio was background noise as Martin and I discussed the meeting we had just left. Suddenly, Martin began to pay attention to the announcer's voice. "He's reporting a statement by Gorbachev, condemning anti-Semitism!" Martin interpreted for me. The intense drama of these words, coming so shockingly soon after our meeting, is something I will never forget.

The following day, Martin and I journeyed to Kiev to watch as the memorial to the Jews of Babi Yar was dedicated. We gazed at the tall bronze *menorah* set at the edge of the ravine and said the *Kaddish* for those who had no one to pray in their memory. Yevtushenko recited his famous poem, and then it was declaimed in English, Hebrew, and Ukrainian by several actors on an outdoor dais, including Cliff Robertson, Tony Randall, Chaim Topol, and the Ukrainian performer B. Stupka.[10] I stood on that hallowed ground, breathed the crisp autumn air and thought how brilliantly the poet had caught the mood of this place:

> *Wild grasses rustle over Babi Yar,*
> *The trees look sternly, as if passing judgement.*
> *Here, silently, all screams...And I myself,*
> *like one long soundless scream,*
> *Above the thousands of thousands interred,*
> *I'm every old man executed here,*
> *As I am every child murdered here...*
> *No fiber of my body will forget this....*[11]

Ukrainian President Leonid Kravchuk spoke to the thousands in attendance, including dignitaries from around the world, acknowledging the complicity of his countrymen in the executions, and asking forgiveness from the Jewish people. "None of us has the right to forget anything," he said, and ended his speech with the words, *"Shalom Yidden."*[12]

A requiem by the much-honored Ukrainian composer, Yevhen Stankovich, had been commissioned for the event, but for me the sweetest music at the ceremony came when Aleksandr Yakovlev stepped onto the platform, and read a statement from President Gorbachev. It was not a mere repeat of the statement announced on the radio the previous evening. On this day, through Yakovlev, Gorbachev acknowledged the suffering of the Jews and admitted the historical complicity of the Soviets in the Holocaust in a way that no Soviet leader had ever dared.

> "The memory of irreparable losses passes from generation to generation... Babi Yar, in the same way as...Buchenwald is not simply a geographical name now, but a frightening symbol...a place of grief...of confession. The Nazis speculated on the lowest feelings of envy, national intolerance and hatred. They used anti-Semitism as a major means to infect peoples' minds with...racism. The Stalin bureaucracy, which publicly disassociated itself from anti-Semitism, in fact used it as a means to strengthen their dictatorial position....Among tens of millions of victims were almost six million Jews, representatives of the great nation dispersed over the whole planet. Babi Yar shows that Jews were among the first Nazi victims both in our country and in the whole of Europe..."[13]

Turning to the subject of contemporary Soviet society, he added, "Babi Yar is now also an appeal to the politicians of our day to be vigilant, to remember everywhere and at all times that they were given the power to serve people, that a policy that is immoral should never have a place in the world."

In a remarkably candid statement that betrayed the government's embarrassment at its Jewish citizens' rush to leave the country, he added, "The right of emigration has been approved. However, to speak frankly, we [regret] that our compatriots are leaving, that the country is losing so many talented people. I accuse those social and administrative structures that could not or did not...create the atmosphere of intolerance and condemnation for all manifestations of anti-Semitism."

And he concluded, "This ceremony in Babi Yar is a mournful event, but it inspires hope that we, our renovating society, are capable of learning lessons from the tragedies and errors of the past." Mikhail Gorbachev had been perceptive enough to see the approach of a new reality for his nation and courageous enough to turn away publicly from the demons of the past. It is for this bravery that I will always remember him.

Opposite page: After we recited the *Kaddish*, I placed a stone on the historical marker, a traditional gesture when one visits a Jewish grave.

Above: President Bush and Prime Minister Rabin announce mutual agreement on loan guarantees for Israel, August 11, 1992. Associated Press photo by Greg Gibson. Reprinted with permission. Opposite page: Prime Minister Yitzhak Rabin addresses the Conference of Presidents, August 13, 1992. Photo by Richard Lobell. Reprinted with permission.

XIII
Problems Resolved

he upheaval in the Soviet Union presented the United States and American Jews another opportunity to fight global anti-Semitism. The repeal of United Nations Resolution 3379, also known as the "Zionism is Racism" resolution, had been an early goal of the Bush administration. Vice President Dan Quayle called for its recision (as repeal is formally known at the UN) as early as 1988, but that seemed a distant possibility until the implosion of the Soviet Union, the original author of Resolution 3379.[1] In the fall of 1991, with this opportunity opening before him and the onus of the loan guarantees issue weighing rather heavily on his approval ratings, President Bush threw the full muscle of the State Department behind a repeal effort.

Secretary of State Baker assigned John Bolton, then Assistant Secretary of State for International Organizations, to be his point man on the issue, and Bolton turned to the Conference of Presidents for assistance. We responded by coordinating a program in which our member organizations intensely lobbied the diplomats from every country with which they had a relationship. In this, the American Jewish Committee and B'nai B'rith International were particularly helpful. Malcolm Hoenlein and his Presidents Conference staff tracked diplomatic contacts daily and kept an ongoing count of positive and potentially positive responses. It was, at the time, the largest, most concerted and concentrated lobbying effort ever mounted at the UN.

Because we had been keeping track, we knew that the repeal was assured when Deputy Secretary of State Lawrence Eagleburger introduced it in the UN General Assembly on December 16. The low-key language of the resolution—"The General Assembly decides to revoke the determination contained in its Resolution 3379 of 10 November 1975"—was carefully crafted to meet the "special needs" of various delegations who did not want to be seen as specifically supporting Israel. Secretary Eagleburger had shown it to me and I assured him it would meet the approval of the American Jewish leadership, many of whom were present to observe the vote. When the final tally of 111 for and 25 against flashed on the electronic board above our heads, applause broke out in the chamber and delegates left their seats to rush over and congratulate Israel's foreign minister, David Levy. We spectators were excited and more than a little relieved, and though we knew even then that this vote provided no assurance that the anti-Israel rhetoric in the UN would diminish, the victory was of immense symbolic importance.[2]

The victory also may have been politically helpful to President Bush, but the matter of the loan guarantees—one far more discomfiting to American Jews—had yet to be resolved. While the Conference of Presidents was helping the administration lobby the nations of the world to repeal Resolution 3379, the Council of Jewish Federations held its General Assembly in Baltimore. Yitzhak Shamir made the customary prime minister's appearance before the CJF General Assembly, using his address to defend the settlement policy that had caused so much friction with the Bush administration. The delegates gave him a resounding welcome and applauded his speech, but a Wilstein Institute poll that was widely reported in the newspapers that day indicated American Jews overwhelmingly disagreed with Shamir's hard line position on negotiations with the Palestinians. The assembly delegates, although generally more hawkish than rank-and-file American Jews, were themselves more deeply divided on the question of whether or not Israel should continue to build settlements in the "occupied territories" than their applause indicated.[3] Many felt that giving up the building of settlements was a small price to pay for the financial assistance Israel sought and so desperately needed. Others believed Israel should behave as though the territory gained through military conflict it did not initiate was its own. The group agreed to disagree; in resolutions approved at the 1991 GA, the Assembly voted to follow its usual policy, which was to let Israel choose its own course.[4]

Israeli Foreign Minister David Levy, Israel's United Nations Ambassador Yoram Aridor, and Deputy Ambassador Ephraim Tari embrace after the UN votes to rescind Resolution 3379, December 16, 1991. This was only the second time in UN history that the General Assembly voted to overturn one of its own resolutions. Associated Press photo by Mark Phillips. Reprinted with permission.

The Israeli press excoriated American Jewry for its division on this question, for a failure of leadership, and for what appeared to Israelis as impotent silence. Most of all, we were skewered for the fact that, by a slight majority, American Jews favored some sort of territorial compromise with the Palestinians. The author of one editorial, Shmuel Katz, a former adviser to Prime Minister Menachem Begin, singled out the Presidents Conference for condemnation, writing that none of our members was elected "because of [our] special knowledge of Jewish or Arab history; or [our] knowledge and experience of Zionist questions; or for diplomatic acumen; or for the firmness of [our] backbone; or for [our] freedom from those 'ghetto' characteristics which have lingered on."[5] The writer concluded that since American Jewry had played a significant role in opening the Soviet floodgates so that the Russian Jews deluged Israel, it was only right that they should make the economic means available for the Israelis to absorb them into society.

Although Katz's criticism was a rather personal slap, I knew it arose from the profound misunderstanding many Israelis exhibit regarding the relationship between American Jewry and the U.S. government. The success of the American Jewish community in national political life comes through organizing groups, raising funds to support candidates and causes, and regularly showing up at the voting booth. Unquestionably, these efforts give us access and influence in government that is disproportionate to our numbers, and we have used that influence to create sympathy in Washington for the only Western-style democracy in the Middle East. Even so, the support Israel has come to expect from Washington—primarily in the military hardware department—is due mostly to our government's wish to protect its long-term global interests, and not from the political might of influential American Jews. We simply do not have the power Israelis seem to believe we have to influence the American foreign policy agenda.

Israel's policies and interests are often in sync with our own, but not infrequently, the two countries disagree. Furthermore, as I often told reporters during the conflict on the loan guarantees, the administration's policies could be the result of circumstances not directly related to the issues at hand. As Israel was requesting $10 billion in loan guarantees, President Bush was dealing with a deepening economic recession, the public's isolationist mood in the wake of the Persian Gulf War, and a serious challenge to his renomination from the right wing of his own party. He desperately needed the political boost he would get from successfully initiating Middle East peace talks.

Over the next several months, the greatest difficulty I faced as chairman of the Conference of Presidents was confronting the despair that was spreading through large segments of the American Jewish community. Many believed we had lost the battle over loan guarantees. "A kind of paralysis has set in" within the community, Henry Siegman, executive director of the American Jewish Congress, told one reporter. "We do not have the political leverage to pass the loan guarantee if settlements continue. That is the conventional wisdom in the community today."[6]

I never accepted the view that loan guarantees were dead in the water, and I did my best to alter that perception in my speeches, interviews, and a series of op-ed pieces. I felt like the coach whose team is losing at halftime. I wanted to rally my players, remind them we had not yet lost the game. I was almost the lone voice of encouragement at that time, and I was quite disturbed that so many other leaders were willing to give up so easily. I traveled the country, visiting communities to encourage them to marshal their resources for the second half, reminding them that another budget year was coming up. I kept saying, "Israel needs the loan guarantees; we have to show the country how important this is. Make them see we're not going to go away."

My view made some people uneasy. I received much negative mail in which the writer would tell me to stop pushing the issue. Even my own rabbi said to me, "Why did you have to pick a fight with the president?" But the way I saw it, I didn't pick a fight with the president; he had picked a fight with me.

I constantly repeated the point that what was meant to be humanitarian aid to refugees coming to Israel had become a misguided political missile, and I always reminded my audiences that the loan guarantees would eventually go to Congress—where they were likely to get a sympathetic hearing—for a vote. The word "eventually" worried me, however. My understanding of the need in Israel was very personal. I knew that some Russian refugees were doing quite well. My friends Igor and Ina Uspensky, for example, both biologists and both in their sixties, arrived in Israel in 1990, after years of being denied permission to emigrate. They were followed a year later by Igor's mother. The family had no resources beyond their academic credentials. The Israeli government provided them with a subsidy for shelter, clothing, and a variety of social services, including language education, and they soon became entirely self-supporting.

But there were many for whom the transition period was much more difficult and outlasted the available subsidies, some of my own family members among them. My cousin Nina, her husband, Pyter, and their sixteen-year-old daughter fled Moscow in the spring of 1991. They had been part of the city's upper-middle-class society, living in a large apartment with access to a number of amenities unavailable to other Russians. When the wave of anti-Semitism that arose as the Soviet Union fell reached my cousins' social circle, they decided that their long-term future should be in Israel. They arrived in Haifa, began studying Hebrew, and accepted the Israeli government-provided subsidies spread out over one year to help them settle—in Israel proper, not the territories. However, Nina and Pyter were unable to find jobs. They lived with another three-person family in a tiny apartment in Haifa, and 60 percent of their monthly allocation went to pay the rent. Then their subsidy stopped before they could be productively assimilated into the economy. Their story was not unusual.

In late January 1992, I met again with Prime Minister Shamir in Jerusalem. I wanted to review with him what had occurred and assure him that despite how things looked, the American Jewish community was still fighting for the guarantees. In addition, I tried once again to make him understand that the settlements really were the key to success: loan guarantees were never going to pass Congress or be approved by the president as long as Israel continued to build settlements. Of course, Shamir showed no signs of slowing down the building. Speaking to me, he blamed his inability to call a halt on political pressure exerted by his hard-line housing minister, Ariel Sharon. But while Sharon, then firmly committed to his own vision of a Greater Israel, was certainly actively encouraging the building wherever and whenever possible, there were additional pressures on Shamir. As

Yitzhak Rabin and the Labor Party mounted a serious challenge to his leadership in the coming elections, Shamir hardened his position to shore up his conservative base. And there were always the Arab countries and the Palestinians to consider. Any concessions to President Bush would be read by them as weakness in Israel's resolve, something that, in Shamir's opinion, must be avoided at all costs if Israel was to head into peace negotiations.

His mind made up, Prime Minister Shamir remained optimistic that the Bush administration would eventually relent on the loan guarantees without Israel changing its policy. Our conversation continued as I tried to convince him otherwise, adding my own belief that the loan guarantees were more important to the long-term health of Israel than the building of new settlements. I made no headway with him, and in the weeks that followed, relations between Washington and Jerusalem frayed rapidly, with the American Jewish community caught in between. By February, Senator Patrick Leahy, the Democratic chairman of the Senate Appropriations Committee's Foreign Operations Subcommittee and a longtime friend of Israel, stated quite emphatically in an op-ed piece that appeared in the *New York Times* that while he strongly supported helping the Israelis absorb new immigrants, he would "not support aid that would be used to finance further expansion of the settlements." He also added a healthy dose of political reality, saying that although there might be enough votes in the Senate "to ram through unconditional loan guarantees over President Bush's opposition, the House probably would not pass such guarantees, but even if it did, a [presidential] veto would be sustained." Two weeks later, Secretary of State Baker testified before the House Appropriations Committee formally linking the granting of loan guarantees to the cessation of construction of new housing in the West Bank and Gaza Strip. Baker was saying that Israel had a choice: settlements or loan guarantees. Or, since the administration already knew Shamir's position, Baker's statement could, as Leslie Gelb suggested in the *New York Times*, be seen to reflect "the White House message—no money for Mr. Shamir."[7]

The rhetoric began to escalate as accusations flew. On March 6, an editorial in the *Wall Street Journal* suggested that the White House "had gone out of its way to pick a fight with Israel. The fight allows Mr. Bush to demonstrate the U.S. drift toward Arabism...but Israel...will not be cowed by crude pressure. Perhaps Mr. Baker has been spending too much time with the despotic likes of [Syrian leader] Hafez Assad." The editors not only denounced the administration for abandoning Israel, they also stated that the president had "shown that he can intimidate American Jewish organizations."[8]

I found that assertion maddening enough to fire off a reply, telling the editorial board that "regrettably, the media has reported erroneously that the Jewish community is less than resolute in its support of the loan guarantees. These distortions…ignore the efforts of the community….Little if any coverage has been given to the fact that American Jews of every political persuasion strongly support Israel's request and insist there be no linkage between the humanitarian need to help absorb the refugees and the political issue of settlements."[9]

On the same day that the *Wall Street Journal* editorial appeared, former New York City Mayor Ed Koch reported in his *New York Post* column that at a recent White House meeting, when the secretary of state was criticized for his harsh language toward Israel, Baker replied, "F*** 'em. They [the Jews] didn't vote for us." Koch wouldn't reveal his source, but he claimed that Baker's "statement was made in the presence of the person who repeated it to me. I have no doubt that Baker made it."[10]

Well, maybe. Malcolm Hoenlein, executive director of the Conference of Presidents, and I met with Secretary Baker that day, and right away he told us, "The story isn't true." Malcolm and I expected the denial, of course, and we had agreed on our way to the meeting that, whatever the truth of the matter, we needed to support the secretary of state—there was just nothing to be gained by pressing the issue. Clearly, the secretary was finding it rough going fighting with the American Jewish community and those members of Congress who wanted Israel to receive the loan guarantees; I could overlook a comment uttered in anger and frustration. As I understood matters, the president and the secretary of state wanted to make peace, and make history. They were looking at the big picture, but their grand vision was being obscured by the complex political realities that always seemed to get in the way. It was their job to try to clear the way, just as it was our job to keep the needs of American Jews—particularly our desire to aid Israelis—within the picture. This might sometimes put us at odds with one another, but we had to continue to communicate. Furthermore, I never accepted the view that Baker held some special hostility toward Jews in general and Israel in particular. I refused to use the Koch column against the administration, and no one who tried to do so in my presence found a sympathetic ear.

Secretary Baker, Malcolm Hoenlein, and I got down to the real business of our meeting. We were there to discuss a compromise position on the loan guarantees proposed by Senate leaders, whereby the United States would reserve the right to deduct any monies from the guarantees that were being spent on settlements. We wanted the administration to know that the Jewish community would support such a compromise. Baker was interested; here was a workable solution in which the government could make funds available to Israel while retaining a measure of control over how they were used. However, I could see that he wasn't fully on board. He wasn't ready to let Israel get what it wanted before giving the United States what it had asked. Baker knew we were disappointed, but he stressed to me with particular feeling that American Jews should not construe the position taken by the Bush administration as an abandonment of Israel. I understood that he meant he was working hard to hold the line on American demands of Israel. The Bush administration had been speaking of "territory for peace;" that they had dropped the call to redefine Israel's borders and were instead willing to consider a halt to building in the settlements as a bargaining chip was thought to be something of a concession on their part.[11]

On March 17, President Bush formally answered the Israeli request for loan guarantees with a refusal. Two days later I held a press conference in the Capital Hilton in Washington, D.C. to address the administration's rejection. The questions from the press covered all of the old, painful ground, trying to pin responsibility for the failure on one of the interested parties—Israel, the Bush administration, or the organized American Jewish community. I refused to play their game and tried to keep the discussion where it belonged—on our differences over policy. I had to accept that Israel and the American Jewish community had lost this round, but we weren't giving up. Instead, we were ready for the next skirmish, keeping the media aware of the facts about the benefits of loan guarantees to the United States, and reminding people yet again that this money for Israel had a humanitarian purpose.

Why didn't the loan guarantees pass in the fall of 1991? Clearly, their failure was due to an intricate combination of forces. Yet if I had to point to a single circumstance, I would say that the loan guarantees got into trouble because of the personal relationship—or lack thereof—between President Bush and Prime Minister Shamir. While President Bush was ready to take a bold step or two into the future, he lacked a subtle understanding of the character of the Israeli prime minister by whose side he would need to tread. So Bush asked of the prime minister something Shamir could not grant.

As I mentioned, when I spoke to Prime Minister Shamir in January 1992, his response to my warning was basically, "Don't worry, it will work out." Not for an instant do I mean to suggest that Shamir was plagued by a bad case of wishful thinking. Neither was he deaf to the nuances of diplomacy, nor ignorant of the demands of geopolitics and the complexities of the relationship between the United States and Israel. However, he was by personal inclination and political affiliation a conservative, and he would never permit himself to make a decision that could in any way drastically alter the status quo in Israel. For Shamir, the potential downside could be too steep. He saw himself as a strict guardian of the Jewish state, and unlike that other Likud hard liner, Menachem Begin, he did not burn with the desire to project himself into the world historical canon through a grand gesture like the Camp David agreement with Egypt. No one looking back at the record would ever be able to say any harm ultimately came to Israel because of a mistake that Yitzhak Shamir had committed on his watch. If settlements were going to be discontinued, if the borders of Israel would be contracted, Shamir wouldn't be the prime minister to make that risky decision.

This analysis of Shamir's character and its impact on the negotiations for the loan guarantees is solely my speculation, but as proof of my argument I offer the following. In June 1992, Prime Minister Shamir lost the election to Yitzhak Rabin. Two months later, Rabin came to the United States to spend a couple of late summer days with President Bush and his family at his vacation home in Kennebunkport, Maine. There, President Bush announced that he was "extremely pleased" to grant the $10 billion in loan guarantees to Israel. Rabin, standing by the president's side, in turn announced that he was building "a relationship of trust and confidence with the president," adding that Israel's "change in national priorities" meant that there would be little or no funds spent on settlements.[12]

The conclusion of my relationship with the Bush administration came a month later in September of 1992. It was a political season. Bill Clinton was running against George Bush, who had seen his approval ratings—sky high in the triumphant aftermath of the Gulf War—sink like the proverbial stone as the economy continued to slide and showed no immediate signs of improving.

The choice for the presidency represented a generational and cultural divide, the baby boomer versus the veteran of the Second World War. The campaign rhetoric was contentious, and, to make matters more difficult for the president, a third-party candidate, Ross Perot, was attracting traditional Republican voters. George Bush could not afford to lose the support of those Jewish voters who had helped to put him in the White House for his first term. Unfortunately for him, despite the resolution of the loan guarantee matter and the warm relationship he enjoyed with Yitzhak Rabin, the rancorous disagreements between his administration and the American Jewish community were far from a distant memory.

In keeping with the Conference of Presidents' regularly scheduled briefings with the administration, we were invited to the White House on the morning of September 24, our last gathering before the general election. We sat in the Roosevelt Room and listened to Dennis Ross of the State Department's policy planning staff outline the current state of affairs regarding U.S. policy in the Middle East. When he was finished, James Baker spoke. He had—reluctantly, if one believed the rumors in Washington—left the State Department to oversee his friend's campaign, and what he said had the unmistakable air of someone trolling for votes.

Baker reminded us that during the last four years, three important goals had been achieved: the rescue of Soviet and Ethiopian Jewry; the approval of the loan guarantees; and face-to-face negotiations between Palestinians and Israelis.

"Don't forget under whose administration these things happened," Baker said. "And it is especially important that we don't lose the momentum in the peace talks."

He ended by saying that right now the United States' relationship with Israel could not be better, a statement I took to mean that he blamed Shamir for the earlier problems.

I shared one final poignant moment with James Baker during a break in the discussion. He pulled me aside and complimented me for being "a most articulate spokesperson for your case and your people." Then he added, "Shoshana, I appreciate your restraint on my behalf when they were trying to skewer me. I'll never forget it."

We left the White House before noon and flew to New York. We were slated to meet with Bill Clinton at the Sheraton so he could air his views and hear our concerns. Setting up a Conference of Presidents meeting with the candidate had been a chore. Clinton had tried mightily to avoid seeing us—a group of people with a variety of political inclinations—preferring a mix of his own supporters and some of our members whose votes he could count on. When I realized the Clinton campaign's intentions, I made it clear this arrangement would never fly, and George Stephanopoulos phoned to offer an apology.

Clinton was late, so the meeting began with Governor Mario Cuomo of New York reporting on his recent trip to Israel. He was an astute observer and wonderful speaker. Then Governor Clinton arrived and spoke to us. He was articulate and knew his facts. Unfortunately, the good impression he made was tarnished when his campaign staff managed to infuriate me. We had told the Clinton people in no uncertain terms that the Presidents Conference does not support specific candidates in an election. This has long been one of the most sacred principles of our organization, and our ability to remain scrupulously outside the fray is, to some degree, responsible for our success. Yet when we were finished listening to Clinton, his staffers ushered us into another room to talk to the press where my attention was immediately drawn to a banner on the lectern that read "Clinton for President." In addition, a number of his prominent Jewish supporters who were not members of the

Presidents Conference were seated in the front row. I could just imagine the pictures in the newspapers and on TV, images that would have made it appear as though I were campaigning for Clinton.

I insisted that the banner be taken down or I would simply inform the press about the problem and then leave. That, of course, would never do during a political campaign, and so the banner was removed. I told the press that the Presidents

Candidate Bill Clinton addressed the Conference of Presidents, 1992. Photo by David Karp. Reprinted with permission.

Conference does not endorse particular candidates, that Governor Clinton had told us he thought the current administration was too tough on Israel, and that he supported the peace process and would ensure it continued. No sparks flew, and the press departed quickly.

My term of office as chairman of the Conference of Presidents of Major American Jewish Organizations ended at the same time as George Bush's administration. It had been exhilarating and tumultuous, at turns satisfying and frustrating. Looking back at how I unhesitatingly waded into the controversies of the day, I am amused at how my younger self thought she wielded real power. Still, I never flinched from saying what had to be said, and had little fear of the far greater power of those to whom I spoke.

Above: Making a point for a UJA audience, c. 1992. Photo by Robert A. Cumins. Reprinted with permission.
Opposite page: Posing with Jerusalem Mayor Ehud Olmert, while on a trip to Israel on behalf of the Jewish Agency for Israel, 1994.

XIV
Challenges of Leadership

I had earned a respite. I was not seeking a new leadership position in the Jewish community upon retirement as chairman of the Conference of Presidents and the NCSJ, even though I might miss the excitement of an international platform. I had previously observed other leaders casting about somewhat desperately for a way to remain relevant once their terms of office were complete, and I had wondered how I would feel when my turn came. I had decided that I would not accept a position at any of the organizations that made up the Conference of Presidents; it would be sufficient to have a seat at the table as a past chairman, a position that entailed attendance at board meetings several times a year. I was sixty-six years old and still had enormous energy to direct toward any work that intrigued me. I was confident I would be called upon to somehow put to use the skills and knowledge I had acquired during my years of service to the community.

The call I answered was from Rabbi Irving (Yitz) Greenberg's National Jewish Center for Learning and Leadership (CLAL). When I agreed to chair CLAL, I made a choice that was unusual—it seemed incomprehensible to some—but was just right for me. CLAL was a small organization with more ambition than resources.

However, I believed strongly in its mission, which was Jewish leadership development. I have often said that anyone who chairs a federation fund-raising campaign can become the leader of a United Way campaign, but the reverse is not true. What distinguishes Jewish leadership is the application of principles taught in Torah and Talmud. The work we do for our community has always been grounded in Jewish tradition, but often, when we make our beliefs explicit, our community splinters because we disagree among ourselves on matters of interpretation and practice. CLAL pitches a large tent, encompassing leaders of all stripes, and fosters a vocabulary of mutual respect. I felt then, as I still do, that this is the kind of leadership our community needs to carry us forward, so I was eager to assist CLAL in achieving its goals, as they were then viewed by Rabbi Greenberg.

Yitz founded CLAL in 1974, at a time when relations between the Reform, Reconstructionist, Conservative, and Orthodox movements were becoming increasingly acrimonious. An Orthodox rabbi with a Ph.D. from Harvard University, he championed the concepts of pluralism and inclusiveness, believing that since "the Jewish polity could ill afford to lose the power that comes with unity," we had better learn to work together. Furthermore, in an era of growing Orthodox fundamentalism, Yitz braved censure from his own stream of Judaism and dared to suggest that it was time to embrace new ways to be Jewish. In particular, he recognized the fund-raising activism of the federation movement as an "inherently sacred" mode of Jewish expression, a stance which reflected my personal experience. One of the first organizations to emphasize Jewish education for adults, CLAL provided courses and other learning opportunities to federation leadership that strengthened the connection between our community-development goals and traditional Jewish teachings.[1] For example, CLAL faculty interpreted the text often referred to as *eilu v'eilu*, "these and these (are the words of God)," to mean that no single stream of Judaism had a monopoly on the truth—classical rabbinic support for pluralism. I found this approach inspiring.

CLAL was at a crossroads when I arrived at the beginning of 1993, and it soon became clear to me that my role during my two-year term as the organization's chairman would be to spearhead a strategic restructuring. Would CLAL become the leading edge of "post-denominational Judaism"—that is, Jewish practice that transcends identification with any of the four established religious movements—based on the principle of respect for diversity that Yitz had been espousing for two decades? Or should CLAL emphasize its mission as an educational organization, dedicated to training Jewish leaders and rabbis of the future? We chose the second, and it became my responsibility to help raise the profile of this growing university without walls.

Beyond the big questions were the day-to-day challenges: as in many young organizations where the strong founding director remained heavily involved, the executive director's office seemed to be entered and exited via a revolving door. Rabbi Greenberg, whose title at CLAL was president, was on sabbatical in Israel as I began my term, and his very able executive director backed a plan for the future that Yitz did not support. I worked hard to get the two of them on the same page, but in the end, thinking he had the board of directors in his corner, the executive director asked us to choose between their two visions for CLAL's future. At the time, we felt that Yitz was more important to the organization than this particular director, however sound his reasoning and however talented he might be, and I was soon without an exec.

CLAL faced additional difficult issues. Its constituency of aspiring leaders was primarily in New York, and it drew its board of trustees primarily from the same community. If CLAL were to achieve its potential as a national entity, we would have to broaden our base of support and the reach of our programs. Intertwined with this problem was our difficulty in fund-raising. CLAL depended heavily on major grants for issues conferences—a primary component of our work—but the grants did not cover many administrative costs. Raising funds became a big part of my task. Luckily, we were able to contract with Herman Markowitz, a seasoned organizational hand who had recently retired as executive director of the United Israel Appeal, to serve as interim executive director and help with our structural overhaul. Soon after that, we hired Donna Rosenthal to be our chief executive, a position she retains to this day.

Yitz dreamed of having a CLAL scholar in every major community. He knew, and I was able to verify in my travels for CLAL, that the American Jewish community hungered for tradition, for learning, and for Torah—more so, I thought, than in previous generations. We offered a well-regarded series of lectures that addressed this craving, but it was a very expensive project for many communities. With a little experimentation, we soon found that having local speakers address most of the series' study questions, with a CLAL scholar on hand to open and close the series, was an equally effective means of inspiring continuing education. This allowed us to spread ourselves widely and reach a broader audience of national leaders. I recommended that CLAL scholars teach CJF professionals at their offices and lead sessions for participants at the General Assembly, to give us more exposure. Soon federations around the country were inviting our faculty to present in their communities, so we began to grow and hired additional faculty.

It wasn't long after Yitz returned from sabbatical that it became clear to me he had outgrown CLAL. He was quite interested when philanthropist Michael Steinhardt offered him the opportunity to help develop the Jewish Life Network, but was not quite ready to cut the knot between him and the organization he had built. We worked out an arrangement in which CLAL and the Jewish Life Network shared Yitz's time for a year, easing his transition and ours. While, just a few months earlier, I had been convinced CLAL could not afford to lose Yitz, he and I now believed that we would survive his departure and use this change to continue our growth. Yitz designated the talented Rabbi Irwin Kula to be his successor. I invited Charles Bronfman—who was actively supporting several of the projects spearheaded by Rabbi Kula—to lead the board in a strategic planning effort.

I hadn't worked with Charles, but I knew he had little patience with the endless "pro-cess" (he pronounced the word with a Canadian accent, giving it a long "o" sound and undertones of disdain) of the Jewish communal world, a reputation for being a talented planner, and deep pockets. Luckily, the challenge intrigued him and by the time I completed my term, the organization was very different from the one I had taken charge of two years before. We had a new president, a new executive director and comptroller, and were poised to address the challenges of Jewish leadership and diversity.

A decade earlier, Yitz had predicted that the next generation of American Jewish leaders would come not from the rabbinate, as it had for previous generations, but from the laity. His words rang in my ears as I left my post at CLAL. While chairman, I had attended many CLAL programs, and I had seen auditoriums filled with those anxious to learn how to fuse today's challenges to yesterday's wisdom. I had also come to realize how many of our otherwise well-educated and sophisticated leaders were lacking in basic Jewish knowledge. I left with a better understanding of the needs of emerging Jewish leaders, and I hoped to make further contributions to the leadership development field.

When I completed my term in 1994, I thought that CLAL would be my last national agency chairmanship. For one thing, I was running out of positions to consider; by then, I had held the leadership of many national Jewish organizations. Also, Jewish communal leadership had begun a generational shift, and I was a member of the "old guard." However, I still held seats on the boards or executive committees of four primary and interrelated philanthropic agencies: the Council of Jewish Federations, United Jewish Appeal, United Israel Appeal, and the Jewish Agency for Israel. These positions could have provided me a ringside seat from which to watch as the volunteer and professional leadership of the community spent

A CLAL portrait from 1997, including (l–r): Morton Kornreich, Ben Zion Leuchter, Marty Stein, me, Rabbi Irving (Yitz) Greenberg and his wife, Blu Greenberg, Nadine Spier, Irwin Kane, and Robert Loup. Photo copyright Steve Friedman Photo. Reprinted with permission.

the last years of the century fighting over a redesign of these major communal organizations. I had been too long in a leadership position, however, to be a mere observer; much as I might have wanted to sit out this conflict, I soon became a key player in the internecine drama that ultimately led to the restructuring of the entire federation system.

An explanation of this saga must begin with a quick review of the "alphabet soup" of Jewish charities that held sway for most of the twentieth century. The first federation of Jewish charities was founded in Boston at the end of the nineteenth century. Its mission was to raise funds for and coordinate the efforts of local social service organizations and also groups that sought to aid Jews in Palestine and elsewhere in the world. It didn't take long for Jewish communities throughout the United States to replicate Boston's model. The Council of Jewish Federations and Welfare Funds (later Council of Jewish Federations, or CJF) was created in 1932 as a kind of trade association for this rapidly growing number of local federations. CJF supported federations' work by undertaking community studies and compiling demographic information, studying and reporting on overseas projects, developing standards and principles of best practice for social welfare programs, and providing a forum for the community to air disagreements and seek consensus on primarily domestic public policy issues that affected the Jewish community. CJF also assisted federations in conducting their local fund-raising campaigns.[2]

There were other early twentieth century groups that focused solely on raising money for overseas needs. Chief among them was the American Jewish Joint Distribution Committee (JDC), which was founded in 1914 to aid European Jews who were suffering the ravages of World War I. In 1925, the United Palestine Appeal (later the United Israel Appeal, or UIA) was created to unify the efforts of several groups working to raise money for Palestine.[3] Shortly afterwards, the organized community realized it also needed an agency to allocate those collected funds to service providers in Palestine, and in 1929, the Jewish Agency for Palestine (later the Jewish Agency for Israel, or JAFI) was born. JAFI doled out money for housing, employment, and education. Before the establishment of the State of Israel, it served as a *de facto* government for Palestine.

Before World War II, donations collected by local federations were pooled into a single fund at the United Palestine Appeal. The Appeal, in turn, allocated the money to JAFI for distribution in Israel, or to the JDC for distribution in Europe.[4] In 1939, United Palestine Appeal and the American Joint Distribution Committee together organized the United Jewish Appeal (UJA) in order to unite the independent fund-raising efforts to aid European Jews after *Kristallnacht*. Now the communal architecture became more complex. UJA decided right from the beginning to utilize the already well-established fund-raising muscle of the local federations to implement its campaign. Soon, it was leading the way to ever-more effective campaigns for a wide variety of domestic and international needs, in which communities raised greater and greater sums of money. The organization added leadership training and other educational programs to its brief, and it wasn't long before UJA became the largest voluntary philanthropy in Jewish history.[5]

During most of my career in the Jewish community, federations paid approximately 3 or 4 percent of their annual campaign receipts to CJF as dues. The system also called for each local federation to negotiate an annual commitment for a "partnership share," or percentage, of its fund-raising campaign to be granted to UJA, and the balance of the funds raised were retained for community use. Partnership share varied widely from city to city—ranging from 40 percent to as much as 70 percent—and, to some degree, from year to year. UJA reserved a portion of the federation-raised funds to pay for its overhead costs and distributed the rest to JDC and UIA. In a similar fashion, UIA (negotiating on behalf of the Jewish Agency) and JDC would come to a contractual agreement on the percentage of the UJA funds each of them would receive.[6] UIA then distributed its share to JAFI, by contract the sole beneficiary of this money. This distribution system evolved to ensure that the money was being spent in accordance with United States regulations governing nonprofit organizations.

The system I have described was complex and unwieldy. As things stood in the 1990s, we had a real need to streamline, to reduce duplication of services, and most of all, to cut costs. After the runaway success of the 1992 Operation Exodus campaign to assist the massive influx of Soviet Jews to Israel, donors were tapped out and local federation campaigns had become flat. This often occurred after communities extended themselves to the hilt for a special campaign, but this time it was a worrisome development because it came on top of sharp cuts in social welfare expenditures by the federal government. Federation agencies were feeling the pinch, and faced with greater needs at home, they began decreasing their commitments to UJA. Reduced partnership share, taken as a percentage of smaller campaign totals, translated into some very real cutbacks for the national agencies. The system needed to economize.

There were other signs that a radical change in the system was in order. Negotiations between federations and UJA had long been tinged with some reluctance and resentment on both sides. Federations chafed at the partnership share sent to UJA and distrusted its opaque accounting procedures. Additionally, by the 1990s, the largest federations had become increasingly independent. They were less likely to see themselves as part of a national system, and CJF had neither money nor clout to enforce the principle of "collective responsibility" among the communities. UIA was having difficulty protecting allocations for overseas needs and the sum of money it sent to Israel was declining dramatically. At the same time, the JDC was attempting to negotiate directly with federations for its allocation, trying to raise money above their partnership share.

Almost everyone felt there was money to be saved in a merger of the national organizations. But what would a merged agency look like? UJA and CJF were very different from one another. UJA was focused on overseas needs, while CJF's expertise lay in the domestic concerns of the North American communities. Furthermore, the two agencies could not have had more widely divergent corporate cultures. At CJF, decision-making was done by consensus while UJA fostered competitive, entrepreneurial drive. UJA's free-wheeling "cowboy culture" often led its directors to set priorities without consulting with the federations at all, while CJF was very responsive to federations but had ceased to lead them. UJA represented the priorities of wealthy donors, while CJF represented a wider range of community interests. UIA was an important piece of this puzzle because its board of directors represented the broadest spectrum of the Jewish community, including the Zionist and religious movements. Under the best of circumstances, it would be difficult to combine these three organizations into an effective single agency. Unfortunately, the process of change was complicated by "unclear expectations, unshared visions, mixed motivations, and multi-layered power games," in the sharply-worded critique of two university professors who examined the transformation.[7] As I saw it, once the executives of the "Big 19" federations (as the group of the largest federations is known) began pushing for a change, UJA went full-court press in a bid for institutional hegemony.

In my opinion, it was a mistake to allow this to happen. I felt that if a merger were to be accomplished, the national community's structure should look more like the structure of a local federation: CJF should be the entity setting the national agenda, and the powerful fund-raising know-how of UJA should be harnessed to that agenda for the good of Jewish communities both at home and abroad. Experience had taught me that some degree of separation and competition among our national agencies was a good thing, so that each acted as a check on the power of the others. Although a relatively small agency, UIA provided much-needed balance by including on its board representatives of organizations outside the federation system.

Discussions about merger were just getting underway when, in 1994, I was asked to consider taking the leadership of UIA. I was a bit wary. I knew the idea to abolish UIA had been discussed repeatedly for over a decade, so I called the executive director of CJF, Marty Kraar, to ask what plans were afoot regarding UIA in the current reorganization movement. When he assured me that "we have to change the way we do things, but dissolving UIA is not on the agenda right now," I agreed to accept the nomination and ultimately became chairman. It would be an intriguing challenge, I thought, to protect and guide the agency through the reorganization minefield.

Despite the view among some leaders that the United Israel Appeal was irrelevant, I felt that the UIA was undervalued by the community, and I hoped to raise awareness of its importance. For one thing, the UIA occupied (and still occupies) a unique and crucial legal niche in our community as the agency that receives U.S. Department of State grants for aid to refugees in Israel.[8] I had strong reservations about what would happen to this grant money if the Jewish community attempted to alter its agreements with the American government.

Second, I was aware of a little-known fact: UIA owned approximately 11,000 public housing apartments in Israel, making it one of the largest landlords in the country. I had discovered this several years earlier, when I was serving as a member of the Jewish Agency Executive. In reviewing agency budgets, I had noted an interesting oddity. I don't recall exactly what it was that tipped me off, perhaps a line item listed as "other income" that seemed much larger than a miscellaneous item should have been. I asked Florida attorney and JAFI board member Alan Shulman to investigate the matter. He spent three years digging into the murky records of land purchases made since the establishment of UIA.[9] In the end, Alan was able to document UIA ownership of thousands of housing units. Ownership of this much property conferred a certain amount of power, enough that when the Knesset voted to increase the rent it charged for subsidized apartments, UIA successfully lobbied for an equivalent increase in the rent it was charging for its apartments. Furthermore, the community would have to take into account the question of title for all that property before UIA could be disposed of.

Thirdly, I knew that UIA was meant to be the "principal arm of the American Jewish community in overseeing the use of funds raised for Israel."[10] By charter, it was UIA's responsibility to advise—in consultation with UJA and CJF—in the selection of the Chairman and Executive of JAFI (and of the World Zionist Organization, as well) and in nominating the American directors to the Board of the Jewish Agency. Federations had the opportunity to influence the selection of JAFI leadership through their twenty-four representatives on the UIA board, but, in my opinion, they had failed to recognize the power of their voting block. Had the federations and the UJA selected representatives who understood the UIA's vital role in overseeing JAFI, there would have been less talk about UIA's "irrelevance." And, had UIA exercised the power of the purse it held as landlord of millions of dollars worth of rental property, we might have found the authority to change the way JAFI did business and quieted some persistent complaints about it.

The Jewish Agency for Israel was battling an unsavory image. JAFI had long been perceived as a "hapless, immobile bureaucracy."[11] In the early 1990s, its reputation was further tarnished by negative publicity from a scandal over the executive's financial improprieties. To counter this image, both for JAFI's sake and, by extension, for the good of UIA, I wanted to bring greater attention to the superb field work JAFI *shlichim* (emissaries) carried out daily. In the former Soviet Union, for example, wonderfully dedicated young Israelis accepted postings to isolated and sometimes downright primitive communities, where they helped the local Jews develop the tools to educate themselves and their children, and establish or enhance communal institutions. This work was invaluable to those Jews who had made up their minds to stay and reinvigorate their Jewish lives in the countries of their birth, as I had predicted many would.

JAFI *shlichim* also staffed summer camps for children in the former Soviet Union. These camps were extraordinarily effective in promoting Jewish identity. The children who attended—including some who may not have been Jewish by *halachic* definition but who were accepted into the program because they wanted to identify as Jews—were transformed in one or two weeks of summer camp: they learned Hebrew songs, Israeli dances, and the *brachot* (blessings), and they went home rested, well-fed, energized, happy, and inspired to be Jewish. Every year, the number of children attending this popular program rose; one could look long and hard to find a more successful model for Jewish continuity. However, in the midst of the tight budgets of the mid-1990s, the JAFI treasurer cut allocations to these camps, a move that seemed to me shortsighted and absolutely wrong. I wanted to convince the board of governors to restore the funding, but did not know how I would accomplish that.

I had been a member of the board of the JAFI since 1984, and in 1995 was serving as the chairman of its Special Unit for Soviet Jewry. A day or two before I was to attend a JAFI budget meeting in Israel, I visited one of the summer camps with a UJA Women's Division mission. We told the children we visited that we would be traveling directly to Israel after leaving the camp, and that they might send with us a prayer or message to God to be inserted between the stones at the Western Wall. We promised to make a videotape of the messages being placed, so they could see that it was done. As we left the camp, we were presented with yellow camper's tee shirts emblazoned with the JAFI logo and the name of the camp in Hebrew and in Russian.

Upon our arrival in Israel, we were scheduled to attend the budget committee meeting prior to going to the Wall. We wore our yellow tee shirts to the meeting, and our bus waited outside the JAFI offices, ready to take us to our destination. When funding for the camps was brought up and the suggestion made to cut the program, I stood up to speak passionately in favor of maintaining the current budget and then said, "Mr. Treasurer, you may not have the money, but we are going to keep our promise to the children." A dozen or more yellow-shirted women walked out of the meeting in protest and boarded the bus. The Israeli media was on hand to record the fulfillment of our promise to the campers. As we placed the notes between the stones, some of our brightly clad protesters were interviewed and our modest demonstration found its way into the papers. The next day, when JAFI's budget request was submitted, the line item for the summer camps was restored.

I was gratified to find I could still prevail in such a skirmish, for by this time the community was engaged in a full-scale battle over reorganization and it was clear that UIA needed protection. Those leading the push for change had lost my support right from the start. When a motion to grant funding to an expensive commission that would study ideas for restructuring was presented at the April 1994 CJF

Above: Our group of yellow tee shirt-clad women at the Western Wall, 1995. Right: Kiev summer campers perform the song *Dovid Melech Yisrael*, with hand motions known to every Jewish camper the world over. They are wearing their yellow camp shirts.

quarterly, I became aware that both the UIA and JDC had been left out of the planning process. I immediately introduced an amendment from the floor calling for consultation with, and approval by, UIA and JDC of any proposals that might emerge from the study. I remember clearly the look of shock on the faces of those standing at the podium. It was their surprise at my interference—as well as the fact that, as incoming chair of UIA, I had not been consulted—that alerted me to the immediate danger brewing for UIA: we were to be sidelined, if not completely eliminated in the effort to streamline.

The study committee, which convened without UIA, issued its first concrete proposal for a new structure a year later, in May 1995. That scenario eliminated UIA completely, with its functions divided between UJA and CJF. UIA flatly refused to go along with it, and the committee went back to the drawing board, this time with a UIA representative present. A second proposal issued two months later was, from UIA's point of view, little better. This one suggested a merger between

UJA and CJF, with UIA subsumed into the new entity. Neither proposal recognized the role of UIA; both of them dismantled the system through which allocations to the overseas agencies were negotiated, and effectively excluded the Zionist and religious movements from those negotiations. Furthermore, the merged UJA-CJF entity, in my opinion, would violate certain principles of the system—specifically, fair (partnership) share and collective responsibility—which balance the natural independence of individual communities. As discussions turned increasingly contentious, Max Fisher—regarded as the dean of American Jewry—called the heads of CJF, UJA and myself, representing UIA, to a meeting at his home in Michigan,

hoping to help us resolve our differences. Unfortunately, we couldn't come to terms. I simply could not condone what I thought was a totally misdirected effort.

I fought hard but lost the battle. It was a bruising fight, not just for UIA, but for me personally, and for a generation of volunteer leaders who had given so much to the community. As the three organizations combined, so too did their governing bodies. Many leaders were left without a portfolio, which effectively denied our community their valuable, highly experienced guidance. CJF and UJA first merged under the name

Max Fisher was a colleague, friend, and mentor for many years. Here, we are on a mission in Israel, in 1990.

"Newco," and in 1999 renamed itself the United Jewish Communities (UJC) in a second restructuring that included UIA.[12] Before I completed my term of office in 1998, I was able to work out a legally binding five-year grace period during which UJC would phase in its governance of UIA. I hoped this would protect our important oversight role while insulating the organization from the worst of the growing pains UJC was sure to experience. Now that the five-year grace period has expired, UIA is a wholly-owned subsidiary of UJC, with an entirely UJC-appointed board. It retains its responsibility for funds allocated to JAFI. JDC, having refused to consider merging, has remained a very effective, independent entity, serving Jews in Israel and eighty countries around the world. Currently, the division of monies from UJC to JAFI and JDC is negotiated between the recipients—as in previous years—and not by UJC, which had attempted to do so.

This meeting was held at the 1999 General Assembly, not long after the merger agreements between CJF and UJA were signed. Participants include (l–r): Steve Solender, Joel Tauber, Charles Bronfman, and Carole Solomon. Photo by Robert A. Cumins. Reprinted with permission.

I had feared that the projected savings on overhead costs that would result from the merger were overblown, and that while economies of scale might eventually be found, it would take years and a period of painful readjustment before we would see real savings. I was right. The benefits were far lower than projected, and the adjustment period has indeed been painful. Eight years on, however, UJC's budget is slightly lower than it was in 1999. Holding the line against constant pressure for budget increases was not a small feat, achieved through difficult decisions and sacrifices.[13] Under the direction of President and CEO Howard Reiger, who brings remarkable vision to his responsibility, UJC has learned to identify with the total community. When UJC successfully led the 2006 Israel Emergency Campaign in the wake of renewed hostilities in Lebanon, it was an effort in which the organization successfully overcame the old divisions between federation fund-raising and UJA campaigns. I am hopeful that the services which CJF used to provide for federations— communal strategy, setting of priorities, demographic research, outreach, and promotion of the federation concept—will soon receive increased attention as well. I am cautiously optimistic that our community is regaining its balance and that UJC will lead us effectively into the future.

Why was this process so painful and fractious? Even after so many years, it is difficult to say what, precisely, went wrong. Perhaps there were just too many players with too great an investment in the way things were for the changes to be anything but painful. However, it seems to me that when the large federations asserted that they were the ones best placed to maintain control over the rising costs of serving the community, and used that assertion as a rallying call for change, they chose an issue that hid the underlying fragmentation of the community. Federations agreed to work together to control costs, while continuing to act independently regarding issues of priorities and policy. This inability to put aside local concerns for greater national and international unity strikes me as a grave failure of leadership. At the same time, other ostensible leaders were too easily led. These people did not know enough about the current system and did not critically examine the proposed changes. Finally, what caused me the greatest disappointment was that some individuals found a means for personal aggrandizement in the merger, forgetting that they were there to serve the interests of the community.

Back home, these lessons of leadership were very much on my mind as the Jewish community concluded the wrangling over structural reorganization and headed into a new century. A new group of leaders was taking the helm, leaders who would need thorough knowledge of the complex issues facing the Jewish community, and a wellspring of Jewish thought to inform their decisions. I turned to my home community, to the local level where new leaders emerge, to address leadership needs.

In Baltimore, Jewish communal professionals had been able to take advantage of the Baltimore Institute for Jewish Communal Service (later renamed the Darrell D. Friedman Institute for Professional Development) since 1971, but there was no complementary training for lay leaders, beyond the system of fund-raising campaign development that usually carries them through the ranks. In 1985, my family approached the Associated with the idea of a Jewish leadership development institute to be established in my name. Plans for this project were dropped when Jerry was indicted. (My children tried again in 1988, this time approaching CJF with the idea of establishing a national leadership institute. Unfortunately, this project never got off the ground, either.) Now, the need seemed greater than ever. Rabbi Joel Zaiman, of Baltimore's Chizuk Amuno Congregation—my congregation—was one of the many professionals concerned about the future of Jewish lay leadership in our community. After several lengthy discussions, he and I and Chizuk Amuno Congregation President Lee Hendler decided to join forces to respond to this communal shortcoming. In 2000, I created the Shoshana Cardin Institute for Leadership (SCIL), which debuted as a program for leadership development at Chizuk Amuno.

SCIL's curriculum was jointly developed by Rabbi Zaiman and Johns Hopkins University professor Dr. Ann-Michele Gundlach. Participants in the pilot program were experienced volunteer leaders who were committed to improving their Jewish literacy. In twelve intense monthly sessions, they studied traditional and contemporary Jewish texts on questions of power, authority, and communal responsibility. They also learned about the history and governing principles of Jewish communal systems, and prepared *divrei Torah*—short sermons, literally, "words of Torah"—as a "graduation" exercise. Since we initiated it, the institute has graduated two classes of leaders, in 2002 and 2003, whose attendance at sessions was stellar and who were passionate enough to demand longer sessions.

Hoping that sessions could be replicated in any community in the United States, I incorporated SCIL and copyrighted its curriculum. However, although the response of the students was enthusiastic, I learned that the team-teaching model is expensive, and the intense sessions are not for everyone. While I remained convinced of the soundness of the SCIL curriculum, I soon became involved in another effort to create a less expensive yet effective Jewish lay leadership development program.

Back in 1999, the Associated had convened a committee to address the lack of a development pipeline for volunteer leadership, to which I was named. Our committee held focus groups with local rabbis and community professionals to answer several questions: Where would we find candidates for leadership development? How could a leadership program serve the broadest segment of the Baltimore community? What skills were of primary interest both to our potential participants and to the organizations most likely to benefit from our "graduates"? Our research came to one particularly interesting conclusion. The community did not trust our federation to refrain from skimming the most talented candidates for its own purposes, so any program we started would need to be an independently chartered nonprofit organization.

I was enthusiastic about initiating another leadership development program, especially one that already had buy-in from the organizations represented by members of the committee and the focus groups. I contributed funds to a pilot program, and secured an additional grant from the Gerson and Sandy Eisenberg Foundation. We established a board of trustees, co-chaired by Ned Himmelrich and Laurie Weitz, hired Debra S. Weinberg to be our part-time director, and selected Dr. David Teutsch, past president of Reconstructionist Rabbinical College, to team-teach the course with Larry Ziffer, executive director of the Center for Jewish Education. *Acharai*: The Shoshana Cardin Leadership Institute, was born in 2005.

Like SCIL, the fourteen-month *Acharai* program ties Jewish philanthropy to traditional Jewish teachings. It is less intense than SCIL, however, and more accessible to a broad spectrum of participants. The first Acharai class graduated in 2007. The organization also administers the Baltimore Jewish Leaders Assembly, a

The Acharai graduating class of 2007. Faculty members Dr. David Teutsch and Larry Ziffer are in the back row, David on the far right, and Larry second from the left. Photo by Debra S. Weinberg. Reprinted with permission.

one-day event formerly sponsored by the Associated, where volunteer and professional leaders of diverse youth and adult constituencies are encouraged to develop a community-wide vision.

The demands on Jewish leaders and the ways in which Jewish leadership is exercised have changed enormously over the span of my career. When I joined Beacon Chapter No. 60, OES in 1949, we had no professional staff to advise us, no paid secretaries to communicate with us, no trained accountants to help us work through our budgets. Today, professional directors with advanced academic degrees develop sophisticated action plans to inform and guide the efforts of volunteers. On the whole, this has been a very effective partnership. As a community, we are raising many millions of dollars and reaching millions more people than ever before, to serve their increasingly complex needs. However, our philanthropic system has a natural tendency to break apart. A lot is riding on our ability to train and encourage a new generation of leaders to maintain it. The future of Israel, the very future of *Klal Yisrael* is at stake.

Above: The greatest reward of a long life: a houseful of grandchildren. Here, they pose as the family gathered at my house for Passover, 2004. Opposite page: Dr. Ismar Schorsch awarded me an honorary doctoral degree from the Jewish Theological Seminary on May 18, 1989. With us in this photo is Dr. Jack Wertheimer, professor of American Jewish history at the seminary.

XV
Reflection and Reward

M ost of the time, I am a person who focuses more on the present and on the future than on the past. I am usually too interested in what is going on around me right now—problems to be solved, new ideas to implement—to consider seriously the question of personal legacy. But one evening the Jewish Agency for Israel Board of Governors staged a tribute to me, and I began to reflect on my career in a new and different way.

It was June 22, 1998. I was not expecting to be recognized that night and was totally unprepared. Charles "Corky" Goodman, then chairman of JAFI, was eloquent in singing my praises, as was Bennett Aaron, who had just succeeded me as chairman of UIA. My vision was clouded by tears when Bennett called me to the podium. I rushed forward, tripped, and lost my left shoe, but continued to the microphone without it. My voice caught as I began to speak and Corky retrieved my shoe. Inevitably, the image of Cinderella flashed through my mind. But was the analogy apt?

I often say that I never planned my career, my public life. At no point did I tell myself, "After being president of the Associated, I think I'd like to be president of CJF," or, "Next, I'll be chairman of the Conference of Presidents." In some ways, I was like Cinderella—or any other fairy tale princess, for that matter—swept along by events to the realization of my dream to somehow change the world. Burning to make a difference in people's lives, my career in the Jewish community and in the wider world was, for me, attendance at the grandest imaginable royal ball. And what a dance it has been! I participated in redrafting the Maryland State Constitution, helped American women gain greater financial security, and led a campaign to give the Baltimore Jewish community financial stability. I traveled the world in the service of Jewish continuity, helped open the way for Jewish emigration from the Soviet Union, and bettered the lives of those who chose to stay. I spoke truth to power and reminded the world that anti-Semitism is unacceptable.

And what of my public realm "prince"? My lifelong love affair has been with *Klal Yisrael* and *Medinat Yisrael*—the Jewish people and the State of Israel. I learned the Zionist dream at my parents' knees, and everything I have seen in my lifetime has reinforced the message. In my generation, the possibility of a homeland gave our people a glimmer of hope at the time of its darkest despair. Now we have a home in Israel; if something were to happen to it, I believe we Jews would not be safe anywhere in the world. But our religion and our culture demand that we go beyond a commitment to nationhood. It is our responsibility to safeguard the future by knowing the teachings of our Torah, our heritage and history, and the remarkable accomplishments of our people. Our posterity lies in sharing with one another the beauty, wisdom, and joy of Judaism.

I had the help of several mentors along the way—all men because at that time there were no women to whom I might have turned. Bob Hiller's effect on my life was quite direct. From our first meeting, when I refused to be pressured into merging the Federation of Jewish Women's Organizations with the Women's Division of the Associated Jewish Charities, Bob quietly marked me as someone to be watched. He tested my skills when, as campaign co-chair of Women's Division, I suggested raising the level of giving among the women. After I passed that test by attracting women to participate at a higher level, Bob invited me to join the Associated's executive committee as a vice president. While there were further tests along the way, it was this step in particular that propelled my voluntary career into a higher orbit. When he moved to CJF, he quietly, and without my knowledge, made certain I was tapped for various roles at CJF as well. Just a few years later, he was directly responsible for my advancement to the top leadership spot.

At the same time, I was watching Bob and I was learning from him. He succeeded Harry Greenstein as director of the Associated Jewish Charities, an out-of-towner replacing a long-admired figure in the community. He quickly earned the respect of the Baltimore leadership with his quiet intelligence, political savvy, and commitment to the city. Bob was one who could put together a broad coalition to address a particular objective and then select the right professional to manage it. He could compromise with others, but knew when to insist that certain standards be met. He was persuasive and pragmatic and always in control, with the best interests of the community uppermost in his mind. I took note of his skills and expertise, lessons to be put to use at the right moment. I even mimicked his largely extemporaneous speaking style and found that it worked well for me. I learned from Bob that a leader needs to radiate poise and self-possession to remain in control. When he validated my efforts to do just that during the disruptive protest at the Toronto General Assembly in 1984, his approval provided me with a much needed boost in confidence.

I needed a different kind of mentor when Jerry's legal trouble was making headlines. At that point, I was not certain that I should or could continue as a spokesman for the Jewish community, and I seriously considered resigning from my positions. I turned to the rabbi of my congregation, Rabbi Joel Zaiman, who told me, "This doesn't have to pull you down." He reminded me that I was an individual and that I was not implicated in the scandal. He gave me the courage to maintain my dignity and carry on with my work. What I was doing was necessary because it was effective, he assured me. I'm not certain that others would have given me the same advice, and I am very grateful that he did.

I must also mention Ambassador Morris Abram, who taught me to operate at the highest echelons of power. I doubted that my experience at the helm of CJF had prepared me for the international challenges I subsequently faced as chairman of the National Conference on Soviet Jewry, but Morris raised my confidence by discussing the issues with me and seeking my opinion. He demystified high-level meetings by including me, prior to my assuming the chairmanship, in several of his appointments with Secretary of State George Shultz. Not only did this signal to Secretary Shultz that I was a trusted confidant and soon-to-be equal partner, it literally positioned me to look over Morris' shoulder as I sat beside him while he conducted his meetings. I learned how to pursue a special kind of agenda, reading along as he took notes on his lined, yellow pad of paper. I learned from him that charm and courtesy could take you far, but a will of steel was needed to ensure your point was made. And in case I needed to be reminded, Morris set an example of confidentiality and integrity. He never quoted the participants after a meeting unless it was for the benefit of the group; comments made to him off-record remained off-record.

Morris Abram, President Ronald Reagan, and I met in 1987. Photo by Rich Lipski. © 1987, the *Washington Post*. Reprinted with permission.

Morris put a lot of time and effort into guiding me, so I felt relieved when Dr. William Korey, a leading American and international authority on the Helsinki Process, East European anti-Semitism, and human rights, gave me his stamp of approval. He made a point of telling me, just as the second year of my term at NCSJ was beginning, "You are a very good student. I was worried when you came in because you hadn't been involved in the Helsinki process [meaning human-rights activism]. I must say, you learned the language and the issues in a hurry."

There were other key lay leaders who served as my advisors and guides. Max Fisher opened all doors to Republican presidents and secretaries of state—he even arranged seating for me at prestigious tables at state events. Rabbi Israel Miller advised me how to present my message at the annual Washington Prayer Breakfast and other national non-Jewish events. Chuck Hoffberger, chairman of the board of JAFI, assigned me many important roles, including a most difficult and potentially explosive diplomatic task: to arrange for JAFI Chairman of the Executive Leon Dulzin to resign his position with dignity. Mendel Kaplan and Simcha Dinitz entrusted me with the chairmanship of the JAFI Special Unit for Soviet Jewry, a five-year experiment that sought to increase *aliyah* from the former USSR while at the same time supporting the Jewish traditions and activities of those who chose to remain. I am deeply appreciative of all those who advised and enabled me to succeed.

Lay leaders do not operate alone. In each organization chairmanship I have held, I was fortunate to partner with outstanding professional executives. Each time

I began a new position, I made it a practice to meet with my CEO to clarify our corresponding expectations and responsibilities. Our conversations were direct and open, and in each case we built relationships of trust and respect. We learned to consult one another closely, and to act in concert so as to avoid surprises or embarrassments. It is my opinion that day-to-day operations are the responsibility and purview of the professional, while the lay leader and board establish policies and directions, with the advice of the professional. I must mention Stephen Solender at the Associated; Carmi Schwartz at CJF; Martin Wenick and Mark Levin at NCSJ; Malcolm Hoenlein at the Conference of Presidents; and Jay Yoskowitz and Rabbi Daniel Allen at UIA. All are consummate professionals and it was a joy to work with them. Without them, little would have been accomplished.

Yes, I think the analogy to Cinderella is appropriate. There are moments of fairy tale unreality to the power and responsibility that come with being a leader, and it is easy to get carried away. To feel an audience respond to your conviction, to speak with a passion that brings them to their feet, is intoxicating. When you think your

A story accompanies this photo, taken on the occasion of a state dinner in Israel marking the end of Seymour Reich's term as chairman of the Conference of Presidents and the beginning of my term. Before the dinner, I missed my plane to Israel. After trying frantically and unsuccessfully to find another flight that would arrive in Jerusalem in time for the event, I finally called Israeli Consul Uri Savir and asked him to advise the Prime Minister's office that I would miss the dinner but would arrive for talks the next day. By the time I was able to confirm a flight, I received word that the prime minister's office decided to postpone the dinner until I could attend. This was a gracious gesture and an unprecedented honor, which I attribute to the importance of the Conference of Presidents of Major American Jewish Organizations. Photo by Isaac Harari. Reprinted with permission.

I introduced former British prime minister Margaret Thatcher at the 1992 Jewish National Fund Ball in Baltimore. Photo by Linda Rosenthal. Reprinted with permission.

words will affect millions of lives, it becomes challenging to maintain a proper perspective about your place in the vast scheme of things.

Life has a way of helping you regain your humility, however. In 1991, a year I might easily describe as "the height of my power," I participated in a JDC mission to Romania to commemorate the Holocaust in Bucharest, fifty years after the fact. Our group flew from Tel Aviv to Bucharest to Iasi, and traveled in a caravan of cars from the Iasi airport to a cemetery deep in the countryside outside of Iasi, where we were joined by Romanian Jews who had arrived there in buses. After the commemoration, I became engrossed in a conversation with a Romanian woman who was delighted to have someone with whom to speak Yiddish. As I bade her goodbye, I turned and watched the last of the buses leave. It was then that I realized my group had gone on to their next stop—a Jewish community center about twenty miles away. They had left without me!

I wasn't truly concerned until the caretaker of the cemetery, with whom I shared no common language, refused for some incomprehensible reason to take me to the center—that's when a form of terror gripped me. A policeman in a car came by but he, too, refused to take me down the road. Finally, the caretaker flagged down a pickup truck headed in the right direction. The two young men inside seemed to find my predicament highly amusing, and agreed with great good cheer to drop me at my destination, which they acknowledged they understood. I climbed nervously into the truck and we headed out.

For the next half hour, I stared intently out the window of the truck, hoping to recognize the right place as we came upon it, while the men beside me laughed and joked (I imagined) at my expense. And then the ordeal was over. With enormous relief, I pointed to the JCC, they dropped me off, and away they went. I collected myself and walked into the community center, expecting a rush of greetings and expressions of concern, but not a single soul asked where I had been. Apparently, they had not missed me at all! I didn't say a word about my adventure, and to this day no one who was on that trip knows what happened. It was a powerful lesson in humility.

I'd like to think I didn't need such a pointed lesson. I have tried to stay grounded, always focusing on issues and objectives rather than on my place in events. I never cared whether credit was assigned to me, and I was quick to recognize the work of others. It was not important that my name or photograph appear in the news. Instead, I was interested in conveying a clear message that got results. I also wasn't overly concerned about appearing to be in the wrong or taking the blame. While I have tried hard to build consensus, I learned long ago that disagreements were about issues, and were not to be taken personally. I concentrated on making a cogent case for my position, knowing that if I were successful, people would follow me. And I formulated my position in concert with my inner moral compass and in tune with what I and many others envisioned as the best future for our people. There were times when I had to tell some very powerful people that I and my organization would not be able to do what was asked: I told Prime Minister Shamir I would not cancel CJF's efforts to derail changes in the Law of Return; I did not heed Secretary of State Baker's request that the Conference of Presidents cancel the loan guarantee Education Day; I told President Bush I could not speak for him to the leadership of the Jewish community; and there were numerous other times when I refused to make deals I felt were not in the community's best interests. It is not easy to say no in these circumstances, and standing up for a principle must be done judiciously and with great care. In my opinion, these are the hallmarks of an effective leader— any leader, whether a man or a woman.

I add that qualifying phrase because people often ask me how it has felt to be a woman in leadership. I have considered this very carefully, and I must assert that while I was often the only woman in a roomful of men, I did not feel isolated. With the exception of the time I was prevented from toasting the king of Morocco, I never felt I was treated differently because of my gender. This will disappoint people, I know, but it is true. While my ascension to several official positions broke precedents and barriers, I waged no wars and stormed no battlements to achieve them. I simply conducted myself in a forthright manner, and I tried to bring to bear on the issues every ounce of preparedness and commitment I had at my disposal. I was focused and pragmatic and down-to-earth. I was not emotional, remaining almost always in control of myself. While I made it a point to dress attractively,

197

aware that first impressions are critical, I was never flirtatious. I made it clear that work relationships were not social relationships. When at work, I rarely thought of myself as a woman, or as a representative of womankind.

This doesn't mean I was unaware that my gender might be on someone's mind (most often, I would be alerted when someone suppressed a vulgarity), or that I didn't recognize how often I was the lone woman among men. I remember with amusement an incident where the tables were turned at a 1987 Department of Labor conference that underscored the gender distinctions I usually overlooked. I was one of a group of women and just a couple of men who were speaking rather intensely together while walking down the hall during a break in the conference. I'll never forget the look on the men's faces when they realized we were headed towards the ladies room. We women continued the conversation as we entered the bathroom, leaving our male colleagues behind. Once inside, we all enjoyed a moment of sisterhood as one of the women tartly noted, "Now they know how it feels!"

Is it "womanly" for me to declare that as important as my work has been to me, my family has always meant more? For that has certainly been a guiding principle of my life. I am grateful to my parents for everything I learned from them, including how to balance passion with moderation, and idealism with pragmatism. Abba died in 1985, disillusioned by all that had befallen Jerry. The public lynching of his son-in-law sent him into a tailspin, and he seemed to fade away before my eyes. I was sorry to lose his good counsel so soon after I had moved into the national spotlight. He was a clear thinker and an ardent Zionist who never let his ideology and affection for the State of Israel cloud his sense of realpolitik. My mother died two years later. Only as a widow was she able to open up and share with me the constant physical and emotional pain with which she lived as a child and as an adult. During the last two years of her life, she spoke about the bitterness with which she viewed the disappointments of her childhood and marriage. I wondered at how well she had hidden all this, or how I had not seen it, and regretted how little I had done to help.

I have only one sibling, my brother Zvi, from whom I learned to be as comfortable and friendly with boys as I was with my girlfriends. As he grew to be a warmhearted man with a great sense of humor, we developed the affectionate relationship that only adult siblings can share. Our families have remained close, and I treasure his friendship and support.

My husband—partner, supporter, father of my children—deserves special attention. I was proud and happy to be able to fashion our home as Jerry envisioned it, a place that could be both a backdrop for his success and a reservoir of love and acceptance. In return, Jerry encouraged me to channel my energies in ways that helped me find my voice, develop my skills, and learn some important lessons in leadership. He became my cheerleader even as my work took me farther and farther away from him, and he generously put the fruits of his financial success at my disposal. Nothing I have achieved would have been possible without him.

Jerry left prison in 1989 a broken man, but he tried hard to reestablish himself in our home in Florida. He maintained an office in Deerfield Beach and drove himself to work each day as he cast about for an activity at which he could succeed. He became a partner in a men's clothing store—something he knew little about; he attempted to go back into construction; he invested in some property in Nevada. Unfortunately, none of these ventures worked out well. When I was home with him, we rarely spoke about my work. Instead, we relaxed together and tried to enjoy the days we had. It was hard for me to watch him struggle for breath and to realize that his mind could not regain its former agility, but he remained independent almost until the end. His downturn was sudden and harrowing, brought on by an emergency visit to the hospital that occurred when I was away, in Baltimore to help his recently widowed father negotiate changes in his own living situation. I returned to Florida to find Jerry on a respirator in the hospital, after a tracheotomy which rendered him speechless. I lost him three weeks later. Jerry's last days were an agony of uncertainty during which he was connected to life support equipment against his wishes. In the end, unable to speak, he was able to indicate to me that he wanted to be taken home to die. It was Chanukah—December 1993; he was only sixty-eight years old

Our children and grandchildren were a joy for both of us, and have continued to be a special light in my life. My close bond with my daughters has included knowing with an uncanny certainty when they were about to give birth to each of their eight children. Ilene was the first to make us grandparents, in 1978. Jerry and I were vacationing in Florida when I turned to him and said, "We have to leave. Ilene's going to have the baby." Jerry knew better than to question my "sixth sense" about these things, so we found a flight to Baltimore and then headed to Washington, D.C., where Ilene and her husband lived at the time. In those days before cell phones, we had received no call from the expectant parents, but we headed directly to Bethesda Naval Hospital from the airport. We arrived just as the new baby headed off to the nursery and our son-in-law was on the telephone trying to reach us. He was very surprised to see us as we walked up to him, but Ilene wasn't surprised at all.

I had a similar experience when my daughter Nina, who then lived in New Jersey, was pregnant with her third child. I called her to say I was coming to stay with her two days earlier than we had planned. "Mom, I'm fine," she told me.

Students Vadim Kashtelyan and Talia Boxman carry Torahs through the congregation during services celebrating the opening of the Shoshana S. Cardin Jewish Community High School on October 15, 2003.

"Don't come." Naturally, I went anyway, and she went into labor that very night saying, "Mom, how did you know?" One or two such incidents could be chalked up to serendipity. However, I was at the hospital just before or immediately after the birth of each one of my daughters' children—this was all the more remarkable when you consider how often I traveled—so I ascribe this ability to my motherly connection with them. My sons and I have also enjoyed special relationships, but in different ways.

It was partly family needs and partly conviction that led me to say "yes" to a new leadership challenge in 2000. By that time, my public career had ended, I was developing health problems, and I was content to stay at home and limit my activities to the local Jewish and general community. When I was invited to co-chair with Stewart Greenebaum, a local businessman and philanthropist, the founding committee of a pluralistic, transdenominational Jewish high school in suburban Baltimore, I was intrigued. I believed strongly in the mission of the proposed school: to create an atmosphere where students of diverse Jewish backgrounds could learn together and barriers between them would be broken down. The fact that two of my granddaughters were then searching for a high school with just such a mission made the project that much more compelling for me.

This start-up project was far more difficult than we imagined. There was no large group of parents clamoring for such a school, nor did the Associated, our Baltimore federation, evince support for us by either backing our mission or providing financial assistance. With a Jewish community close to 100,000 strong, Baltimore was already lucky enough to support a number of excellent Jewish day schools, and many people did not understand why we were seeking to found yet another. To those of us committed to pluralism within Judaism, however, the reason was obvious, and luckily our most vocal partners were a group of three Conservative and Reform rabbis whose congregations had K–8 day schools and religious schools. Together, we held a series of meetings to which every synagogue was invited to send a representative to hear about our concept. In September 2001, we judged we had sufficient support to incorporate as the New Jewish Community High School of Greater Baltimore.

Just as we were turning to private Jewish foundations for funding, the financial markets took a serious nosedive. We saw promised grants shrink by a factor of ten, but we soldiered on. We recruited an energetic board of trustees, hired a head of school, and secured offices. And in our 2001 mission statement, we put our vision on paper in a fashion that was easy to understand:

> We will build and sustain a community where Jewish and secular cultures not only co exist but are interwoven aspects of an organic whole. Students will learn of our past and be active members of our present in order to be leaders of our future. Jewish youth face the challenges of the complex world of the 21st century. They must emerge from their secondary education with a sophisticated vision, one based not only on knowledge and scholarship but on an obligation to the ethical principles of our tradition …a commitment to the cultural, spiritual and religious traditions of the Jewish people, and a strong sense of identity as American Jews.

In the winter of 2002, with fund-raising moving along slowly and the target date for opening, in fall of 2003, approaching rapidly, my phone rang. I picked it up and couldn't quite believe the words I heard. Stewart Greenebaum was calling to inform me that he was recommending to the board that they rename the school the Shoshana S. Cardin Jewish Community High School.

When I found my voice, I told him "No, thank you." Forty years of laboring in the tangled vineyards of the philanthropic world had taught me that in a serious fund-raising campaign, the most attractive and effective request for a large gift offers the potential donor a "naming opportunity." Jerry and I had always been generous givers, but we were not in the rarefied league of those who have institutions or buildings named in their honor. I told Stewart that we ought to save the name of the school for a later date and for someone capable of making a sizable gift. No, he told me, he and the board disagreed with that reasoning; the time had come to acknowledge an international leader—because of her lifetime of service, not the size of her check. The school was renamed.

The school opened on time, and in 2007 we acquired a property for a campus to be located in the heart of the Owings Mills area, near Garrison Forest Road, Ruxton School, and the Torah Institute. In 2007, we also graduated our first class of twenty-nine bright, enthusiastic, and committed students. I am proud to say that they were admitted to fine colleges and universities, and I fully expect that they will each contribute in significant ways to the future of America and the Jewish community. We are on our way to fulfilling our mission.

During my career as a volunteer working for a variety of political and philanthropic groups, my work has not gone unnoticed. I'm the proud owner of some three dozen humanitarian and woman-of-the-year awards, and I hold a collection of honorary degrees from institutions around the world. I have gone to dinners at the White House and held discussions with presidents, secretaries of state, ambassadors, and prime ministers. I have appeared on local and national television numerous times, and I have been praised and criticized in print and on TV. But this Jewish high school which bears my name is my proudest achievement—bar none. It is the reward of a blessed lifetime.

List of Abbreviations

The following list of acronyms, which those of us working in the community often refer to as "alphabet soup," is meant to assist readers of this book.

ADL: Anti-Defamation League
AIPAC: American Israel Public Affairs Committee
AJC: American Jewish Committee
CHAI: Comprehensive Housing Assistance, Inc.
CIVIC: Council of Independent Voters for an Improved Constitution
CJF: Council of Jewish Federations
CLAL: National Jewish Center for Learning and Leadership
CSCE: Conference on Security and Cooperation in Europe
GA: General Assembly (annual meeting) of the Council of Jewish Federations and United Jewish Communities
HIAS: Hebrew Immigrant Aid Society
HRD: Human Resources Development
JAFI: Jewish Agency for Israel
JCC: Jewish Community Center
JDC: American Jewish Joint Distribution Committee
JEA: Jewish Educational Alliance
JTA: Jewish Telegraphic Agency
MSSIC: Maryland Savings-Share Insurance Corporation
NCSJ: National Conference on Soviet Jewry
NJCRAC: National Jewish Community Relations Advisory Council
OES: Order of the Eastern Star
PTA: Parent-Teacher Association
SCIL: Shoshana Cardin Institute for Leadership
UCLA: University of California at Los Angeles
UIA: United Israel Appeal
UJA: United Jewish Appeal
UJC: United Jewish Communities
WZO: World Zionist Organization
YMCA: Young Men's Christian Association

Appendix:
Shoshana Shoubin Cardin
Curriculum Vitae

Place of Birth: Tel Aviv, Israel

Marital Status: Widowed (husband was Jerome S. Cardin)

Children: Steven H., Ilene M. Vogelstein, Nina B. Reisner, Sanford R.

Grandchildren: 13

Education:
Baltimore City Schools
Johns Hopkins University, McCoy College, 1942–1945
University of California at Los Angeles, B.A., 1945–1946
Fellow in Organizational and Community Systems,
    Johns Hopkins University, 1976–1977
Wharton Entrepreneurial Center, Management Seminar, 1978
Antioch University, Baltimore, Maryland, M.A. in Planning and Administration
    for Nonprofits, 1979

Profession:
Teacher, Secondary Schools, Baltimore City, 1946–1950
Director, Calvert Telecommunications Corporation, 1976-1981
Career Volunteer
Organizational Consultant

Current Service:
Executive Committee, NCSJ
Board of Trustees, *Acharai*: Shoshana Cardin Leadership Institute
Board Member, JTA: The Global News Service of the Jewish People
Board of Trustees, United Jewish Communities
Board Member, CLAL—The National Jewish Center for Learning and Leadership
Committee Member, AJC Task Force on Peoplehood
Board Member, The Associated: Jewish Community Federation of Baltimore

Advisory Committee Member, Sadat Lecture For Peace

Board Member, Shoshana S. Cardin Jewish Community High School

Board Member, Jewish National Fund

Leadership Positions Held:

Chairman, Jewish In-Marriage Initiative, 2005–2006

Vice Chairman, Wilstein Institute, 2005–2006

Vice President, Jewish National Fund, 1999–2005; Executive Committee, 2006–2007

Chairman, Shoshana S. Cardin High School, 2003–2007

Executive Committee, America-Israel Friendship League, 2004–2005

Chairman, "Press Ambassadors," The Israel Project, 2003–2004; Board Member, 2003–2005

Vice President, Chizuk Amuno Congregation, 2002–2004; Board Member, 2005–2007

Board of Trustees, Uriah P. Levy Chapel and Jewish Center at the U.S. Naval Academy, 2000–2006

Chairman, Jewish Telegraphic Agency, 1999–2001; President, 2001–2003

Chairman, United Israel Appeal, 1994–1998; Director (Board Member), 1984–1988, 1990–1999; Executive Committee, 1999–2003

Vice Chairman, United Jewish Communities, 1999–2001

National Vice Chairman, United Jewish Appeal, 1992–1998

Board Member, Jewish Agency for Israel, 1985–2000; Chairman, Former Soviet Union Unit, 1990–1996; Chairman for Long Range Planning, 1987

National Chairman, Jerusalem 3000 Committee, 1995–1996

Chairman, CLAL—The National Jewish Center for Learning and Leadership, 1992–1994

Vice Chairman, Governor's Volunteer Council of Maryland, 1985–1993

Chairman, National Conference on Soviet Jewry, 1988–1992

Chairman, Conference of Presidents of Major American Jewish Organizations, 1991–1992

President, Council of Jewish Federations, 1984–87, Executive Committee Member, 1980–1984

Chairman of the Board, The Associated: Jewish Community Federation of Baltimore, 1983–1985; Executive Committee, 1981–2005; Vice President, Social Planning and Budgeting, 1977–1979, 1980–1981; President of Women's Division, 1975–1977

Director, Goldseker Foundation, 1984–1985

Board Member, United Way of Central Maryland, 1983–1985

Board Member, Health and Welfare Council of Central Maryland, 1980 1985

Chairman, Maryland Volunteer Network, 1980–1982

Chairman, Maryland State Employment and Training Council, 1979–1983

Commissioner, Maryland Commission on Human Relations, 1976–1982

Participant, Copenhagen '80: The Washington Conference for Women, 1980

Board Member, Loyola/Notre Dame Library, 1980–1984

Board Member, Junior League of Baltimore Resource, 1980–1983

Board Member, Baltimore Hebrew College, 1979–1982

Member, Governor's Task Force on Title XX Planning, 1978–1979

Member, Maryland State Board of Higher Education, Advisory Committee,
    Title 1A, 1978–1988

Chairwoman, Maryland Commission for Women, 1974–1979

Board Member, Goucher College, Advisory Committee, National Policy Studies
    Institute, 1978–1979

Board Member, Goucher College Volunteers, Practicum Advisory Committee,
    1978–1979

Board Member, Antioch University, Yellow Springs, Ohio, 1977–1978

Vice Chairman, Maryland Delegation, National Women's Conference, 1977

Vice Chairman, Maryland Women's Conference, 1977

Board Member, National Association of Commission for Women, Education
    and Research Fund, 1976 1977

Board Member, Maryland Association of Parliamentarians, 1976–1977

Delegate, National Conference of Volunteerism and Citizenship, 1976

Board Member, National UJA Women's Division, 1975–1977

Co-Founder, Women Together, 1973; Executive Committee, 1973–1976

Board Member, College of Notre Dame of Baltimore, Continuing Education,
    Advisory Committee, 1974–1975

Secretary, Voluntary Action Center of Central Maryland, 1973–1975;
    Executive Committee, 1971–1976

Board Member, Baltimore County General Hospital Auxiliary, 1972–1974

Board Member, National Retinitis Pigmentosa Foundation, 1971–1987

Board Member, Jewish Community Center of Baltimore, 1970–1976

Co-founder and President, Jewish Community Center, Volunteer Associates,
    Baltimore, 1969–1971; Executive Committee, 1969–1976

Coordinator, Women's Fair of Baltimore, 1975

Board Member, Brandeis University Women of Baltimore, 1967–1969

Board Member, Park School Parents' Association, 1966–1971

Board Member, March of Dimes, Baltimore Chapter, 1966–1968

Secretary, Baltimore Jewish Council, 1967–1970; Board Member, 1963–1970; 1980–1982

President, Federation of Jewish Women's Organizations of Maryland, 1965–1967; Board Member, 1960–present

Co-Chairman, Maryland Interfaith Conference for Peace, 1966

Board Member, Maryland Association for Mental Health, 1965–1966

President, Chizuk Amuno School P.T.A., 1964–65; Member of School Board, 1963–1965

Board Member, National Council of Jewish Women, Baltimore Section, 1963–1965, 1968–1972, 1973–1974

Board Member, Levindale Ladies' Auxiliary, 1961–1965

Worthy Matron, Beacon Chapter No. 60, O.E.S., 1959–1960

Co-Chairman, High Holy Day Campaign, Israel Bonds, 1959

Elected Position:

Delegate, Maryland Constitutional Convention, 1967

Publications:

Strategies for Success—Surviving the New Federalism, Maryland Volunteer Network, 1982, Co-Editor

Volunteerism: Moving into the 1980's, Voluntary Resources Coalition, 1979, Co-Editor

Decade of Progress, Maryland Commission for Women, 1976

Women: Where Credit is Due, Maryland Commission for Women, 1976

Getting It Together? How to Run A Fair, Women Together, 1974, Co-Author

Leadership Logic, Federation of Jewish Women's Organizations of Maryland, 1974, Co-Editor

Papers Given:

Jews, Judaism and Community—A Look at Tomorrow, Milender Fellow, Benjamin Hornstein Program in Jewish Communal Service, Brandeis University, March 7, 1987

The Center and the Community, Jewish Welfare Board Biennial Convention, May 1980

Professionalization of the Volunteer, National Conference of Jewish Communal Service, 1978

Honorary Degrees:

Gettysburg College, Doctor of Humane Letters, May 2007

Baltimore Hebrew University, Doctor of Humane Letters, May 1996

Syracuse University, Doctor of Humane Letters, May 1994

Hebrew College (Boston), Doctor of Humane Letters, June 1993

Touro College, Doctor of Humane Letters, May 1993

Bar-Ilan University, Doctor of Philosophy, April 1993

Jewish Theological Seminary, Doctor of Humane Letters, *Honoris Causa*, May 1989

Western Maryland College, Doctor of Humane Letters, May 1986

Awards:

Torch of Liberty Award, NCSJ, Advocates on Behalf of Jews in Russia, Ukraine, the Baltic States and Eurasia, June 2006

Humanitarian Award, Federation of Jewish Women's Organizations of Maryland, May 2006

State of Maryland Governor's Citation for Outstanding Leadership Locally, presented by Maryland Governor Robert Ehrlich, 2006

Senate of Maryland Resolution in recognition of service to Federation of Jewish Women's Organizations of Maryland, Presented by Senator Paula Hollinger, 2006

Inductee, Maryland Women's Hall of Fame, 2005

Resolution, Maryland Senate, 2005

International Lion of Judah Award, UJC National Women's Philanthropy, 2004

Dedicated Publication, Journal of Jewish Communal Service, as Exceptional Volunteer Leader, November 2004

Maryland's Top 100 Women, *The Daily Record*, May 2003

Andrew White Medal, Loyola College of Maryland, 2002

Resolution for Leadership, Maryland Senate, 2001

Resolution for Leadership, Maryland House of Delegates, 2001

The State of Israel, Exemplary Leadership Award, 1998

Woman of Achievement, Federation of Jewish Women's Organizations of Maryland, 1997

Tribute, Project Interchange, 1997

Governor's Citation, presented by Maryland Governor Paris Glendenning, 1995

Official Citation for Devoted Leadership, Maryland House of Delegates, 1994

Resolution for Leadership, Baltimore County Council, awarded by Melvin G. Mintz, 1994

Victorine Q. Adams Humanitarian Award, Fuel Fund of Central Maryland, 1995

Henrietta Szold Humanitarian Award, Hadassah, 1994

Keter Shem Tov, Reconstructionist Rabbinical College, 1993

CLAL Yisrael Award, *In Concert for One People*, 1992

Zvi Hirsch Masliansky Award, Hebrew Immigrant Aid Society, 1992

Rita V. Fishman Human Relations Award, Anti-Defamation League, 1992

The Mathilde Schechter Award, Women's League for Conservative Judaism, 1992

Myrtle Wreath Award, Baltimore Chapter Hadassah, 1991

Governor's Salute to Excellence, Governor William Donald Schaefer, 1991, 1992

Yeshiva University, Women's Organization, 1991

AMIT Women, Distinguished Service Award, 1991

Golda Meir Honoree, State of Israel Bonds, Maryland, 1991

Distinguished American Jewish Communal Leadership Award,
    Brandeis University, 1990

The Defender of Jerusalem Award, Jabotinsky Foundation, 1990

Lifetime Achievement Award, Women's Division, Council of Jewish
    Federations, 1990

Justice Louis D. Brandeis Award, ZOA, 1990

Golda Meir Human Relations Award, Na'amat, U.S.A., 1989

Certificate of Appreciation for Devoted Service, American Jewish Joint
    Distribution Committee, Inc.

The Menorah Award, Maryland Women's Division, State of Israel Bonds, 1988

Outstanding Woman Volunteer, Junior League of Baltimore, 1987

Humanitarian of the Year Menorah Lodge, B'nai B'rith, Baltimore, 1985

Jimmie Swartz Medallion, 1983

Exemplary Campaign Leadership, Associated Jewish Charities and
    Welfare Fund, 1983

Certificate of Appreciation for Service, Women Together, Inc., 1983

Governor's Citation, awarded by Maryland Governor Harry R. Hughes, 1982

Inductee, Maryland Jewish Hall of Fame, Jewish Historical Society of
    Maryland, 1979

Congressional Certificate of Merit—Outstanding Citizenship, Barbara A.
    Mikulski, 1979

Congressional Commendation—Outstanding Leadership, Clarence D. Long, 1979

Shoshana S. Cardin Day, Proclamation by the County Executive, Baltimore County,
    Theodore Venetoulis, 1978

First Hilda Katz Blaustein Award—Outstanding Woman in Community Service, American Jewish Committee, Baltimore Chapter, 1978

Outstanding Citizen of Maryland, Department of Maryland Jewish War Veterans, 1978

Elkan Myers Award, Associated Jewish Charities and Welfare Fund of Baltimore, 1977

City Council of Baltimore President's Citation, presented by Council President Walter Orlinsky, 1977

Citation of Honor, Jewish Community Center of Greater Baltimore, 1977

Leadership in the 1977 Campaign, Associated Jewish Charities and Welfare Fund of Baltimore, 1977

Hannah G. Solomon Award, Baltimore Section, National Council of Jewish Women, 1976

Outstanding Women of Baltimore County, American Association of University Women, Towson Branch, 1976

Women of Distinction, Fashion Group of Baltimore, Inc., 1975

Distinguished Citizen Citation, City of Baltimore, presented by Mayor William Donald Schaefer, 1974 and 1975

Certificate of Appreciation, Baltimore County General Hospital, 1974

Louise Waterman Wise Award, American Jewish Congress, Women's Division of Maryland, 1970

Certificate of Distinguished Citizenship, State of Maryland, 1969, presented by Governor Marvin Mandel

Outstanding Citizen Honor, City of Baltimore, 1969, presented by Mayor Thomas D'Alesandro, III

Certificate of Appreciation for Generous and Meaningful Support, March of Dimes, 1969

Meritorious Service as Constitutional Convention Delegate, Teachers' Association of Baltimore, Maryland, Inc., 1968

Citizenship Civics Affairs Award, Morris I. Feld Lodge, B'nai B'rith, 1968

Woman of the Year, B'nai B'rith Women of Maryland, 1967

Notes

Introduction

1   These words, which name key concepts in Jewish life, may be translated as keeping the Sabbath, observing the dietary laws, performing the commandments and deeds of loving kindness, and worshiping God.

Chapter 1

1   My mother's two older sisters, Shoshana and Chaya, moved with their families to the United States in 1925. Her younger sister, Rachel, remained in Palestine to raise a family there. I am still in touch with my cousins' families, who remain in Israel.

2   Uncle Label went into hiding to avoid conscription. The Turkish authorities jailed my grandfather in an attempt to pressure Uncle Label to report, but a bribe of a bushel of watermelons—or perhaps it was eggplants, the family lore is unclear on this point—secured his release. Then Uncle Label was found and arrested. On the advice of others who had been in the same predicament, he ate unripe figs and became deathly ill. The Turks released him rather than have him die in jail, and after that he managed to escape their notice.

Chapter 2

1   Achad Ha-Am was the pen name of Asher Ginsberg (1856–1927). For more details of his life and thought, see *Encyclopedia Judaica*, 2nd ed. s.v. "Ahad Ha-Am." Elieazer Schweid.

Chapter 6

1   The Federation of Jewish Women's Organizations was not then related to the Jewish federations of charitable organizations found in many communities across North America. They were frequently confused because of the word "federation" in their name. For a history of the Federation of Jewish Women's Organizations of Maryland, see their website at http://www.jewishwomensfed.org/index.html.

2   NGO status of the Federation of Jewish Women's Organizations at the United Nations is confirmed by documents in the archives of the Jewish Museum of Maryland. See MS 82 (Federation of Jewish Women's Organizations of Maryland Records), Box 5, Folder 102.

3   See "U.S. Inactive on Route 40," Baltimore *Sun*, March 30, 1962.

4   To see the names of all Maryland state senators from Baltimore prior to 1967, go to http://www.msa.md.gov/msa/speccol/sc2600/sc2685/senate/html/basenate.html.

5   Archives of Maryland, "Historical List, Constitutional Convention, 1967–1968," found online at http://www.msa.md.gov/msa/speccol/sc2600/sc2685/html/conv1967.html.

6   A publication titled *A Decade of Progress: A Report to the Governor (1976)* details the history and achievements of the commission and gives credit to the many women who contributed to its success. Shoshana S. Cardin Archives.

7   Commercial Credit's efforts were highlighted by the *Christian Science Monitor* in an article by Guy Halberson, dated November 1, 1977.

Chapter 7

1   During these years, I also served as a commissioner for the Maryland Commission on Human Relations (1979–1982); was chairman of the Maryland State Employment and Training Council (1979–1983); and was chairman of the Maryland Volunteer Network (1980–1982).

2   Jacob Berkman, "Future Funding," *Baltimore Jewish Times*, November 16, 2007.

3   For example, see Simcha Jacobovici, "Ethiopian Jews Die, Israel Fiddles," *New York Times*, September 15, 1984. See also a series of op ed pieces and letters to the editor of the *Chicago Tribune*: Monroe Anderson, "Hope a Stranger to Ethiopian Jews," November 16, 1984; Steven B. Nasatir, "Israeli Help for Ethiopian Jews," November 26, 1984; and Emanual Zippori, "Israel and Ethiopian Jews," December 3, 1984.

4   The conference was held November 12–16, 1984, and the airlift began on November 21 of that year. See History/ "Operation Moses," on the website of the Israel Association for Ethiopian Jews, at http://www.iaej.co.il/pages/history_operation_moses.htm. See also "Airlift to Israel I Reported Taking Thousands of Jews From Ethiopia," *New York Times*, December 11, 1984. For more detail on events at the conference, see Mitchell G. Bard, *From Tragedy to Triumph: The Politics Behind the Rescue of Ethiopian Jewry* (Westport, CT: Praeger Publishers, 2002), 150–51.

Chapter 8

1   The Law of Return and its amendments can be read on the Knesset's official website at http://www.knesset.gov.il/laws/special/eng/return.htm. For a historical discussion of legal and social implications of the law, see Mark J. Altschul, "Israel's Law of Return and the Debate of Altering, Repealing, or Maintaining its Present Language," *University of Illinois Law Review*, 2002 (April 2003): 1345–72.

2   Council of Jewish Federations, *Report of Committee on Religious Issues in Israel to General Assembly*, November 12, 1982. Shoshana S. Cardin Archives.

3   A copy of the resolution titled "Religious Pluralism," dated November 1986 and passed at the CJF General Assembly in Chicago, may be found in the Shoshana S. Cardin Archives.

4   See the excellent summary of the issues, titled *Submission: The Law of Return*, by United Israel Appeal of Canada (Summer 1987) in the Shoshana S. Cardin Archives.

5   For a discussion of American reactions to the flap, see Ari L. Goldman, "Who Is a Jew? Debate in Israel Attracts Leading Figures of U.S. Judaism," *New York Times*, December 3, 1988.

6   The prime minister followed his verbal promise with a letter dated March 8, 1989. Shoshana S. Cardin Archives.

Chapter 9

1   To better understand how the Savings and Loan crisis of the 1980s unfolded, see the Federal Deposit and Insurance Corporation's "The S&L Crisis: A Chrono-Bibliography" at http://www.fdic.gov/bank/historical/s&l/.

2   Gary Klott, "Old Court's Fast Growth, But High Risk-Taking," *New York Times*, May 20, 1983.

3   Joe Nawrozki, "Cardin transferred, serving term in city," *Baltimore Evening Sun*, January 4, 1987.

4   Several others who associated with Levitt were caught in the scandal. See "S&L Charge Dropped After Defendant Dies," *Washington Post*, August 1, 1987; "Md. Thrift's 'Good Soldier' Sentenced to 2 Years," *Washington Post*, March 31, 1987.

5   Brian Sullam, "Jerome S. Cardin Convicted in S&L Theft," Baltimore *Sun*, December 4, 1986.

6   Jef Feeley, "Cardin Seeks Post-Trial Relief," *Daily Record* (date unknown). The clipped article is in the Shoshana S. Cardin Archives.

7   Jon Morgan and Robert Hilson, Jr., "Schaefer aided Cardin's release," *Baltimore Evening Sun*, November 30, 1989.

Chapter 10

1   For immigration numbers in Baltimore, see Associated Jewish Charities Executive Committee minutes, December 13, 1977, and November 29, 1978. For the number of Jews to leave the Soviet Union during the 1970s, Soviet Jewry Research Bureau, National Conference on Soviet Jewish Aliyah, cited in "Appendix," Clive A. Jones, *Soviet Jewish Aliyah 1989–1992: Impact and Implications for Israel and the Middle East* (Portland, OR: Frank Cass & Co., LTD, 1996), 221.

2   Jones, 221. For a discussion of Soviet policy regarding Jewish emigration in the 1980s, see Theodore H. Friedgut, "Passing Eclipse: The Exodus Movement in the 1980s," in *Soviet Jewry in the 1980s: The Politics of Anti-Semitism and Emigration and the Dynamics of Resettlement*, ed. Robert O. Freedman (Durham, NC: Duke University Press, 1989), 3–25.

3   See the article "Soviet Jewry in the Postwar Period," on the NCSJ website: http://www.ncsj.org/AuxPages/history.shtml.

4   CJF did due diligence on the activities of NCSJ and NJCRAC through a committee chaired by CJF Vice President Dan Shapiro. Then, after lengthy debate about the committee's findings, the CJF board voted in June 1988 to give the National Conference on Soviet Jewry the mandate to spearhead all federation activities regarding Soviet Jewry. However, I learned that NJCRAC never meant to abide by the board's decision. One day, after a conference call intended to clarify each entity's areas of responsibility, I hung up and the other participants in the conversation continued to talk. Through some quirk in technology, my answering machine recorded that discussion, and later, when I picked up my messages, I heard the NJCRAC representative say that his director intended to continue to conduct business as usual, ignoring the specific agreement that had been negotiated. It pained me to learn this, as my concern was for the Soviet Jews and NJCRAC's goal was to protect their turf and their allocation for "Soviet activities." A thorough account of this conflict may be found in chapter 7, "The Conflict Over Turf in the American Soviet Jewry Advocacy Movement: The Dominance of the CJF," of Fred A. Lazin's excellent and scholarly history of the movement, *The Struggle for Soviet Jewry in American Politics: Israel Versus the American Jewish Establishment* (Lanham, MD: Lexington Books, 2005).

5   Andrew Rosenthal, "March by 200,000 in Capital Presses Soviet on Rights," *New York Times*, December 7, 1987.

6   Soviet Jewry Research Bureau, in Jones, 221.

7   All of these references can be found in *Arab Opposition to Jewish Immigration to Israel*, an extraordinary document prepared in 1990 by David A. Harris for the American Jewish Committee. See also Robert O. Freedman, *Soviet Policy Toward Israel Under Gorbachev* (New York: Praeger, 1991), xiii–xiv.

8   Terence Smith, "Guerillas Seize 3 Soviet Jews on Train, Then Release Them in Austrian Deal," *New York Times*, September 29, 1973.

9   For more on the issue of "dropouts," see Henry L. Feingold, *"Silent No More": Saving the Jews of Russia, The American Jewish Effort, 1967–1989* (Syracuse: Syracuse University Press, 2007), 149–186.

10 For a vivid account of the "dropout" situation that conveys the urgency felt by the agency most directly responsible for providing for the refugees, see The American Joint Distribution Committee, Inc, *1989 Annual Report*, 19–21. The figure for per day costs for refugee maintenance, which was furnished in consultation with Sherry Hyman, archivist of the JDC, is approximate and includes a small amount that was spent on providing for Jewish refugees from places other than the Soviet Union. Email message to editor, May 28, 2008. Additional information was provided by the *HIAS Financial Report 1990*, HIAS Archives, New York.

11 Peter Golden, *Quiet Diplomat: A Biography of Max M. Fisher* (New York: Cornwall Books, 1992), 471–73.

12   See Esther B. Fein, "Office in Moscow Opened by Israelis," *New York Times*, January 4, 1991; John M. Goshko, "Soviet Union Opens Ties with S. Korea," *Washington Post*, October 1, 1990.

13   See the data provided by the Jewish Agency for Israel and the Ministry of Immigrant Absorption at http://www.jewishvirtuallibrary.org/jsource/Immigration/FSU.html (The American-Israeli Cooperative Enterprise); see also "Soviet Jewry in the Postwar Period," on the NCSJ website: http://www.ncsj.org/AuxPages/history.shtml

14   *Newsbreak* (National Conference on Soviet Jewry), February 28, 1990. Shoshana S. Cardin Archives.

Chapter 11

1   Steven L. Spiegel, *The Other Arab-Israeli Conflict: Making America's Middle East Policy, from Truman to Reagan* (Chicago: University of Chicago Press, 1985), 59.

2   Joel Brinkley, "Israel Bristles Over U.S. Loan-Guarantee Terms," *New York Times*, October 4, 1990; Jackson Diehl, "Status of Jerusalem Looms Anew," *Washington Post*, October 18, 1990.

3   George H. W. Bush, "Address Before a Joint Session of the Congress on the Cessation of the Persian Gulf Conflict," March 6, 1991, found online at George Bush Presidential Library and Museum Archives, Public Papers, 1991, March (http://bushlibrary.tamu.edu/research/public_papers.php?id=2767&year-1991&month-3).

4   Dan Raviv and Yossi Melman, *Friends in Deed: Inside the U.S.- Israel Alliance* (New York: Hyperion, 1994), 420–21.

5   Because of the way events unfolded, it is worth reiterating the areas of responsibility and intentions of the Conference of Presidents and AIPAC. The Conference of Presidents generally communicates privately with the president and members of his cabinet, advocating for Israel and other matters of importance to the Jewish community. AIPAC advocates directly to members of Congress, often about the same issues, utilizing the political tools the rules of Congress put at its disposal. In other words, it lobbies Congress for votes favorable to Israel. The education committee was convened by the Presidents Conference rather than AIPAC specifically to avoid the appearance of lobbying. Although AIPAC was a member of the committee and helped to produce our press releases and other materials, our intent was purely to put the facts about the loan guarantees in the hands of members of Congress and the public, in order to counteract the many misconceptions held on the issue.

6   AIPAC handouts September 6, 1991. Shoshana S. Cardin Archives.

7   *Near East Report*, February 18, 1991.

8   "Israel Plans to Expand Settlements," Jackson Diehl, *Washington Post*, September 7, 1991; "Baker Sees Shamir, but Deadlock Over Loan Guarantees Continues," Thomas L. Friedman, *New York Times*, September 17, 1991; "U.S. Tells Israelis Aid Cannot Fund New Settlements," Thomas L. Friedman, *New York Times*, January 25, 1992; Raviv and Melman, 415–16.

9   American Jewish Committee, James Rudin to Carolyn Green, memo, September 11, 1991. Shoshana S. Cardin Archives.

10   For a similar analysis of Shamir's motives, see Stephen S. Rosenfeld, "Resisting a Friend," *Washington Post*, September 13, 1991. For an account of these events from Shamir's perspective and in his own words, see Lally Weymouth, "The View from Israel: Why Shamir Won't Compromise," *Washington Post*, September 29, 1991.

11   Raviv and Melman, 425.

12   Raviv and Melman, 426.

13   Mayer Mitchell letter to Shoshana S. Cardin, August 30, 1991, Shoshana S. Cardin Archives.

14   Raviv and Melman, 425.

15 Transcript, News Conference with President George Bush, September 12, 1991. Shoshana S. Cardin Archives. All quotes from this news conference are drawn from this transcript.

16 George H. W. Bush, "Remarks to the Supreme Soviet of the Republic of the Ukraine," August 1, 1991. Shoshana S. Cardin Archives. Also available online at George Bush Presidential Library and Museum Archives, Public Papers, 1991, August (http://bushlibrary.tamu.edu/research/public_papers.php?id=3267&year=1991&month=8).

17 William B. Quandt, *Peace Process: American Diplomacy and the Arab-Israeli Conflict Since 1967* (Washington, DC: Brookings Institution/Berkeley: University of California Press, 1993), 386–88; Raviv and Melman, 426.

18 Shoshana S. Cardin to George H. W. Bush, letter, September 13, 1991. Shoshana S. Cardin Archives.

19 Clyde Haberman, "Israeli Loan Dispute Turns Ugly; Rightist Calls Bush 'Anti-Semite'," *New York Times*, September 16, 1991; see also "Chairman of Presidents Conference Assails 'Slur' by Israeli Against President Bush," Conference of Presidents Major American Jewish Organizations press release, September 16, 1991. Shoshana S. Cardin Archives.

20 George H. W. Bush to Shoshana S. Cardin, letter, September 17, 1991. Shoshana S. Cardin Archives. See "Bush's Letter to U.S. Jews," *New York Times*, September 21, 1991.

21 Raviv and Melman, 432.

22 Jewish Telegraphic Agency *Daily News Bulletin*, November 13, 1991. See also Dennis Hevesi, "Bush is Said to Hold Off on Israeli Loan Backing," *New York Times*, November 14, 1991.

Chapter 12

1 Richard Rhodes, *Masters of Death: The SS-Einsatzgruppen and the Invention of the Holocaust* (New York: Alfred A. Knopf, 2002), 170–178; "A Monument Over Babi Yar," William Korey, in *The Holocaust in the Soviet Union: Studies and Sources on the Destruction of the Jews in the Nazi-Occupied Territories of the USSR, 1941–1945*, ed. Lucjan Dobroszycki and Jeffrey S. Gurock (Armonk, NY: M.E. Sharpe, 1993), 61–64.

2 Michael Ajzenstadt, "Poetic Justice," *Jerusalem Post*, March 14, 1997.

3 See *Newsbreak* (National Conference on Soviet Jewry), October 11, 1991, Shoshana S. Cardin Archives; William E. Schmidt, "Today at Babi Yar the Sprits Will Rest," *New York Times*, October 5, 1991; *Jewish Bulletin of Northern California*, December 6, 1996; and *Encyclopedia of the Holocaust*, New York: Macmillan Publishing Company, 1990, 135.

4 William Korey, "Fear of Pogroms Haunts Soviet Jews," *New York Times*, January 25, 1990; Mary McGrory, "Anti-Semitism, Soviet Style," *Washington Post*, April 19, 1990; Francis X. Clines, "Gorbachev Condemns Anti-Semitism, Past and Present," *New York Times*, October 7, 1991; Yevgeny Yevtushenko, interview by Eleanor Wachtell, Writers and Company, CBC, 1995, http://lightning.prohosting.com/~zhenka/writersco.html.

5 Max M. Kampelman, *Entering New Worlds: The Memoirs of a Private Man in a Public Life* (New York: HarperCollins, 1991).

6 *Newsbreak* (National Conference on Soviet Jewry), October 11, 1991. Shoshana S. Cardin Archives. See also Fred Hiatt, "Gorbachev, U.S. Jews Meet," *Washington Post*, October 3, 1991.

7 In recalling my meeting with Gorbachev, I relied on my memory and my notes, along with two publications that interviewed me soon after the meeting: *Newsbreak* (National Conference on Soviet Jewry), October 11, 1991; *Daily News Bulletin* (Jewish Telegraphic Agency), October 3, 1991. Both publications are in the Shoshana S. Cardin Archives. See also Fred Hiatt, "Gorbachev, U.S. Jews Meet," *Washington Post*, October 3, 1991.

8   It was well known that Edgar Bronfman had met with President Gorbachev while on a business trip to the Soviet Union. Bronfman raised the question of anti-Semitism with the president at that time. See also, "Jews are Cautious After Soviet Visit," *New York Times*, December 14, 1985.

9   In his State of the Union address on January 31, 1990, President Bush declared, "Every one of us must confront and condemn racism, anti-Semitism, bigotry, and hate, not next week, not tomorrow, but right now—every single one of us." President George H. W. Bush's full speech, Address Before a Joint Session of the Congress on the State of the Union, is available online at George Bush Presidential Library and Museum Archives, Public Papers 1990, January (http://bushlibrary.tamu.edu/research/public_papers.php?id=1492&year=1990&month=01).

10   *Newsbreak* (National Conference on Soviet Jewry), October 11, 1991. Shoshana S. Cardin Archives.

11   A translation by Benjamin Okopnik of Yevtushenko's poem, *Babi Yar*, may be found online at http://remember.org/witness/babiyar.html.

12   Kravchuk's remarks are quoted in part in "Massacre of 30,000 Jews recalled," *Houston Chronicle*, October 6, 1991; Chrystia Freeland, "Ukrainian Role Admitted In '41 Babi Yar Massacre," *Washington Post*, Oct 6, 1991; and *Newsbreak* (National Conference on Soviet Jewry), October 11, 1991. Shoshana S. Cardin Archives.

13   Francis X. Clines, "Gorbachev Condemns Anti-Semitism, Past and Present," *The New York Times*, October 7, 1991. See also Speech of Mikhail Gorbachev delivered by Aleksandr Yakovlev, October 5, 1991, translated by Judy Turkeltaub, National Conference on Soviet Jewry. Shoshana S. Cardin Archives.

Chapter 13

1   Paul Lewis, "Quayle Says U.S. Seeks Repeal of U.N. Condemnation of Zionism," *New York Times*, December 12, 1989. For background on the passage of Resolution 3379 in 1975, see "Zionism as Racism (1975)," in *Great Debates at the United Nations: An Encyclopedia of Fifty Key Issues, 1945–2000*, Robert F. Gorman (Westport, CT: Greenwood Press, 2001), 263–66.

2   John R. Bolton, "Zionism is *Not* Racism," *New York Times*, December 16, 1991; Paul Lewis, "U.N. Repeals Its '75 Resolution Equating Zionism With Racism," *New York Times*, December 17, 1991.

3   Mark Matthews, "Shamir, U.S. Jews at odds," Baltimore *Sun*, November 21, 1991; Bradford Jacobs, "A Valiant Battler—but Obsolete," Baltimore *Sun*, November 30, 1991.

4   Documents in the Shoshana S. Cardin Archives, "Council of Jewish Federations, 60th General Assembly."

5   Shmuel Katz, "A Failure of American Jewish Leadership?" *Jerusalem Post*, December 13, 1991.

6   Larry Cohler, "Don't Call Us…," *Washington Jewish Week*, January 2, 1992.

7   Senator Patrick J. Leahy, "It's Israel's Choice," *New York Times*, February 11, 1992; Leslie H. Gelb, "Treeing Mr. Shamir," *New York Times*, February 24, 1992; Senator John Chafee of Rhode Island, The Israeli Loan Guarantee Program, 102nd Congress, 2nd sess., *Congressional Record*, February 25, 1992, S2131.

8   Editorial, "The U.S. vs. Israel," *Wall Street Journal*, March 6, 1992.

9   Shoshana S. Cardin, unpublished letter to the *Wall Street Journal*, March 9, 1992. Shoshana S. Cardin Archives.

10   Edward I. Koch, *New York Post*, March 6, 1992; "Koch Accuses Baker of Slur on Jews," *New York Times*, March 7, 1992. See also Marianne Goldstein, Cathy Burke and Don Broderick, "Baker's 4-Letter Slam at U.S. Jews," *New York Post*, March 6, 1992, 2.

11   To see the evolution of these positions, see Raviv and Melman, 406–434; For Malcolm Hoenlein's and my meeting with Baker, see Mark Matthews, "Baker Assures Jews of Continuing Support for Israel," Baltimore *Sun*, March 7, 1992.

12   Raviv and Melman, 440–41.

Chapter 14

1   See CLAL's mission statement on its website: http://www.clal.org/ac_index.html.

2   Gerald B. Bubis and Steven F. Windmueller, *Predictability to Chaos?? How Jewish Leaders Reinvented Their National Communal System* (Baltimore: Center for Jewish Community Studies, 2005), 9; *Encyclopaedia Judaica*, 1972, s.v. "Council of Jewish Federations and Welfare Funds."

3   Bubis and Windmueller, 9.

4   Today, groups such as Hadassah and Jewish National Fund raise money in separate fund-raising campaigns.

5   Bubis and Windmueller, 10–11.

6   Typically, UIA received 88 % of the funds, with the balance going to JDC.

7   Bubis and Windmueller, 3.

8   Aid for refugee resettlement in Israel is granted through the U.S. Department of State's Bureau of Population, Refugees and Migration.

9   It may seem incredible to Americans that it was so difficult to disentangle these ownership records, but deeds were often poorly recorded in the Palestine and early statehood periods. Then too, it was to JAFI's advantage to allow matters to remain undefined while it acted as owner and landlord and collected the rent. This research could not have been concluded successfully without the "inside" assistance of a land records employee I had known when he was at the Jewish Agency. He had left JAFI in some frustration, and I knew he would be happy to cooperate in our investigation.

10   Daniel J. Elazar, "Developments in Jewish Community Organization in the Second Postwar Generation" in *American Pluralism and the Jewish Community*, ed. Seymour Martin Lipset, (New Brunswick, NJ: Transaction Publishers, 1990), 186–7.

11   In support of this popular perception, I quote this trenchant observation found at http://en.wikipedia.org/wiki/Jewish_Agency_for_Israel.

12   "Operational Plan: Integration of United Israel Appeal into Newco." February 3, 1999. Shoshana S. Cardin Archives.

13   United Jewish Communities, Draft Proposed Budget FY 2006–07, Executive Summary. Shoshana S. Cardin Archives.